This Kindred People

This Kindred People

Canadian-American Relations and the Anglo-Saxon Idea, 1895–1903

EDWARD P. KOHN

McGill-Queen's University Press
Montreal & Kingston · London · Ithaca

© McGill-Queen's University Press 2004
ISBN 0-7735-2796-6

Legal deposit fourth quarter 2004
Bibliothèque nationale du Québec

Printed in Canada on acid-free paper that is 100%
ancient forest free (100% post-consumer recycled),
processed chlorine free.

This book has been published with the help of a grant
from the Canadian Federation for the Humanities and
Social Sciences, through the Aid to Scholarly Publications
Programme, using funds provided by the Social Sciences
and Humanities Research Council of Canada.

McGill-Queen's University Press acknowledges the
support of the Canada Council for the Arts for our
publishing program. We also acknowledge the financial
support of the Government of Canada through the Book
Publishing Industry Development Program (BPIDP) for
our publishing.

National Library of Canada Cataloguing in Publication

Kohn, Edward P. (Edward Parliament), 1968–
    This kindred people: Canadian-American relations and
    the Anglo-Saxon idea, 1895–1903/Edward P. Kohn.

    Includes bibliographical references and index.
    ISBN 0-7735-2796-6

    1. Canada – Relations – United States. 2. United States
    – Relations – Canada. 3. Anglo-Saxon race. 4. Canada –
    Foreign relations – 1867–1918. 5. United States – Foreign
    relations – 1865–1921. I. Title.

FC249.K63 2004   327.71073'09'034   C2004-902684-4

Typeset in Sabon 10/12
by Caractéra inc., Quebec City

Contents

This Kindred People

Introduction:
The Anglo-Saxon Mirror

The Anglo-Saxon leads the van.
And never lags behind,
For was he not ordain'd to be
The leader of mankind?

> Alexander McLachlan, "The Anglo-Saxon"

At the end of the nineteenth century, English-speaking North Americans discussed race as later generations might discuss the weather. The same subjects found a ready audience on both sides of the border. In the press, in speeches, and in their letters to one another, Canadians and Americans discussed the common issues of immigration, "Indians," Jews, blacks, and French Canadians. In his *The Winning of the West*, Theodore Roosevelt made no effort to conceal his contempt for the "savages," who were destined to be "displaced" on the continent.[1] The editor of *Queen's Quarterly* welcomed Americans to the Canadian west because "they will help to give an Anglo-Saxon character to the social, economic and political development of the west."[2] France's "Dreyfus Affair" incited anti-Semitism in much of North America. A frequent resident of Paris, Henry Adams wrote to his good friend John Hay about "Wall Street Jews," and to his brother Brooks wrote simply, "I loathe the Jew."[3] Writing from Toronto to a friend in 1898 Goldwin Smith urged sympathy for Spain because "she burned a good number of Jews."[4] Men in each country also discussed the unique racial makeup of their neighbour. Theodore Roosevelt expressed alarm to Francis Parkman about the number of French Canadians "swarming into New England with ominous rapidity" and speculated that "their race will in many places supplant the old American stock."[5] For their part, Canadians often argued against union with the United States because of America's racial conflict. "There is no conflict of races in Canada," J. Schurman wrote in 1889, arguing against political union with the republic. "For that, in its most hopeless aspect too," he noted, "you must go to the southern States."[6] Canadians and Americans at the end of the nineteenth century could not avoid questions of race.

At the end of the nineteenth century, English Canadians and Americans faced each other across the border with old animosities. Many Canadians adhered to familiar ideas of Loyalism, imperialism, and anti-Americanism to differentiate the Dominion from the republic. In the United States, lingering notions of anglophobia and "Manifest Destiny" caused Americans to look upon the British colony to the north as a dangerous and unnatural entity. America's rise to world power status and the Anglo-American rapprochement, however, forced Americans and Canadians to adapt to the new international reality. Emphasizing their shared language, civilization, and forms of government, many English-speaking North Americans drew upon Anglo-Saxonism to find common ground. Americans and Canadians often referred to each other as members of the same "family" who shared the same "blood." As many of the events leading to the rapprochement had a North American context, Americans and Canadians often drew upon the common lexicon of Anglo-Saxon rhetoric to undermine the old rivalries and underscore their shared interests. Racial ideology did not cause the rapprochement, but racial rhetoric provided Americans and English Canadians with a device with which to adapt to the changing context of Canadian-American relations.

Historians Barbara Tuchman, Carlos Fuentes, and Ronald Takaki have suggested that history is a "mirror" in which we see ourselves and our society reflected. In terms of racial ideology, the historical "mirror" in which Canadians and Americans viewed themselves was race.[7] For many English-speaking North Americans the discussion about other races merely served to reflect their assumed innate superiority as Anglo-Saxons. Blacks, natives, Jews, and French Canadians were "the Other" against which Canadians and Americans interpreted their place and mission. Such Anglo-Saxonism represented a common strand of thought throughout the English-speaking world. By 1850 this ideology had imbued Americans with a sense of "racial destiny" to spread good government, commercial prosperity, and Christianity across the continent.[8] Moreover, success over "lower" or "backward" races provided further proof of Anglo-Saxon superiority. Such an idea was not limited to the United States. Great Britain and the English-speaking colonies also took part in what might be called the "Anglo-Saxon tautology": Anglo-Saxon superiority justified racial conquest, which in turn proved Anglo-Saxon superiority. Moreover, by the end of the nineteenth century, Anglo-Saxonism rested upon an apparently solid intellectual foundation of English-language scientific and historical writing. Both British and American writers extolled the virtues of the Anglo-Saxons in medieval history.[9] In 1885 the Reverend Josiah Strong published *Our Country*. In this book, as well as in his 1893 *The New Era*, Strong proclaimed the superiority of the Anglo-Saxon and asserted that "North America is to be the great home of the Anglo-Saxon, the principal seat of his power, the center of his life and influence."[10] Strong used the term "Anglo-Saxon" loosely, and stated that he intended "to include all English-speaking peoples."[11] Strong's vague use of the term "Anglo-Saxon" represented the flexibility, and therefore one of the strengths, of Anglo-Saxonism.

White North Americans could justify genocidal wars against natives, the exclusion of Asian immigrants, and the subjugation of blacks and Hispanics by citing the self-evident superiority of Anglo-Saxons to give scientific cachet to their actions. The English-speaking world drew selectively and often mistakenly from Charles Darwin's 1859 *The Origin of Species*, the publication of which represented a watershed in the development of modern scientific thought. Despite meeting resistance in much of the English-speaking world, evolutionary Darwinism and scientific rationalism swept through universities and academic journals.[12] "Ten or fifteen years ago," Whitelaw Reid stated at Dartmouth in 1873, "the staple subject here for reading and talk ... was English poetry and fiction. Now it is English science. Herbert Spencer, John Stuart Mill, Huxley, Darwin, Tyndall, have all usurped the places of Tennyson and Browning, and Matthew Arnold and Dickens."[13] Writers throughout the English-speaking world seized upon Darwin to explain competition between classes, nations, and races. Victorians pointed to the subtitle of *The Origin of Species*, "The Preservation of the Favoured Races in the Struggle for Life," as justification for wars of conquest in Africa and Asia. Anglo-Saxonism justified both the conquest of the American continent and the British imperial wars of the nineteenth century. In turn, Anglo-Saxon success proved Anglo-Saxon superiority, a notion shared throughout the English-speaking world.

British writer Herbert Spencer coined the term "survival of the fittest" and applied it to industrial society. Spencer was the first to apply Darwin's ideas on biological evolution to society, developing the notion of "Social Darwinism." If species competed with each other for survival, by analogy one could discuss individuals in society in Darwinian terms. Just as Darwin's ideas sparked a scientific revolution in the English-speaking world, Spencer's ideas caught the imagination of an American society deep in the disquieting and dislocating experience of rapid industrialization and the taming of the continent. His ideas helped to breathe life into an American individualism fitted both for the frontier and for the teeming cities. It did not take long for other writers to take the next logical step and argue that nations were organisms that fought one another directly and competed for the same resources. Biologically and "scientifically" these nations could be organized by race, and only the strongest would survive. Thus, in the coming struggle for global dominance, only the fittest would survive, and Anglo-Saxons, whether in Canada, Great Britain, or the United States, were not merely natural allies, but actually members of the same "species" or components of a single "organism."

Such quasi-scientific theories had transformed the conception of "nationalism" by the end of the nineteenth century. Ethnicity and language became, according to Eric Hobsbawm, "the central, increasingly the decisive or even the only criteria" for nationality.[14] The international situation only exaggerated this trend to identify nations by racial criteria. Anglo-Saxonism played an important role in establishing a community of identity throughout the British Empire. "Imperialists were imperialists," Douglas Cole writes, "in large measure because they were acutely conscious of ethnic ties and ethnic differentiation." English Canadians drew the United States into the sphere of this racial pride, and Americans reciprocated in kind. Canadians and Americans came to view their common racial heritage as indicating membership in the global English-speaking family. It has been noted that ethnicity can be viewed as "extended kinship," as members of a race proclaim the superiority and special rights of their ethnicity just as they would of their family.[15] Indeed, English-speaking North Americans used kinship language to discuss their common heritage. Canadians and Americans referred to each other as "cousins" or "brothers" who shared the common "mother" of Great Britain. After the Venezuela Boundary crisis Canadians and Americans declared that an Anglo-Saxon war would constitute "fratricide," while Anglo-Saxon harmony would represent a "family reunion." The ensuing Anglo-American rapprochement resulted in the apex of Anglo-Saxonism, with North Americans lacing their discussions of war, empire, and annexation with the theme of their common Anglo-Saxon interests.

By the end of the nineteenth century, the ideology of Anglo-Saxon superiority had become established as a reaction to a radically changing world, and its advocates applied it to both domestic and international problems. In 1894 British civil servant Benjamin Kidd published his *Social Evolution*, which became a bestseller on both sides of the Atlantic. In the United States Theodore Roosevelt gave Kidd's advocacy of "social imperialism" a positive appraisal in the *North American Review*.[16] *Social Evolution* was "a book of its time," a reaction to the social upheaval of rapid modernization and industrialization, and both Kidd and Roosevelt viewed increasing state involvement in business and society necessary to stave off socialism and revolution. Their view represented a common theme of this "Era of Reform," when many middle- and upper-class writers, politicians, and social reformers adopted a paternalistic attitude toward the ills of society. Imperialists had long adopted familial language, referring to primitive peoples as "children" while assigning a "paternal" role for colonial government. Now many such as Kidd and Roosevelt adopted similar language when discussing the poor classes and the paternal role of government at home. As historian Greta Jones writes, "typifications of race and class were interchangeable."[17] Classifying groups of people by class as well as race points to another dimension to Anglo-Saxon affinity: its advocates were very often of the same class. As Canadians and Americans might feel bound together by race, the advocates of Anglo-Saxonism could also feel bound together by common ideas of wealth and privilege. Anglo-Saxonists were not members of the working-class, but were the political, business, and intellectual leaders of their day.

That Kidd's work was a "book of its time" – a reaction to the problems of a specific era – gives an indication of who used Anglo-Saxon rhetoric and how they wielded it. Mainly older, white, upper-class, Protestant Americans and English Canadians used Anglo-Saxonism as a way of reasserting control on a rapidly changing world. In the United States, the Northeast, especially New York and Boston, were the centres of American Anglo-Saxonism. North of the border Toronto was clearly the capital of Canadian Anglo-Saxonism, which was concentrated in Ontario and to a lesser extent in the Maritimes. The geography of racial ideology reflected the concerns of the era. At home, Americans used the language of racial superiority to combat the increasing "disorder" of the "Negro problem" in the south and immigrant poverty and political power in the cities. In Canada, Ontario lumberman and Member of Parliament John Charlton used Anglo-Saxon rhetoric to assert the "Englishness" of the Dominion. Charlton's advocacy of Sabbath observance in his lumber camps and seduction laws in Parliament indicated how Charlton also used ideas of religion and gender to combat the perceived trend toward immorality. Abroad, Canadians and Americans were faced with rising Russian and Japanese empires that threatened more than just British and American economic interests. American intellectual Brooks Adams, descendant of presidents and brother of historian Henry Adams, warned his countrymen that the coming struggle with Russia was "war to the death…One organism, in the end, will destroy the other."[18] If blacks, Asians, Jews, and Slavs could not be allowed to dominate politics and society at home, they certainly must not be allowed to dominate the world. Yet the racial response to these internal and external threats was relatively fleeting. Massive waves of immigration and the potency of French-Canadian nationalism made racial rhetoric rapidly anachronistic in the first years of the twentieth century. The Anglo-Japanese Alliance, Russo-Japanese War, and completion of the Anglo-American entente made a racially motivated foreign policy unnecessary and nonsensical, if not downright danger- ous. The rhetoric of Anglo-Saxon superiority quickly died off, while its aged advocates simply died.

In viewing each other and their relations with other nations, Canadians and Americans utilized racial rhetoric as a way of making sense of a rapidly changing world. Anglo-Saxonism did not cause the Anglo- Saxon rapprochement, but it helped foster it by giving North Americans a common lexicon, the rhetoric of Anglo-Saxon kinship and Anglo- Canadian-American affinity. The Anglo-American rapprochement of 1895–1914 resulted from an identity of interests created by an altered international situation.[19] Throughout the nineteenth century the Amer- ican and British economies had become intertwined through increased trade and exchanges of capital. Moreover, the rise of new powers in Europe and Asia presented challenges to British and American inter- ests, including the maintenance of free trade with the lucrative China market. With America's rise to world-power status coinciding with threats to the British Empire, much of the rapprochement was one- sided, with Great Britain acquiescing to American assertions of hegemony over the western hemisphere. Historians have noted that Canadian- American relations played an extensive role in the rapprochement, yet they usually point to the years 1902–14, or the "cleaning of the slate" era of Anglo-American relations.[20] Many of the central episodes of the early rapprochement, however, played themselves out in a North American context, such as the 1895 Venezuela Boundary crisis, the 1898–99 Anglo-American Joint High Commission, and the Alaskan Boundary dispute. These events illustrated that Canadians and Amer- icans had to find a way to moderate their hostile attitude to each other and adapt themselves to the changed international situation. For many, the answer lay with Anglo-Saxonism. American anglophobia and Canadian Loyalism were still strong, but increasingly anachronistic in a world discussing Anglo-American affinity, unity, and alliance. For many North Americans, Anglo-Saxon rhetoric provided a way to mod- erate resentment and to emphasize their common destiny upon the continent and their common mission throughout the world.

During the rapprochement the United States asserted its new world- power status by claiming hegemony over the western hemisphere as a prelude to overseas expansion and the building of a navy and isthmian canal to protect its new territories. In asserting American hegemony in the western hemisphere through their broadened interpretation of the Monroe Doctrine, Grover Cleveland and Richard Olney included Canada. Americans accepted this implicitly. Initially, American hostil- ity toward Canada resulted from anglophobia and the movement for political union. Yet with British acquiescence and the dawning of an Anglo-American understanding, Americans modified their view toward their northern neighbour. As the United States turned its attention toward the Caribbean and the Pacific, the rapprochement rendered actual occupation of Canada unimportant and irrelevant. Canada's association with a friendly power and the domination by Anglo-Saxons gave the United States hegemony over a continent unified ideologically if not politically. After the Venezuela crisis Americans accommodated Canada to their new world view through the medium of Anglo-Saxonism, stressing Canada's autonomy from England and its natural connection with the United States. As the rapprochement played itself out on the continent, Americans viewed Canadian representation at the Joint High Commission and the sending of a Canadian contingent to South Africa as the undertakings of a fellow Anglo-Saxon nation.

Canadians initially responded to American hostility during the Venezuela crisis with exclamations of defiance and loyalty to the empire. Yet British acquiescence and the resulting rapprochement placed Canada in a new position on the continent. Some Canadians were threatened by Canada's apparently inferior position and angry with Great Britain for abandoning them to a grasping Uncle Sam. Yet many Canadians were exceedingly pleased with the rapprochement, seeing it as a step toward Anglo-Saxon friendship and unity, and as giving Canada increased security on the continent. Canadians did not view themselves as passive spectators in the relations between the two Anglo-Saxon powers, however. Instead, drawing upon a common lexicon of racial superiority, English Canadians believed they had a unique and active role to play in helping secure Anglo-Saxon harmony. This Anglo-Saxon version of what historians would come to call the "linch-pin" theory pre-dated its usual historical placement by at least twenty years.[21] Moreover, though one would expect Canadians to feel threatened by an American war in the hemisphere, expansion, and their quest for hemispheric hegemony, most English Canadians supported the United States as fellow Anglo-Saxons. Indeed, Canadians actually shared in American military endeavours and annexation debates. English Canadians urged American involvement in Cuba and their annexation of the Philippines. If Great Britain could not right Spanish wrongs or bring civilization to the Filipinos, many Canadians believed, then the other Anglo-Saxon power must. When viewing the exploits of the British Empire, English Canadians may have felt an imperial "sense of power," but when they viewed the United States undertaking the same endeavours, they felt an Anglo-Saxon "sense of power."

Anglo-Saxonism also helped alter Canada's place in Anglo-American relations. While rarely finding its way into diplomatic dispatches, Anglo-Saxonism provided a general framework for relations among the nations of the North Atlantic triangle during the rapprochement. With the United States accepting Canada's right to exist as a fellow and semi-autonomous Anglo-Saxon nation, and Great Britain happy to allow the United States to maintain the status quo in the western hemisphere, Canada achieved a new position of prominence in Anglo-American relations. Prime Minister Wilfrid Laurier, who came to power with the Liberal victory of 1896, often exploited the circumstances of the rapprochement, pressing Canadian views and demands to an extent no prime minister had previously. During this era Canadian-American relations became increasingly compartmentalized within Anglo-American relations. The Canadian government followed its own trade policy, sounding out the Americans on reciprocity with informal diplomacy and establishing imperial preference. During the Anglo-American Joint High Commission of 1898–99, four of the five representatives were Canadian. Laurier strongly pressed Canada's position on the Alaska boundary and the abrogation of the Clayton-Bulwer treaty, often creating obstacles for Anglo-American harmony. While often frustrating for American and British diplomats, Canada's actions illustrated the Dominion's new national voice within the English-speaking world. Anglo-Saxonism helped provide the rationale for Laurier's assertion of Canadian autonomy, both on the North American continent and within the British empire.

Wilfrid Laurier's prominence in Anglo-Canadian-American relations during the rapprochement raises the question of French Canada's attitude toward Anglo-Saxonism. Clearly French Canadians were not Anglo-Saxonists. Yet the rhetoric of Anglo-Saxon superiority had penetrated the French-speaking world by the end of the nineteenth century. In 1897 the French economist Edmond Demolins published in Paris a study of *Anglo-Saxon Superiority* which went through five editions in two months.[22] The book received favourable reviews throughout the English-speaking world. Theodore Roosevelt wrote admiringly of the book to his British friend Cecil Spring-Rice, and read the volume on the way to Cuba with his Rough Riders. Neither the French nor French Canadians, of course, shared this view. Yet as a brilliant politician and masterful public speaker, Laurier often adopted Anglo-Saxon rhetoric, noting that Canadians and Americans had the same blood and belonged to the same family. Laurier used such public rhetoric not because he was an Anglo-Saxonist, but because he knew such language would be readily understood and accepted by his English-speaking audience, whether in the United States, Canada, or Great Britain.

North American Anglo-Saxonism existed in a very definite context, that of the zenith of Anglo-Saxonism in the English-speaking world. The years 1895–1903 formed the framework of shared Canadian-American racist ideology, just as they formed the framework of the Anglo-American rapprochement. The same distinct events that shaped Anglo-American relations during this time shaped Canadian-American relations. These events were the Venezuela boundary crisis, the Anglo-American Joint High Commission, the Spanish-American War, the annexation of the Philippines, the South African War, and the Alaska boundary dispute. The Alaska boundary crisis represented the unique continental context of the rapprochement, with Canada directly affected by American claims of hemispherical hegemony. The resulting Canadian bitterness ended much of the rhetoric of Anglo-Saxon continental unity. The years 1903 to 1914 found Canada claiming more independence from both Great Britain and the United States, and defending its national interests without resorting to previous imperial or Anglo-Saxon rhetoric. The vision of Canada as a bridge between the two Anglo-Saxon powers would have a hiatus until after the World War, as Anglo-Saxonism in general became increasingly anachronistic. With waves of non-Aryan immigrants arriving in North America, the rise of French-Canadian nationalism, and the anti-American reciprocity election in 1911, Anglo-Saxon rhetoric melted away. Moreover, with the 1903 Panamanian Revolution, the building of the isthmian canal, and the 1904 Roosevelt Corollary to the Monroe Doctrine, Canada diminished in Americans' world view. The realities of the new century severely challenged the racist ideology of the old.

North American Anglo-Saxonism represented a short-lived and often ephemeral phenomenon. The brief juncture of racial ideology and the rapprochement may explain why it has received so little attention, leading historians to adhere to traditional assumptions. Namely, historians have focused on the "imperial" interpretation of North America at the turn of the century. The United States is seen as having been preoccupied by the Caribbean and Pacific, with Canada playing no part in the new relevance of the Monroe Doctrine. Canada, on the other hand, is depicted as remaining true to its Loyalist tradition and preoccupied by the South African War. Moreover, historians have had difficulty looking beyond traditional American anglophobia and Canadian anti-Americanism, treating these trends of thought as unquestionable constants of their respective national histories. Finally, there has been a tendency to treat Canadian-American relations of this period either as a mere subset of Anglo-American relations, or a continentalist blending of borders. A study of North American Anglo-Saxonism may put some of these fallacies to rest. English Canadians and Americans responded to the rapprochement by employing a common racial ideology. In doing so, they altered the way they perceived each other and their shared continent. For a time at least, English-speaking North

Americans viewed their relations and the great events of the turn of the century as bringing about a reunion of the Anglo-Saxon family.

To summarize briefly, Anglo-Saxon rhetoric gave turn-of-the-century English-speaking North Americans a common point of reference in adapting to the Anglo-American rapprochement. To put it another way, Anglo-Saxonism was an ideological device by which Canadians and Americans could negotiate the rapprochement. Anglo-Saxonism provided a rationale that could compete, and often coincide, with traditional elements of national identity, such as Canadian imperialism and American anglophobia. Canadians and Americans utilized Anglo-Saxon rhetoric in responding to Anglo-American crises and their resolution, as illustrated in chapter 1 on the Venezuela Crisis. Yet Anglo-Saxonism had limits to its persuasive powers, as John Charlton discovered in the failure of reciprocity negotiations and in the 1898–99 Joint High Commission (chapter 2). In 1898 many Canadians initially displayed traditional suspicion of American expansionist motives both in North America and in the West Indies. Yet following the British lead, Canadians accepted America's rise to imperial power, using Anglo-Saxon rhetoric to portray the war with Spain and the annexation of the Philippines as part of a common Anglo-Saxon mission, as depicted by Rudyard Kipling's "White Man's Burden" (chapter 3). America's carrying of the Anglo-Saxon mission to Cuba and the Philippines provided many English Canadians with an example to emulate on the eve of the Empire's war in South Africa. Moreover, Anglo-Saxon rhetoric and the rapprochement offered Canada the opportunity to play a unique role in Anglo-American relations, as a go-between or "linch-pin" for the two powers. Prime Minister Wilfrid Laurier took advantage of this new status to press for Canadian rights regarding the *modus vivendi* for the Alaska boundary and the abrogation of the Clayton-Bulwer treaty. The result was increased Canadian control of the Dominion's external affairs, and the compartmentalization of Canadian-American affairs within Anglo-American relations (chapter 4). Laurier, however, pressed Canada's position on Alaska to little avail. As with reciprocity, Anglo-Saxonism could not overcome the reality of North American power politics, President Theodore Roosevelt's manoeuvrings, or the British need for American friendship (chapter 5). After the Alaska decision, Anglo-Saxon rhetoric waned, yet Canadian-American relations solidified on a new level, with Canadians and Americans largely accepting their common destiny on the continent. For a brief period, racial rhetoric and Canadian-American relations intersected, creating a nexus of intellectual and diplomatic history.

1 The Venezuela Crisis, Canada, and American "Hemispherism": The North American Context of the Rapprochement and the Anglo-Saxon Response

We are much interested in the outcome of the Venezuela matter. I earnestly hope our government do'n't back down. If there is a muss I shall try to have a hand in it myself! They'll have to employ a lot of men as green as I am even for the conquest of Canada.

Theodore Roosevelt to William Sheffield Cowles, 22 December 1895[1]

Let us pray that Canada will interpose no captious and unnecessary obstacles to the realization of a state of concord, peace, and good will among all the Anglo-Saxon States of the world, and especially between the two great representative nations of that race.

John Charlton in *Canadian Magazine*, January 1897[2]

The Venezuela boundary crisis served as an important and necessary first step in America's rise to world power status. At the end of 1895, Great Britain backed its colony Guiana in a border dispute with neighbouring Venezuela. Americans responded by claiming British actions violated the 1823 Monroe Doctrine's prohibition on territorial expansion in the New World by any European nation. During the crisis the United States asserted hegemony over the western hemisphere, placing the nation in potential conflict with Great Britain. After a few weeks of war-talk, Great Britain quickly backed down, essentially acknowledging American dominance on the American continents. America's warning to the European powers actually served British interests. Worried about the threat that other European powers posed to British interests in Africa, Asia, and the Middle East, British statesmen viewed American hegemony in the western hemisphere as a guarantee of the status quo, and thus as a guarantee of British interests. With the United

States holding the British flank in the New World, the British could turn their attention elsewhere, namely towards a brewing conflict in South Africa. During the Venezuela crisis, the unsuccessful coup by a British subject in the Transvaal Republic, known as the Jameson Raid, as well as the German Kaiser's congratulatory telegram to the Boers underscored the importance of American friendship. The crisis marked the first step in the rapprochement that began the century-long "special relationship" between the United States and Great Britain.

The crisis resulted from the state of the "American Mind," as Henry Steele Commager called it, at the turn of the century. Anglophobia, partisan politics, and the Roosevelt-Lodge-Mahan school of "vigorous" · foreign policy all found an outlet in the dispute over the Venezuelan border. Claiming hegemony over the entire hemisphere was a new and bold assertion, yet Americans cloaked the idea in the old and familiar words of the Monroe Doctrine. According to Dexter Perkins, the Venezuela crisis elevated the Monroe Doctrine to a new prominence in American political thought and resulted in a much broader interpretation. Focusing primarily on Latin America, however, Perkins almost completely overlooks the place of Canada in the new interpretation of the Monroe Doctrine. Indeed, Perkins asserts that, "In general, the question of the relationship of Canada to the American dogma was hardly broached in the nineteenth or the early-twentieth century."[3] Perkins's view is a common one. Most historians have treated the Monroe Doctrine as though it only related to Latin America and have labelled Canada an "exception" in the American view.

During the Venezuela crisis, however, Americans focused on Canada in two related ways. Americans believed that in any conflict with Great Britain, Canada would either be the field of battle or a "hostage" against British belligerence. For a war-hungry anglophobe like Theodore Roosevelt in 1896, a war with Great Britain would provide the opportunity to remove the British from North America once and for all and unite the continent above the Rio Grande under American rule. In 1895 and 1896, Americans did not speak only of Latin America but of the entire western hemisphere falling under the purview of the Monroe Doctrine. When Secretary of State Richard Olney addressed the British on Venezuela, he stated: "The states of America, South as well as North, by geographical affinity, by natural sympathy, by similarity of governmental constitutions, are friends and allies, commercially and politically, of the United States." Though historians have called Olney's interpretation of the Monroe Doctrine highly flawed, the overwhelming majority of Americans in December 1895 agreed with the Secretary of State. Canada was "an American nation," and Americans claimed an interest in Canada's political fate.

The Venezuela crisis quickly abated. The threat of disrupting the voluminous Anglo-American trade caused the American stock market to crash, while both the United States and Great Britain faced more serious crises on the international front. Another rebellion in the Spanish colony of Cuba focused American attention on a decades-old problem. In South Africa, Great Britain faced a restless Boer population that attracted the sympathies of a belligerent Germany. The crisis resulted in trans-Atlantic declarations of friendship, the call for Anglo-Saxon unity, and speculation about an Anglo-American alliance. The Venezuela crisis also illustrated that North America would be the theatre for much of the Anglo-American rapprochement. Separated by three thousand miles of ocean, Anglo-American relations would play themselves out where their interests came into conflict and their territory came into contact. The corresponding Canadian-American rapprochement would be more problematic, facing as it did a long history of American anglophobia, Canadian Loyalism, and a new assertion of the Monroe Doctrine.

Many English-speaking North Americans adapted Anglo-Saxon ideology to the new reality of American hegemony on the continent and Anglo-American relations. Through the prism of Anglo-Saxonism, Americans came to view Canada as a racial exception to the foreign nations referred to in the Monroe Doctrine. Not only did Americans stop viewing Canada as a threat; they actually viewed the Dominion – a fellow Anglo-Saxon state – as a good and trusted friend on the republic's northern frontier. Moreover, Americans began distinguishing Canada from Great Britain and the Empire. No longer did Americans view Canada as an outpost of a hostile European power. Instead, the Venezuela crisis and the ensuing rapprochement led Americans to see Canada as a distinct, Anglo-Saxon nation with which the United States could share the continent in harmony. Indeed, many Americans stressed the essential unity of the United States and Canada. In an era of aggressive American hemispherism and expansion, Americans used racial rhetoric to adapt to the Anglo-American rapprochement, altering their view of Canada in fundamental ways.

American assertions of the Monroe Doctrine, the republic's rise to great power status, and the Anglo-American rapprochement also challenged Canadians' perception of their place on the continent. Although English Canadians initially bristled at American aggressiveness during the Venezuela crisis, and responded with knee-jerk avowals of loyalty, British acquiescence forced Canadians to accommodate themselves to the new international reality. While some English Canadians responded with shrill anti-Americanism or intense imperialism, many others viewed America's new role as world power as being of benefit to Canada.

English Canadians viewed Americans as "cousins" within a larger Anglo-Saxon family, and welcomed the rapprochement as a "family reunion" of the Anglo-Saxon race. Canadian journalists and politicians took their cue in part from their British counterparts who filled the pages of the British press with calls for Anglo-Saxon amity. Yet English Canadians did not merely ape the British. Instead, Canadians felt their country had a special role to play as a fellow Anglo-Saxon state in fostering Anglo-American friendship. Like their American cousins, English Canadians used the common rhetoric of Anglo-Saxonism to alter their view of their nation, their neighbour, and their shared continent.

THE VENEZUELA CRISIS AND AMERICAN "HEMISPHERISM"

The dispute over the boundary between Venezuela and British Guiana dated from the 1840s. As would occur in the Alaska boundary crisis between Canada and the United States a few years later, the discovery of gold in the disputed region in 1886 caused a rupture between the British and Venezuelan governments. The crisis simmered without resolution for several years until the Venezuelan government hired the former American minister to Caracas, William Scruggs, to influence American opinion in Venezuela's favour. In October 1894, Scruggs published a small pamphlet, "British Aggressions in Venezuela, or the Monroe Doctrine on Trial." The pamphlet was widely read by leading Americans, and in early 1895, the Senate and the House of Representatives unanimously passed a joint resolution recommending arbitration to settle the boundary dispute. Although Democratic president Grover Cleveland signed the resolution, the Republicans sought to use the Venezuela issue as a weapon in their continued attack on the President's foreign policy.

Leading the attack on the President was Massachusetts Senator Henry Cabot Lodge. In March Lodge wrote an article for *Forum* magazine entitled "Our Blundering Foreign Policy." Lodge took up the popular, and politically beneficial, undertaking of assailing Cleveland's rejection of the annexation of Hawaii. Yet Lodge also revealed a number of ideas that would guide him and other proponents of the "large policy" of American expansionism. Lodge did not simply outline a program of overseas annexation and expansion. Instead, he argued in favour of what has been called "hemispherism." Lodge asserted American hegemony over the western hemisphere, and especially North America. This territory constituted, in Lodge's words, "our citadel of our power and greatness as a nation." Pacific islands such as Samoa and Hawaii he referred to as the "outworks essential to the defense of that citadel." Great Britain held a central place in this formulation of America's future. By failing to annex Hawaii, the United States was "throwing the Hawaiian people into the arms of England." Lodge extended his fear of the British Empire to its outpost in North America, Canada. "The Government of Canada is hostile to us," Lodge wrote. "They lose no opportunity of injuring us." According to Lodge the United States should give Canada no access to American markets, unless the dominion "unite with us either entirely or as to tariffs." Indeed, Lodge asserted that "from the Rio Grande to the Arctic Ocean there should be but one flag and one country."[4] The annexation of extraterritorial possessions, the construction of an isthmian canal, and the building of a large navy, then, would only serve to ensure American hegemony in this hemisphere. This transitional stage between insularity and expansionism was, as the historian William Widenor says, "an important landmark on the road to an imperial future."[5]

Only a few months later, in June 1895, Lodge published an article in *The North American Review* entitled "England, Venezuela, and the Monroe Doctrine." In this article Lodge repeated a number of themes from his *Forum* article of March, and presented the Venezuela boundary crisis as a test case of American hegemony in the hemisphere. If Great Britain were allowed to take even a square foot of territory in Venezuela, Lodge argued, "there is nothing to prevent her taking the whole of Venezuela or any other South American state." If the United States allowed Great Britain a free hand in the crisis, the republic would become increasingly "hemmed in by British naval posts and European dependencies." Taking up the theme of Scruggs's pamphlet and of the American press since early that year, Lodge sought to make the hallowed Monroe Doctrine the handmaid of American hemispherism. "The American people are not ready to abandon the Monroe doctrine," Lodge declared, "or give up their rightful supremacy in the Western Hemisphere." Asserting the Monroe Doctrine now would end British "territorial aggressions" and prevent any future European encroachments. "The supremacy of the Monroe doctrine should be established and at once," the senator concluded, "peaceably if we can, forcibly if we must."[6] Lodge's two articles illustrated that America's bold assertion of the Monroe Doctrine and American hemispheric hegemony during the Venezuela Crisis did not materialize out of thin air, or mere party politics, but occurred within a firm ideological context and broader agenda of strengthening America's hand on the world stage.

With Lodge and the Republicans threatening to make a firm stance on Venezuela a strong position from which to attack the Democrats, President Cleveland and his new Secretary of State, Richard Olney, set out to prove themselves equally stout defenders of the Monroe Doctrine.[7]

In July Olney, possibly influenced by Lodge's June *Review* article, sent a message to the British government via the American ambassador in London, Thomas Bayard.[8] The message, which has since been criticized by historians as tactless and historically inaccurate, remains a remarkable example of the ideological underpinnings of American foreign policy on the eve of attaining great power status. Olney's note, which was heartily approved by Cleveland, boldly asserted American hegemony in the western hemisphere and declared "unnatural" any connection between a European power and an American nation. As justification of this policy, Olney offered a wider interpretation of the Monroe Doctrine. While Lord Salisbury and some American political scientists of the day criticized Olney's misinterpretation of the 1823 doctrine, Olney simply dusted off an old argument and adapted it to America's new position at the end of the nineteenth century. As President Cleveland stated in justifying the invocation of the Monroe Doctrine in his December 17 message to Congress, the doctrine "was intended to apply to every stage of our national life, and can not become obsolete while our Republic endures." Indeed, American foreign policy makers tinkered with the Monroe Doctrine as the ideological underpinnings of a continually changing American policy well into the next century.[9]

Taken together, Lodge and Olney's 1895 writings on American hemispherism offer a strikingly unified view of American foreign policy at the end of the nineteenth century. Moreover, both writers made perfectly clear that Canada was no exception to American hegemony in the hemisphere. In Lodge's March *Forum* article he had asserted that "from the Rio Grande to the Arctic Ocean there should be but one country." Race figured prominently in this vision of American greatness, including the old theory that white men were poorly adapted for southern climes. The United States did not seek to extend American territory to the south, Lodge wrote, "for neither the population nor the lands of Central or South America would be desirable additions to the United States." These same factors, however, offered no barrier to the absorption of Canada. "Neither race nor climate forbids this extension," Lodge stated, "and every consideration of national growth and national welfare demands it."[10]

Olney, too, included Canada under the umbrella of the Monroe Doctrine and hemispheric hegemony. Not only did Olney declare the connection between Canada and Great Britain to be "unnatural and inexpedient," but he asserted that the people of the western hemisphere shared naturally inherent interests: "The states of America, South as well as North, by geographical proximity, by natural sympathy, by similarity of governmental constitutions, are friends and allies, commercially and politically, of the United States. To allow the subjugation of any of them by an European power is, of course, to completely reverse that situation and signifies the loss of the advantages incident to their natural relations to us." Of course, by no stretch of the imagination could the Latin American republics be called "allies" of the United States. Nor could Olney truly claim that his nation and those to the south were linked by "natural sympathy" or a "similarity of governmental institutions." Yet as Dexter Perkins has rightly pointed out, Olney was not penning a "historical tract," but a rhetorical text meant to pressure the British and win favour at home. "To-day the United States is practically sovereign on this continent," Olney affirmed in one of the more striking passages of his "diplomatic" note, "and its fiat is law upon the subjects to which it confines its interposition." Finally, Olney flexed the newly developed muscles of American power, stating that America's "infinite resources combined with its isolated position render it master of the situation and practically invulnerable as against any or all other powers." The United States stood ready to defend its hegemony in the western hemisphere against all comers.

Together, Lodge and Olney had resurrected the Monroe Doctrine and put it into the service of American hemispherism. Moreover, both men explicitly included Canada within America's sphere of power. Before Cleveland made the message public in December, its contents provoked strong reactions from those who read it. Clearly Cleveland supported the bold assertion of the Monroe Doctrine. Upon reading a draft of Olney's note to the British, Cleveland wrote to his Secretary of State a glowing endorsement: "I read your deliverance on Venezuelan affairs the day you left it with me. Its [sic] the best thing of the kind I have ever read and it leads to a conclusion that one cannot escape if he tries – that is if there is anything of the Monroe Doctrine at all. You show there is a great deal of that and place it I think on better and more defensible ground than any of your predecessors – *or mine.*"[11]

When Bayard expressed his misgivings about the belligerent tone of the note, Cleveland expressed incredulity and affirmed his support of the Monroe Doctrine. "I am entirely clear that the Doctrine is not obsolete," Cleveland wrote, "and it should be defended and maintained for its value and importance to our government and welfare, and that its defense and maintenance involve its application when a state of facts arises requiring it."[12] Long before Cleveland made the message public, the President, his Secretary of State, and the administration's harshest critic were in near-total agreement concerning the Monroe Doctrine's sanction of American hegemony in the western hemisphere.

CANADA AND THE MONROE DOCTRINE

When Prime Minister Salisbury received Olney's note, he regarded it as a low priority and delayed replying. When he did reply, the British Prime Minister wrote with a lecturing and dismissive tone that grated on Cleveland and Olney. Salisbury dismissed Olney's reference to the Monroe Doctrine, stating it had no standing in international law and, furthermore, had "no relation to the state of things in which we live at the present day." Salisbury also took umbrage at Olney's labelling as "unnatural" the connection between an American nation and a European power. "The necessary meaning of these words is that the union between Great Britain and Canada," Salisbury stated "[is] 'inexpedient and unnatural.'" Salisbury informed the United States government that London did not understand America's interest in a border dispute miles from American territory, and that the British government would not submit the problem to arbitration. Salisbury replied to Olney's undiplomatic note with an equal lack of diplomatic tact. Moreover, by his complete refusal of arbitration, without leaving open the possibility of future discussion on the matter, Salisbury placed the President in an embarrassing and politically untenable position. To save face with the Republicans, Cleveland was left with only one choice. He took the matter to the country.

On 17 December 1895, Cleveland sent to the Congress a message detailing the American demand, and British refusal, of arbitration on the Venezuela boundary. The President outlined Salisbury's objection to American interference and the British Prime Minister's dismissal of the Monroe Doctrine. Cleveland ended his message by asking Congress to make an appropriation for an American commission to investigate the Venezuela boundary dispute. Upon the report of the commission, Cleveland said, "it will in my opinion be the duty of the United States to resist by every means in its power as a willful aggression upon its rights and interests the appropriation by Great Britain of any lands or the exercise of governmental jurisdiction over any territory we have determined of right belongs to Venezuela."[13] When Cleveland finished reading the message, raucous applause broke out in both the House and the Senate. The next day the House unanimously approved a bill to establish a commission to investigate the Venezuela boundary.

Although at the time many American historians and political scientists firmly stated that Cleveland had misinterpreted or misapplied the Monroe Doctrine, the great bulk of the American press and public supported the president.[14] As the *Atlantic Monthly* told its readers concerning the president's message, "whether he was historically correct has ceased to be a matter of practical importance. The American people ... have accepted and approved his understanding of the doctrine. It is the Monroe Doctrine now, whether it was so before or not."[15] Certainly Cleveland and Olney's view of American power in the hemisphere coincided with that of the advocates of a "vigorous" foreign policy. Theodore Roosevelt wrote his friend Henry Cabot Lodge and declared himself "very much pleased with the President's or rather with Olney's message" and called it a "vindication" of Lodge's position.[16] Henry Adams wrote to Olney the night of Cleveland's message to Congress, and said, "I pray you to be assured that your message of this day commands my strongest possible approval and support."[17] The press echoed the president in declaring the United States willing to fight over apparent British encroachment in the western hemisphere. The Atlanta *Constitution* printed a cartoon of Uncle Sam and Lord Salisbury facing off across the Venezuela boundary. "Salisbury, we've had fooling enough," Uncle Sam says to the portly prime minister, "If you cross that line I'll shoot." Behind Uncle Sam the ghostly apparition of James Monroe urges, "Go it, Samuel, my boy."[18] The New Orleans *Times-Democrat* asserted that "Great Britain must accept the Monroe doctrine in regard to all American territory."[19] The New York *Tribune* also approved of the President's interpretation of the Monroe Doctrine, calling it, "simply a notice to all monarchies to keep off the grass," while the United States was "the big policeman with a club standing by to enforce the notice."[20] The *New York Times* printed a ditty entitled "John Bull's Cheap-Jack Show," depicting Great Britain as a carnival hustler, grabbing land in the hemisphere through sleight-of-hand. "Your tent, cheap lion, and show must go," the *Times* said. "The law for thieves is rather rough/And tough, you know."[21] Lord Salisbury had made a grievous mistake in misjudging the feeling of the American people and the Cleveland administration. The President, his political opponents, and the national press presented to the British a near-uniform front in the American assertion of hemispheric hegemony.

The outburst of nationalism and jingoism should not be dismissed as a mere political stunt, for it represented a key way-station on the road to American great-power status. A unanimous assertion of American hegemony in the hemisphere necessarily preceded the Spanish-American War and the annexation of Hawaii, Guam, Puerto Rico, and the Philippines. Moreover, Americans did not limit the application of the Monroe Doctrine to Latin America only. Far from viewing Canada as an exception to the doctrine, Americans explicitly included Canada in both the talk of a possible war and in considering America's rights in the hemisphere. American newspapers referred to Canada as a "hostage" to British good behaviour, as the American army could overrun the Dominion in a matter of days. "It is not likely," the Atlanta

Constitution declared, "that England would be willing to exchange Canada for any two or three South American Republics."[22] The *New York Times* printed General Miles's comment that he needed only ten days of preparation before taking Canada, "and intimated that he would do so." General Lew Wallace of Indiana welcomed a scrap with England, for at its conclusion, "we would own everything on this side of the globe from the Gulf of Mexico to the north pole." The *Times* also drew a connection between the Venezuela boundary dispute and the Anglo-Canadian dispute over the Alaska boundary. "Venezuela to-day," an editorial stated, "Alaska tomorrow. It is well to remember that an English boundary line always extends just far enough to include gold fields ... There are gold fields in Alaska."[23] Canada, then, figured very prominently in the American conception of the hemisphere. The Dominion represented the outpost of a hostile European power, a potential battlefield in the fight for hemispheric hegemony, and the potential source of future conflict between the United States and Great Britain. The dispute over British Guiana gave new prominence to the destiny of the Anglo-Saxon territory to the north, in which Americans were ultimately much more interested.

One leading American who made clear his view of the connection between American hemispherism and the place of Canada was the editor of the *American Monthly Review of Reviews*, Dr. Albert Shaw.[24] Shaw, a native of Ohio and a graduate of Iowa College, had received his doctorate in political science from Johns Hopkins University. William T. Stead, the founder and editor of the British journal *Review of Reviews,* chose Shaw as editor for an American version of the same journal in 1891. Shaw was a prominent Republican and a frequent correspondent of many leading politicians, namely his good friend Senator Albert Beveridge.[25] Most revealing, however, were his letters to his friend and employer, Stead. In writing to Stead, Shaw revealed himself to be an American nationalist, who argued strongly in favour of American hegemony in the hemisphere. His view closely paralleled that of Henry Cabot Lodge in seeing British possessions in North America both as unnatural and as a threat to American interests. As with Lodge, such an attitude can not be dismissed simply as anglophobia. After all, Shaw penned his letters to his British employer. Rather, Shaw regarded American hegemony in the hemisphere as necessary to American interests.

While Americans waited to hear from the British government prior to Cleveland's December 1895 message, Shaw's employer, William Stead, made a public stand in his British journal declaring Great Britain an "American power" due to British possessions in the hemisphere. Canada, said Stead, had as much a right to grow and prosper as any

American republic. To hemispherists such as Shaw and Lodge, such an assertion was anathema to their ideas of American hegemony, and Shaw made clear his attitude in a letter to Stead.

The Dominion of Canada may be a sovereign member of the family of nations whenever the people of the Dominion of Canada so ordain. But the present link between the Government at Ottawa and the Government at London does not serve to make the United Kingdom of Great Britain and Ireland an American power. You claim for British Guiana or Canada as much a right to grow and extend in this Hemisphere as any of our full-fledged American Governments. But our contention is that Canada and British Guiana have no right to extend their domain in the Western hemisphere by getting a big European power to put its military force back of their feeble colonial pretensions.[26]

Shaw clearly differentiated between the immature colonial possessions of Great Britain and the "full-fledged" nations of the western hemisphere. While Canadians viewed the sobriquet of "Dominion" as conferring autonomous status, Americans found the title a grating reminder of Canada's connection to Great Britain. Indeed, only when Canada no longer tied itself to the Empire would the Dominion become a "sovereign member of the family of nations." Shaw repeated this assertion in the December 1895 issue of his journal. If the Dominion would sever its connection to Great Britain, "Canada may become an 'American power.'" Yet the imperial connection did not make Great Britain an American power, Shaw stated, "any more than those relations make Canada a European power." Moreover, Shaw confirmed Olney's view of the unnatural connection between American and European states. "To any right-minded American," Shaw wrote, "this whole system of European colonies within the bounds of the Western hemisphere is a strife-inciting and a vexatious thing."[27] On the eve of the Venezuela crisis Shaw stated a primary facet of American hemispherism at the turn of the century: Not only should American policy prevent any European encroachments in the western hemisphere, but it should challenge the very idea of colonial possession in the American hemisphere. Primary among those possessions was the Dominion of Canada.

A few weeks later, following the Jameson Raid, the Kaiser's telegram, and British acquiescence in the Venezuela affair, Shaw wrote again to the British writer and editor. Shaw widened his discourse into a discussion of the future of all Anglo-Saxon nations. Once again Canada figured prominently in his reasoning. Shaw told Stead that his attitude toward Canada and the other Dominions reflected "no malevolent design against the British Empire." Instead, Shaw wrote, "I merely hold to the view, which, as I always understood, was your own view;

namely, that British North America would never reach a position of stable or political equilibrium until federated with the United States." For Shaw such a federation would be the natural outcome of the Dominions attaining true autonomy, while all Anglo-Saxon nations would continue to be drawn toward each other by the bonds of blood. While Canada's continued unnatural attachment to England served to divide the United States from Great Britain, the true independence of all the English-speaking nations would bind all together into a single family. Shaw wrote at length on this subject:

I believe as strongly as all the facts will justify in the great destiny of the English-speaking areas, and in the value of all the real binds which hold the American, the Australian, the Canadian and the South African alike in close and dear relationship with England, the common mother of us all. But as I look to the future, it seems to me perfectly sure that Canada, Australia and South Africa, let us say twenty, thirty or forty years hence, would grow faster and amount to more if they were independent countries, while their political independence would make such an alliance between England, the United States and these other English-speaking regions as would amount virtually to one federation.

Shaw's attitudes appeared formed much more by racial ideology than by anglophobia. Using the familial terms of Anglo-Saxonism he referred to England as "the mother of us all." Moreover, he looked forward to the day when all English-speaking nations would form a single federation, with political independence for the Anglo-Saxon dominions a necessary prerequisite.

Shaw's vision of an Anglo-Saxon federation was a common one at the turn of the century. Many men in the United States, Great Britain, and the English-speaking dominions held the notion that loyalty to the race existed on a higher plane than loyalty to one's nation. Such a union would serve to ensure the peace of the world and the onward march of civilization and Christianity. The idea took hold among many Social Gospellers (Christian reformers who preached the brotherhood of man) who gave turn-of-the-century Anglo-Saxonism a millennial quality. With the dawn of a new and uncertain century, many believed that English-speaking people across the globe must band together to continue God's mission. Shaw's correspondent, William Stead, shared many of the same ideas. In 1902 he published a volume entitled *The Americanization of the World; or, the Trend of the Twentieth Century*. Stead warned his fellow countrymen that the empire risked losing its place among the great powers of the world. "Unless we can succeed in merging the British Empire in the English-speaking United States of the World," Stead wrote, "the disintegration of our Empire, and our definite displacement from the position of commercial and financial primacy is only a matter of time, and probably a very short time." Stead made clear that racial affinity constituted the foundation of such a federation: "If, on the other hand, we substitute for the insular patriotism of our nation the broader patriotism of the race, and frankly throw in our lot with the Americans to realize the great ideal of Race Union, we shall enter upon a new era of power and prosperity the like of which the race has never realized since the world began." Stead cited the emergence of the United States as "the greatest of world-Powers" as the greatest phenomenon of the time. Instead of constituting a threat to the empire, America's new status actually created new and greater opportunities for the British. Together, the United States and Great Britain would form a unified entity with unlimited power for good. "We shall continue on a wider scale," Stead wrote, "to carry out the providential mission which has been entrusted to the English-speaking Race, whose United States will be able to secure the peace of the World."[28] For Stead, a powerful Anglo-Saxon United States indicated a means by which Great Britain might maintain its status among nations. By utilizing Anglo-Saxon rhetoric, a possible threat became a natural benefit.

Just as the British used Anglo-Saxonism to alter their ideas of the United States, so, too, did many Americans employ Anglo-Saxon rhetoric to alter their view of Great Britain and Canada. Shaw conveyed to Stead his understanding of their basic agreement upon the Anglo-Saxon apportionment of the world: "When the "Review" was founded, and you and I proceeded to apportion the earth, you assured me, as I understood it, that so far as Anglo-Saxon institutions were concerned you fully conceded to the United States the priority and the essential hegemony of the Western Hemisphere. You have more than once assured me personally, and if I mistake not have said in print, that you would welcome the day when the North American republic extended from the Arctic ocean to the isthmus of Panama."[29] Few British Anglo-Saxonists sought American rule over Canada, however, and few Americans wished to extend American rule over tropical climes assumed to be inhabitable by white men. Yet Stead and Shaw, among others, would agree that American hegemony in the western hemisphere would protect British interests and "Anglo-Saxon institutions." Shaw employed the Anglo-American journal as an apt metaphor for the Anglo-American rapprochement, "apportioning" the earth between the two great Anglo-Saxon powers.

CANADA'S REACTION

Just as Americans reacted to the Venezuela crisis with the expected outburst of anglophobia, English Canadians responded with traditional exclamations of Loyalism. Canadians declared their unbending loyalty to Great Britain, vowed to defend against any attack by the United States, and rejected President Cleveland's extension of the Monroe Doctrine. Yet only the most Tory of the Loyalist press took an explicit anti-American stand. Of these the Halifax *Herald* was most virulent. In an editorial on December 21, the paper derided the citizens of the United States. "The American people send missionaries to the heathen," the *Herald* observed, "but we venture to assert that there are more people who have all the vices of the heathen in the United States than in any country on the face of the globe."[30] Most of the English-Canadian press took a more moderate tone. Canadian editors urged their readers to take no offensive action that might lead to hostilities. Certainly this may have resulted from Canadians realizing their untenable position in the event of an Anglo-American war. Yet the press also stressed Canadian-American ties and the unity of the Anglo-Saxon family. Such expressions of Anglo-Saxon rhetoric constituted an important step in Canadians accepting an Anglo-American rapprochement based upon American hegemony in the hemisphere, and envisioning a common destiny for the Anglo-Saxon family of nations.

An influential proponent of Canadian moderation during the Venezuela crisis was the Very Reverend George M. Grant, the Principal of Queen's University and the editor of *Queen's Quarterly*.[31] Grant had long been an advocate of Anglo-American solidarity. Indeed, Grant believed that Canada stood at the nexus of the British and American peoples, and had a "divine mission" to be a "living link" between the two great Anglo-Saxon nations. As early as 1887 Grant had proclaimed that Canada "was American because the atmosphere, climate and other physical conditions under which people grew up, determined to a great extent their character and place in history. But it was also British, because we have inherited from Britain not merely that which the United States has inherited, language, literature, laws and blood, and the fundamental principles of civil and religious life, but also continuity of national life."[32] Throughout the Anglo-American rapprochement Grant would interpret Canada's mission via such Anglo-Saxon rhetoric. Grant advocated Canada acting as a "linch-pin" between the United States and Great Britain based upon Canada's unique British-American heritage. Although most historians place the date of the linch-pin theory of a Canadian national mission after World War I, clearly an Anglo-Saxon version of the theory existed some time before.

Grant received much attention during the Venezuela crisis, with his words and writings appearing not only in *Queen's Quarterly*, but also in *Canadian Magazine* and *Methodist Magazine*, both of which supported the Social Gospel. The *Free Press* reprinted a sermon of Grant's in which he said that Great Britain should "put up with almost everything from the United States short of a direct attack."[33] In the January issue of *Queen's Quarterly* Grant repeated his plea that "no provocation must come from our side."[34] Grant, a believer in the Social Gospel and a hater of war, obviously sought to err on the side of caution in preventing a conflict with the United States. And he was happy with the results. In the February edition of *Methodist Magazine* Grant noted that Canadians had responded to American jingoism with great moderation. "There was no outcry," Grant observed, "no boasting; no word indicating hatred of our neighbours; no retorts."[35] Canadians dismissed American spread-eagle-ism as mere political manoeuvring and went quietly about their business.

Like many other Canadians, Grant declared that Great Britain, Canada, and the United States were inextricably linked together and would not go to war. A number of papers pointed to the great volume of trade.[36] Much more significantly, the English-Canadian press affirmed the impossibility of war between the United States and the British Empire because of the bonds of race. In doing so, journalists and editors took their lead in part from the British press. After President Cleveland's message, the New York *World* cabled leading British men in politics, the royal family, and religion to comment upon the prospect of war between the United States and Great Britain. Their answers had an immediate calming effect in the United States, and set the tone for much of the Canadian press. Not surprisingly, the British decried the possibility of war because of, as the Prince of Wales said, the "warm feeling of friendship which has existed" between the two countries for so long. Yet the British went beyond merely wishing for peace; they employed Anglo-Saxon rhetoric that underscored the natural bonds between the United States and Great Britain and their common mission in the world. Lord Rosebery, the Liberal leader, said such a war would be "the greatest crime on record" especially as the "two mighty nations of the Anglo-Saxon race" appeared ready to "overshadow the world in [the] best interests of Christianity and civilization." The leading men of English religion especially underscored the familial relations between Great Britain and the United States and the two nations' civilizing mission. "Our common humanity and our Christianity would sternly condemn a fratricidal war," Cardinal Vaughn said. "We are too closely bound to America by blood, respect and affection." The Bishop of Manchester stated that an Anglo-American conflict would be "a civil war" and a "crime against civilization." Finally, the Archbishop of Armagh called such a war "unnatural strife between mother and daughter, the leaders in [the] progress [of] Christianity and civilization."[37] Such public overtures from leading British figures might be said to have been the opening movements toward the Anglo-American rapprochement, coming even before the turmoil in South Africa and the Kaiser's menacing telegram. While such Anglo-Saxon rhetoric did not, in the end, cause the rapprochement, it certainly provided the ideological justification. Moreover, when the British spoke of "fratricidal war" and the progress of "Christianity and civilization," they drew upon language and ideas common throughout the North Atlantic triangle.

The English-Canadian press echoed the Anglo-Saxon sentiments of the British. No American or Englishman would go to war, said the *Free Press*, "especially over such a wretched question as this Venezuelan boundary."[38] "Settle It," a headline in the same paper demanded, for the present crisis did not merit risking "the goodwill of the United States." The citizens of the United States and Great Britain were essentially one people, and the paper looked toward the day when "the Anglo-American people will be masters of the world."[39] For Principal Grant, too, the racial unity of the Anglo-American people prohibited any "fratricidal strife."[40] The Americans and the British were not about to "slaughter kinsfolk," Grant stated in a December sermon. In *Queen's Quarterly* he wondered at the "mad fever for war" in the United States. Such an outburst "on the part of a Parisian mob" would be understandable, but not "on the part of English-speaking men, of their race, religion and business habits." Despite President Cleveland's strongly worded message, Grant did not believe that the American president would allow a war and thus "sacrifice civilization."[41] *Canadian Magazine* noted Grant's comments in the *Week* where he stated, "I believe that the child is born who will see a moral reunion of the English-speaking race, commercial union based on free trade, a common tribunal and a common citizenship, if not more." Moreover, the journal called Grant "one of Canada's representative men" whose views reflected "the hopes of many Canadians."[42]

Many periodicals repeated the idea of the essential unity of all English-speaking men. The Toronto *Globe* even quoted the French-Canadian Liberal leader, Wilfrid Laurier, who said, "The best feeling in Canada and in the United States to-day would regard a war between Great Britain and the United States as being as fratricidal as that in which thirty years ago were shed pools of blood."[43] Although clearly not Anglo-Saxon himself, Laurier was a master of rhetoric and would often employ Anglo-Saxonist language to underscore his desire for Canadian-American harmony. The *Globe* also quoted the British politician Arthur Balfour who stated that "the British people have a pride of race which embraced every English-speaking community in the world, and an Anglo-Saxon patriotism." Indeed the *Globe*, the leading organ of the Liberal party in Canada and the paper with the widest circulation in Ontario, utilized much Anglo-Saxon rhetoric in its response to the Venezuela crisis. Moreover, the paper noted the affinity between Canadians and Americans, and viewed the future of the continent in racial terms: "There is surely room on this North American continent for the peaceful development of two nations of English-speaking people, and peaceful development is the only ambition of the people of Canada."[44]

Only days later the *Globe* expanded upon the theme of Anglo-American affinity, expressing shock that Americans would ponder "war with a country to whom they are everlastingly bound by blood, religion and literature." "It is inexplicable," an editorial entitled "The War Cloud" stated, since "Americans speak the English tongue, welcome English capital, read English books, witness English plays, listen to English lecturers, and buy and sell more with England than with any other country in the world."[45] On Christmas Eve, a week after President Cleveland's message to Congress, the paper included interviews with some of Ontario's leading men. Some, such as O.A. Howland, former mayor of Toronto and a member of the provincial legislature, urged Canada to make the necessary preparations for a conflict. Yet he also cautioned Canadians to refrain from "unnecessary language" that would excite the situation and lead, not merely to war, but to the "ruin of civilization." The paper noted that most of those who had expressed opinions believed that there would be no war "between the two nations so closely allied to each other." Included among these was Dr. Withrow, editor of the *Methodist Magazine*. "What is to be feared worse than war with all its bloodshed and barbarism," he wrote to the *Globe*, "is kindling the fires of hate between kindred people and creating a bitter feud which would outlast a century." The paper's editorial page continued to address the crisis and in an editorial entitled "Spurious Patriotism" sought the reasons behind American anglophobia, which caused Americans to be "ill-disposed towards their kindred on the other side of the Atlantic."[46]

The theme of an Anglo-American war being a war between kin was a common one, and taken up by other periodicals. The Montreal *Daily Star* had initially responded to the crisis with avowals of loyalty and even offered to outfit a regiment and support the men's families while they were in the field. Yet almost simultaneously the paper offered a moderate tone, praying that "western civilization may be spared this unnatural scourge."[47] "No Canadian wishes a war with the United States," the paper stated. "It would present the spectacle of the two leading columns of civilization pausing in the march forward to fire upon each other."[48] The *Canadian Magazine* printed a poem entitled "Fratricide" by a London, Ontario, author: "War with our brother? –

sooner let our hands/Fall paralyzed forever by our sides;/Forbid it, Heaven, that these fair fields run red/With blood we deem no other than our own."[49] While the English-Canadian press initially responded to President Cleveland's message with outrage and calls for the preparation of Canada's defence, within a week the newspapers' tone had become much more moderate. While Canadians would do their duty and stand by the Mother Country, they abhorred the thought of a "fratricidal" war with the United States. With the crisis coming only thirty years after the end of the American Civil War, many English-Canadian writers made the implicit point that an Anglo-American war would really be an Anglo-Saxon war. A war with the United States, as the above poem stated, would be a "war with our brother."

During the Venezuela crisis, many Canadian public men studiously avoided making statements in order to avoid complicating Anglo-American relations. Sir Charles Tupper's comment on December 27 that no "fratricidal war" would occur between "the two great Anglo-Saxon nations of the world" was a rare one.[50] The Christmas holiday may have also played a role in Canadian politicians' initial lack of comment. Such reticence proved wise since by the time the House of Commons reconvened in February, the situation had altered significantly. Tensions in the Cape had reached a new high with Colonel Jameson's botched coup attempt on December 29, and the entire British Empire bristled upon hearing of the German Kaiser's congratulatory telegram to President Paul Kruger. The Kaiser had applauded the Boers' ability to put down the rebellion "without appealing to the aid of friendly powers." Now England found itself faced with international crises on two fronts. Unwilling to risk a serious breach with the Americans while facing possible German interference in the Cape, Lord Salisbury agreed to put the Venezuela boundary question to arbitration. Moreover, leading British politicians, writers, and even the Prince of Wales, filled the pages of the British press with declarations of goodwill and affection for their American cousins. Threatened by European rivals, the British essentially conceded American hegemony in the western hemisphere, viewing American preservation of the status quo in the Americas as a benefit to imperial policy.

Such was the situation when the Canadian House of Commons reconvened and entered a motion addressing the recent crises with both the United States and Germany. The motion consisted of two parts. The first part assured the imperial government of Canada's "unalterable loyalty and devotion to the British Throne and constitution," and promised that in the case of conflict, "from no other part of the Empire than the Dominion of Canada would more substantial sacrifices attest the determination of Her Majesty's subjects to maintain unimpaired the integrity and inviolate the honour of Her Majesty's Empire." Such a declaration of loyalty offered little that was new, stating only that Canada stood with the Mother Country no matter what crisis arose. While slightly belligerent in tone, the object of the motion appeared to be Germany and not the United States, since the second part of the motion expressed the "desire of the people of Canada to maintain the most friendly relations with their kinsmen of the United States." Simultaneously expressing loyalty to the Empire and friendship with the United States, the Commons motion illustrated that Canadian imperialism did not always mean anti-Americanism. At the end of the nineteenth century, loyalty to the Empire and identity of interest with the United States were not mutually exclusive, but actually co-existed quite easily. Indeed, many Canadians viewed friendly and profitable Canadian-American relations as serving imperial needs. The ability of English Canadians to identify simultaneously with their British and American cousins was reflected by the motion's reference to Canadians' "kinsmen of the United States." Although openly discussing war with the republic only a few weeks earlier, Canadians quickly reconciled themselves to the reality of the rapprochement through the medium of race.

One after the other Canadian Members of Parliament stood to support the motion and proclaim friendship with the United States. In part many of these men may have simply been copying what their British counterparts had been saying publicly for weeks. Yet the Canadian MPs did more than merely ape British politicians. Instead, through their support of the motion the Canadian MPs illustrated that they possessed a unique conception not only of the empire's relations with the United States, but also of the role that Canada could play in bringing about Anglo-American goodwill. Louis Davies of Prince Edward Island expressed "horror" at the possibility of Canada being threatened by "her own kin." "Commercially and socially," Davies said, "our relations are intertwined and united, and are becoming yearly more so." Davies pointed out the essential unity of the British and American peoples: "Largely speaking the same language, largely drawing inspiration from the same sources, and worshipping at the same altars, I believe in the sentiment ... that, after all, blood is thicker than water, and that the man or the nation who precipitates a war and all its horrors between these two great English-speaking nations, would be committing a crime against humanity."[51] George Cockburn repeated Davies's point about the common Anglo-Saxon heritage of Canada and the United States. "They are no doubt," Cockburn said, "peoples whose national roots go down deep into the same past as our own; we draw from the fountain the same literature; we have the same science, the same arts, the same language; we worship ... at the same altars; our institutions are to a great extent similar."[52] With such characteristics transcending national boundaries, Cockburn suggested that Canadians "rise to the conception of a higher patriotism," one above the "domestic patriotism" of "the Canadian for Canada" or the "Imperial patriotism for the Imperial Empire." Cockburn painted a picture of the English Canadian as having an ever-increasing circle of loyalty, first to Canada, then to the greater empire, then to the even greater Anglo-Saxon race. Anglo-Saxonism allowed Canadians to have sympathy and even identify with Americans without undermining their loyalty to either the nation or the empire.

After Cockburn, Sir Richard Cartwright continued the discussion of Anglo-Canadian-American relations using the racial theme. Cartwright noted the "tremendous consequences" of a "collision unhappily ever occurring between the two great Anglo-Saxon nations." He stated that "such a war would be a fratricidal war," and evidently meant it both figuratively and literally. "[T]here is scarcely one family in ten in the Dominion of Canada," Cartwright pronounced, "which has not a son or a brother or a near relative in some part of the United States." The cultural, business, and familial ties between the two nations were so great in fact, that, according to Cartwright, "Canada and the Northern States, at any rate, are more closely knit together in a great many ways than the North and the South were before the war."[53] Cartwright made clear that he viewed the recent Venezuela crisis in racial terms, expressing disbelief, as many Canadians and Americans had, that Great Britain and the United States would go to war over something so trivial as a few acres of South American swamp. "I think it would be a thousand pities," Cartwright said, "were a single drop of Anglo-Saxon blood shed for the sake of all those murderous man-monkeys in South America." For Cartwright, one of the Liberal leaders and a future Cabinet member, viewing Anglo-American relations through the prism of race made the choice for Canada clear. Canadians had much more in common with Americans and their "Anglo-Saxon blood" than with the "murderous man-monkeys" of British Guiana.

Cartwright's comments about Anglo-Saxon unity were coloured by the international situation. The United States had asserted hegemony in the western hemisphere, and Great Britain, threatened with belligerent Boers and a sabre-rattling Kaiser, acquiesced. The speeches of the Canadian politicians, then, moved logically from affirmations of friendship with the United States and the unity of the English-speaking world, to the possibility of Anglo-American cooperation. The simultaneous Venezuela and South Africa crises underscored for many the isolation of the British Empire amidst numerous rivals. An alliance between the United States and the British Empire would not only protect Canada, but would constitute a "family reunion" among the Anglo-Saxon nations. Made highly aware of the Empire's precarious position by recent events, many of the Canadian MPs showed themselves eager to foster such an alliance.

Louis Davies made explicit the connection he viewed between threats from European powers and the desire for closer Anglo-American cooperation. Davies spoke of British interests in the Cape being "menaced by the German autocrat." He then declared himself to be in favour of an Anglo-American alliance in the strongest terms. "An alliance between Great Britain and the United States would be the guarantee of the world's peace, no nation and combination of nations is strong enough to withstand a union between the greatest Empire in the world and the greatest republic in the world." Davies referred to a recent, highly publicized speech by Arthur Balfour, who hoped to see Great Britain and the United States work together "to promote and extend the Anglo-Saxon ideas of liberty," and by doing so "fulfill the duties Providence had entrusted to her." Davies called Balfour's remarks "noble words," and the religious overtones evidently struck a chord with this leading Liberal and future Minister of Fisheries. Davies simply repeated a frequently expressed sentiment about Anglo-American relations; that a war between the two Anglo-Saxon nations would be a crime against God and humanity, while an alliance between them would bring peace, extend liberty, and fulfill the duties of Providence. Like many of the English-Canadian commentators during the crisis, especially George Grant, Davies believed Canada had a special duty to foster such an alliance. "[E]very Canadian who helps forward such a blessed consummation," Davies said, "makes a substantial and national offering to the Empire." With his reference to a "blessed consummation" between the United States and Great Britain, Davies called upon Canada to act as matchmaker between the Anglo-Saxon powers.

In his comments Richard Cartwright also linked an Anglo-American alliance to the present international situation. England, he said, "stands in a state of splendid but dangerous isolation." An alliance between the "140,000,000 English people," Cartwright said, evidently meaning English-speaking people, would not only place the empire in a more secure position; through such an alliance "a very great security would be given to the peace and welfare of the world at large and to the future progress of the world at large." Cartwright concluded by agreeing with Davies that all Canadian men "who can aid and help, and who do aid and help, in promoting that, will render the greatest service that can be rendered to Canada in the first place, and the British Empire at large, in the second place." Just as a number of English

Canadians had proposed a "larger loyalty" to the Anglo-Saxon race, Cartwright and other MPs discussed the overlapping and mutually supporting loyalties of Canadians. A Canadian might take an action that benefited Canada, England, the British Empire, and the Anglo-Saxon race, including the United States. Clearly for the Canadian representatives, none of these loyalties excluded the other.

By means of Anglo-Saxon rhetoric, with its emphasis on familial ties, racial affinity, and a common mission, English Canadians greatly modified their initial response to the Venezuela crisis. Cries about American "spread-eagle-ism" or "jingoism" were quickly replaced with expressions of friendship and caution. Fears about an American attack were replaced by fears of an apocalyptic war between the Anglo-Saxon powers. Canadian "loyalty" during the crisis initially meant providing a unified front to the Americans and shouldering a fair, Canadian share of the British defence burden. However, Canadian loyalty soon came to mean doing nothing to irritate Anglo-American relations, and even helping to foster those relations by whatever means available. To English Canadians, their national identity had moved from that of an outpost of the British Empire to a country that was both British and American, as well as Anglo-Saxon. Such themes would be repeated during the events that constituted the Anglo-American rapprochement and America's rise to world power. By early 1896, Canadians had already significantly altered their perception of the United States by way of Anglo-Saxon rhetoric. The United States was not some foreign menace that threatened Canada's very existence, but a member of a global Anglo-Saxon family. With threats to the British Empire on a number of fronts, Canadians would rejoice in the Anglo-Saxon affinity of their southern neighbours.

THE AFTERMATH: ANGLO-SAXONISM ENTRENCHED

Faced with the failed Jameson Raid in the Transvaal and the Kaiser's congratulatory telegram to President Kruger, the British government quickly chose acquiescence in the Venezuela matter over facing crises on two fronts. Through the intermediary of Lord Playfair, a former Liberal Cabinet minister, Salisbury suggested to Ambassador Bayard not only "friendly arbitration" of the Venezuela boundary, but also a conference of the European powers with colonies in the western hemisphere to "proclaim the Monroe Doctrine."[54] Given Salisbury's previous rejection of arbitration and his pedagogical dismissal of the Monroe Doctrine, the British government's new position represented a near-complete about-face. Although Bayard favoured such a conference,

Olney quickly rejected that idea, explaining that the United States was "content" with the "existing status of the Monroe Doctrine."[55] By the end of the month, the British and Americans had agreed upon an Anglo-American commission to arbitrate the line.

Ambassador Bayard had long worked to bring about a better Anglo-American relationship, and often utilized Anglo-Saxon rhetoric. Yet many blamed him personally for the Venezuela crisis, for not having made America's position clear to the British. "If the American feeling had been properly represented to Lord Salisbury by the American Ambassador," Senator Lodge wrote Henry White, whom Olney had used as an unofficial agent during the Venezuela crisis, "all this trouble could have been avoided."[56] Indeed, Bayard had been unhappy with Olney's provocative missive to the British Government, and both the President and the Secretary of State had chided the ambassador for his stance. Bayard's case illustrated the limits of Anglo-Saxon rhetoric. Although the American ambassador to Great Britain used such rhetoric to foster better Anglo-American relations, his ideal differed significantly from that of those who sought to assert American hegemony and flex America's new world-power muscles. Bayard's Anglo-Saxonism did not help bring about the Anglo-American rapprochement. Indeed, it may have precipitated an Anglo-American conflict by causing Bayard to dilute the force of American feeling regarding Venezuela and the Monroe Doctrine. The settlement of the Venezuela crisis came as a relief to Bayard, and, as he wrote to President Cleveland, accomplished "the maintenance of friendly competition in the onward march of civilization of the two great branches of the English-speaking people."[57] Only after the crisis did Bayard's Anglo-Saxonism coincide with the new friendly feeling between the United States and Great Britain.

In the Capitol, Senator Wolcott reciprocated the Anglo-Saxon expressions of goodwill from the other side of the Atlantic. In a speech that received much comment, the Senator from Colorado thanked God he was of the Anglo-Saxon race, and spoke at length of the Anglo-Americans' common blood and common mission. "Everywhere upon the earth," he said, "it is our mission to ameliorate, to civilize, to Christianize, to loosen the bonds of captivity, and point the souls of men to noble heights." The advancement of the human race meant "the spread of the religion of Christ and the dominance of the English-speaking people, and wherever you find both, you find communities where freedom exists and law is obeyed." Once the applause had died down, Wolcott continued along the familiar Anglo-Saxon line: "Blood is thicker than water, and until some quarrel divides us, which Heaven forbid, may these two great nations, of the same speech and lineage and traditions, stand as brothers, shoulder to shoulder, in the interest of humanity, by their union compelling peace, and awaiting the coming of the day when nation shall not lift sword against nation, neither shall they learn war any more."[58] Wolcott spoke in the familial, biblical, and millennial terms of Anglo-Saxonism. He repeated the old refrain that "blood is thicker than water," and referred to Anglo-Saxons as "brothers." Finally, Wolcott expressed the popular view that an Anglo-American combination could dictate not only the spread of civilization, but the end of war itself. Already Americans understood that Anglo-American relations had entered a new phase, and they viewed it through the prism of Anglo-Saxonism.

Of course, not everyone held such views. In a January 26 letter to his sister Anna, Theodore Roosevelt called Wolcott's address "a very foolish pro-English and anti-American speech." Roosevelt still harboured old Anglophobic feelings that had only been exacerbated by the Venezuela matter. In the same letter Roosevelt praised Olney as "far more of a man than the president," high praise from the masculinity-minded Dakota "dude," and criticized American diplomat John Hay as "more English than the English."[59] Yet the outbreak of renewed rebellion in Cuba and the prospect of war in South Africa began to alter Roosevelt's view of the British. Two months later he wrote to Henry White his view that American foreign policy "should emphatically be vigorous," and blamed England's current crisis in the Transvaal on Gladstone's "cowardly retreat" in the Cape and his previous "magnanimity" to the Boers. Roosevelt did not express Anglophobic glee that England might get her nose bloodied by the Boers, but great regret that "the English had serious trouble ahead of them at the Cape and in South Africa generally." "I am very sorry for this," Roosevelt told White, "for though I greatly admire the Boers, I feel it is to the interest of civilization that the English-speaking race should be dominant in South Africa, exactly as it is for the interest of civilization that the United States themselves, the greatest branch of the English-speaking race, should be dominant in the Western hemisphere."[60] Roosevelt's words summed up the view of many Americans at the time. While many viewed the Boers as a righteous and oppressed people standing firm in the face of a distant colonial power, the world's needs mandated that Anglo-Saxon peoples, and not those of Teutonic, or even Dutch extraction like Roosevelt himself, rule in Africa. Roosevelt used the rhetoric of Anglo-Saxonism liberally in his letter to White, citing the needs of "civilization," and referring to the United States as a "branch of the English-speaking race." Moreover, Roosevelt used Anglo-Saxon rhetoric to accommodate his views to the changing international situation, with the world divided into Anglo-Saxon spheres of influence. Though an American nationalist beyond compare, Roosevelt also defined

America's future within the context of the Anglo-Saxon race, and viewed his nation as the leading member of a related family of nations.

The Venezuela crisis entrenched Anglo-Saxonism in the rhetoric of Anglo-American relations, and in the way Americans viewed Canada. In February the industrialist Andrew Carnegie published an article in the *North American Review* entitled "The Venezuela Question."[61] In the article Carnegie explained the crisis using Anglo-Saxon rhetoric. While some Anglophobes had seen Great Britain's Venezuela stance as typical British land-grabbing, Carnegie called such "land hunger" a "leading characteristic of the English-speaking race." As fellow members of the Anglo-Saxon family, Americans shared in the divine mission of spreading justice and liberty throughout the world. "The English-speaking race is the 'boss' race of the world," Carnegie wrote. "It can acquire, can colonize, can rule. It establishes law and administers justice everywhere it settles, where before there was neither the one or the other. It tolerates all religions and encourages a free press; it makes free men in free states." As a new crisis faced the British in South Africa, such a statement from one of America's leading men served as a staunch defence of British hegemony in the Cape. Moreover, with a renewed rebellion in Cuba against Spanish autocracy, Carnegie reflected the belief of many that the Anglo-Saxon was particularly fit to colonize and govern distant lands. Like Roosevelt, Carnegie viewed all Anglo-Saxons as having united overseas interests.

Carnegie also employed the old rhetoric of family relations when describing the United States, Great Britain, and her Dominions. "Her office is that of mother," Carnegie said of England, reiterating the old metaphor. Like Albert Shaw, Carnegie believed in the inevitability of self-government for the maturing dominions, just as the independence of the thirteen American colonies had been inevitable. "[S]he begets numerous children," Carnegie said, "nurses them tenderly, is a most generous parent, but all her care leads to one inevitable end – her children obtain maturity and leave the household. All that there was of this Republic was once hers; it is now all lost. Canada remains only nominally hers, a wayward child, unjust and tyrannical to her mother because bursting into manhood." Carnegie cited Canada's growing claims of autonomy, including taxing British products, opting out of the British imperial copyright laws, and engaging in disputes with the United States over Bering Sea seals and the Alaskan boundary. Instead of finding fault with Canada, Carnegie rejoiced in the Dominion's show of independence. "All these restless revolts against authority prove that the days of her dependence upon the old land pass quickly," Carnegie wrote. Carnegie did not view Canada as a British threat to American security and an obstacle to its Manifest Destiny, but as an increasingly independent nation sharing the same continent. Again like Shaw, Carnegie placed great emphasis on the residents of the maturing Dominions being of the same self-governing race – or "family" – as Americans:

We should be greatly sorrowful for Britain if it were not clearly seen that this growth of colonies to maturity, and thence to independence, was favorable to the increase, enterprise and power of our English-speaking race as a whole. One cannot help feeling sorry for the mother who sees her children successively leave her to start in life for themselves, and we bow before this wonderful, small but mighty old mother England in reverence and sympathize deeply with her in the wrenches which she is compelled to undergo in the course of nature. Nevertheless, it is better for our race that it should be so. If her offspring were content to live as colonists, we could no longer be proud of our blood.

Canada, then, was not some "unnatural" outpost of monarchism and imperialism; the Dominion's relationship to Great Britain was as natural as that of mother and child. Moreover, instead of a threat to the United States, these increasingly autonomous Anglo-Saxon dominions were cause for joy as they were "favorable to the increase, enterprise and power of our English-speaking race as a whole." In looking at Canada Carnegie broadened his view beyond the dominion's attachment to England and instead saw her attachment to and advancement of the Anglo-Saxon race.

Like so many in the English-speaking world Carnegie employed the missionary rhetoric of Anglo-Saxonism in his discussion of Anglo-Saxon colonization. Carnegie dismissed the "agencies" of this colonization as unimportant, for "over all there rests this source of satisfaction that, upon the whole, the management of the land acquired by our race has been best for the higher interests of humanity." Carnegie also utilized explicit Darwinian rhetoric. "It is an evolution," he wrote, "the fittest driving out the least fit; the best supplanting the inferior; and the interests of civilization rendered the acquisition of the land necessary." Anglo-Saxon rhetoric seemed to bridge the late nineteenth century conflict between the sacred and the scientific. Carnegie could readily speak of the divine mission of the race, acting "in the best interest of humanity," while giving the same rhetoric a scientific veneer by calling Anglo-Saxon colonization "an evolution." While Anglo-Saxonism may have been vaguely defined, it was this very flexibility that gave it such a broad appeal. With Anglo-Saxonism well established as an American ideology by the end of the nineteenth century, Carnegie could safely use its rhetoric to appeal to a large audience.

Political scientists and economists also took up the standard of Anglo-American unity. Writing in the *Political Science Quarterly* the economist and industrialist Edward Atkinson noted that "the great groups of the English-speaking people of all sections of the world are becoming more and more interdependent." Atkinson, an anti-imperialist, pacifist, and advocate of free trade, argued for "commercial union among the English-speaking people," but also advocated the establishment of an International Court of Law, shared Anglo-American control of interoceanic canals and waterways, and the joint protection of "islands in midocean," such as the Hawaiian Islands. In the same issue writer Sidney Sherwood also argued for an Anglo-American alliance.[62] Such a combination would "make most strongly for progress in civilization." Sherwood had no doubt as to the superiority of Anglo-Saxon institutions and practices. "By a firm union between all English-speaking peoples," Sherwood wrote, "their supremacy in industrial methods, in free government, and in moral living would be made unassailable." Sherwood recognized his assertion of Anglo-Saxon superiority as "an arrogant pretension," yet in Darwinian terms said "history justifies it." "To live with us the rest of the world would be forced to live like us," Sherwood concluded. "And that is a fair definition of progress." For Sherwood and other writers, the Darwinian aspect of an Anglo-American alliance had a dual nature. Not only did the two nations represent the highest level of civilization, but the Anglo-American way of life was in a contest with those of other nations and racial groups. The continued progress of the world depended upon an Anglo-American union, and a victory for the Anglo-Saxon way of life.

Not all Americans favoured an alliance with Great Britain, however, especially as it contravened George Washington's hundred-year-old entreaty for the United States to avoid "entangling alliances." Yet the resolution of the Venezuela crisis had fired the American imagination with another medium for Anglo-American cooperation: arbitration. Many American writers proposed the establishment of a permanent Anglo-American Court of Arbitration to settle peacefully any dispute among the Anglo-Saxon nations of the world. For some this represented a logical and practical step that took advantage of the recent rapprochement. For others, however, arbitration constituted a first step toward increasingly intimate Anglo-American relations and the ultimate union of all Anglo-Saxons. Moreover, many Americans gave special prominence to Canada in suggesting arbitration. After all, Canadian-American disputes appeared to be the leading cause of Anglo-American hostility and thus an obstacle to Anglo-Saxon harmony. E.J. Phelps, a law professor and one-time United States minister to Great Britain, made this point in his *Atlantic Monthly* article, "Arbitration and our Relations with England." Phelps wrote that "Great Britain may perceive the importance of so far repressing the conduct of Canada towards us as to guard against the sort of injustice that irritates, perhaps, even more than it wrongs." With the Venezuela crisis behind the two powers, Phelps wrote, "That is the only quarter in which any serious trouble between England and the United States is reasonably to be looked for."[63] The journal *Arena* also called for the establishment of a "court between England and America," that would "practically include all English-speaking nations, since Australia, Canada, and South African states" were "integral parts of Great Britain."[64] By establishing a court of arbitration, the Anglo-Saxon states of the world would take a giant step in the progress of their race specifically, and of mankind generally. As a fellow English-speaking nation and member of the British Empire, Canada was included as part of the Anglo-Saxon family.

Unlike those writers who included Canada under the purview of England, however, Albert Shaw once again made a distinction when considering Canada and any scheme of arbitration. In doing so, Shaw took up the old themes of Canadian-American irritation, and the natural affinity of the North American peoples. Shaw saw little need for an Anglo-American tribunal when all outstanding and potential disputes involved distinctly North American affairs. "On account of the contiguity of the United States and Canada," he wrote in *Review of Reviews*, "there are always likely to arise some questions of minor consequence that affect solely our people and those of the Dominion." Indeed, Shaw continued his theme of distinguishing Canadians from the British and did so in the Anglo-Saxon rhetoric of kinship. "[T]he Canadians are related to us by virtue of constant intercourse," Shaw wrote, "and also by virtue of ties of blood across the boundary line, very much more intimately than they are related to England." Shaw stated the need for a tribunal of arbitration made up solely of Canadians and Americans for questions "which affect merely the people of Canada and the United States in their capacity as occupants of North America." In stating his belief in the need for a distinctly North American tribunal, Shaw reemphasized his position that England should not be considered an American power. Separating Canada from the mother country through arbitration would further dilute the already tenuous bonds between Great Britain and her North American Dominion. Yet Shaw also believed that just as North Americans shared a distinct relationship, so too their problems should be resolved in a distinct tribunal. Only a "clear recognition of the fundamental and complete distinction between questions of a strictly North American character, and questions properly arising between the United States and the United Kingdom *per se* would allow for a permanent treaty of arbitration."[65]

Just as he viewed Anglo-American relations through the prism of Anglo-Saxonism, Shaw interpreted Canadian-American relations through the medium of North American racial affinity. When a Manitoban wrote Shaw to disagree with the editor's view of Venezuela and "certain international questions," Shaw placated the Canadian by appealing to their shared heritage. "From what you say of your own connections and ancestors," Shaw wrote, "I find that we have the same racial blood in our veins, and probably hold identical opinions upon almost all practical subjects."[66] Just as Canadian and American politicians and journalists frequently did, Shaw appealed to his correspondent by drawing upon the pervasive rhetoric of Anglo-Saxonism. Public men and writers like Shaw used Anglo-Saxon rhetoric to appeal to a broad audience, and to bridge the gaps between diverse groups, or to use Shaw's words, to illustrate that all English-speakers held "identical opinions upon almost all practical subjects." Such rhetoric was, quite literally, the common language of English-speaking North America.

In Canada as well, the aftermath of the Venezuela crisis found Anglo-Saxonism entrenched as the rhetoric with which to assess North American and Anglo-American relations. In January 1896, Canadians responded warmly to Senator Wolcott's Anglo-Saxonist speech, with the Conservative organ *The Daily Mail and Empire* leading the way. In an editorial entitled "A Speech True to the Language" the paper called Wolcott's speech the "bravest, worthiest utterance made by an American public man upon the Venezuelan boundary dispute." The editorial gave special prominence to "the noble sentiments to which he gave utterance when speaking of the civilizing and Christianizing work that he believed the two English-speaking nations are called to do." The paper concluded by contrasting Wolcott's position with Senator Lodge's "jingoism," and giving the Colorado Senator's speech possibly the highest praise it could muster: "Senator Wolcott's speech could not be more fair-minded and British if it had been delivered in the British House of Lords instead of in the American Senate."[67] Even the most imperialist and conservative of the English-Canadian papers, it seemed, could reciprocate American hopes of a common Anglo-Saxon future. Most English Canadians agreed that the English-speaking peoples of the world shared a common "civilizing and Christianizing" mission.

The recent scare in South Africa had underscored the empire's vulnerability, and English Canadians interpreted Anglo-Saxon relations within that context. In January the Canadian journal *Saturday Night* noted that "Russia, Germany, and France seem almost upon the point of casting themselves upon Great Britain," and contrasted British opinion toward the European powers on one hand and the United States on the other. The British were much more willing for a "single-handed" fight against the European powers than "for the spilling of brothers' blood in North America." The journal noted the expression of goodwill sent by the Prince of Wales to New York, saying that even "the dignity of the throne has to give a little because of the British desire for peace with kinsfolk." Unlike many of its fellow periodicals, *Saturday Night* noted that relations of the Prince of Wales sat on both the German and Russian thrones, but that the Prince had not interposed when the Kaiser "set Great Britain ablaze by outraging diplomacy." The Anglo-Saxon kinship rhetoric clearly applied to the racial makeup of nations, but not to the royal family tree that branched throughout Europe. The journal also asserted that "the English-speaking countries should be allied together," for the "the mother of nations does not forget her offspring." Just as the South African crisis led Canadians to find common cause with their American cousins, so *Saturday Night* sought to present the Transvaal as a problem facing all English-speaking peoples: "Out in the Transvaal there are probably thousands of Americans, for there are hundreds of Canadians. In the eye of the Boers all are alike English, are alike wondering how they can procure the liberties that are enjoyed wherever the English language is the tongue of the people. Our cause is common wherever trade or pleasure takes us, and all the jingoes alive cannot undo what nature does in this respect. If the United States were allied with Great Britain for mutual interest and peace – for they are the two powers that fatten in peace – they could command at will."[68] The common race of Canadians and Americans not only precluded the possibility of war, therefore, but made alliance between English-speaking peoples a natural prospect. The near-simultaneous crises in Venezuela and South Africa forced English Canadians to appeal to their American kinsmen to join with the British "for mutual interest and peace."

The settlement of the crisis was received with relief in other quarters of Canada. *Canadian Magazine* reiterated the unity of the English-speaking race, stating that the Venezuela question would not "endanger the measure of good-feeling which obtains between two great nations with a common language, the same blood, a joint literature and a civilization which is essentially indivisible."[69] The actual settlement of the Venezuela question came about in November 1896 with a treaty signed by Venezuela and Great Britain (and ratified the following February), based on the ruling of the American boundary commission. The treaty sent the dispute to a board of arbitration, but greatly favoured Great Britain by exempting land held by either party for over fifty years. With the rapprochement now in place, the British cooperated gladly with the commission, and the American ruling favoured England. Only some "arm-twisting" of the Venezuelans by Secretary Olney made the treaty acceptable to Caracas.[70] For the most part the English-Canadian press welcomed the settlement as further proof of the friendly feeling now existing between the United States and Great Britain and the effectiveness of arbitration. Moreover, Canadians welcomed America's new role as "protectorate" of the Latin American republics, less than a year after disputing the relevancy of the Monroe Doctrine. Just as the United States had come to distinguish Canada from the other states of the western hemisphere based on race and self-government, now Canadians used much the same language to distinguish themselves from their Latin American neighbours. The *Globe* welcomed the treaty as binding the United States to "guardianship over the semi-civilized little republics of Central and South America." The United States would undertake "police duty" to keep "the ragged little beggars" in line, and thus prevent future crises. The Toronto paper asserted that the original Anglo-American arbitration treaty would "probably provide for the submission of all disputes to a similar tribunal" to prevent a matter such as the Venezuelan boundary becoming the cause of Anglo-American friction.[71]

In *Queen's Quarterly* George Grant also welcomed American hegemony in the western hemisphere, saying that "every English speaking man ought to hold up both hands for such a principle on more grounds than one." After all, American hegemony of Latin America "does not touch Canada," Grant said, but only the "quarrelsome, semi-bankrupt, semi-civilized Spanish-American states."[72] Like the *Globe*, Grant, who had previously called the Monroe Doctrine "like the handle of a jug – all on one side," now accepted American hegemony as a boon for all Anglo-Saxons. Canada could share in America's power as part of the English-speaking family, and quite distinct from the "semi-civilized" states of Latin America. The Manitoba *Free Press* printed a cartoon of the equally-stout Lord Salisbury and President Cleveland walking arm-in-arm over the caption "Anglo-Saxon Unity For Ever!"[73] The *Mail and Empire* declared themselves to be "Satisfied All Around" in an editorial that welcomed the "growth of friendship between the two great branches of the Anglo-Saxon family."[74] The editor of *Canadian Magazine* also welcomed the "prospect of a peaceful and speedy settlement" to the Venezuelan dispute. "The Anglo-Saxon race," the paper continued, "holds in its hand, at present, the destiny of the world, for no other race at all equals it in intellectual power and progressive civilization. Though that race may be divided into two parts politically, there is no reason why it should not be united for material and intellectual progress."[75] When the English-Canadian press celebrated the

ANGLO-SAXON UNITY FOR EVER!

SALISBURY – "I do not believe I am using unduly sanguine words when I declare any belief that this –"

CLEVELAND – "Ends it; that's right. Set, my boy!"

In November, 1896, the tribunal of arbitration reviewing the Venezuela boundary dispute handed down a judgment largely favourable to Great Britain. Many viewed the decision as disposing of a nettlesome Anglo-American problem, as well as establishing a precedent for settling future disputes. In this *Globe* cartoon, the equally corpulent President Cleveland and Prime Minister Salisbury walk arm-in-arm carrying the "Basis of Arbitration" and "Olney's Happy Thoughts," while leaving behind them "War Talk" and "Cleveland's Venezuela Message." (Toronto *Globe*, 12 November 1896)

referral of the Venezuelan dispute to arbitration, they did so by marking it as a step in the progress of Anglo-Saxon civilization. For many, arbitration was both a result and a proof of Anglo-Saxon superiority, and a necessary step in the reunion of the Anglo-Saxon family. All that was desired now, many believed, was an arbitration treaty between Great Britain and the United States "to settle," as George Grant said, "all disputed questions between [the British people] and their kinsfolk."

Grant did not have long to wait. In January of the next year, Great Britain and the United States concluded a general arbitration treaty. Once again, the English-Canadian press welcomed the Olney-Pauncefote Treaty as an advance in civilization and in the Anglo-Saxon rapprochement. The *Free Press* announced the treaty with a front-page headline: "MILLENNIAL DAWN! Beginning of a New Epoch in Civilization – Of Universal Peace." The treaty would, the paper believed, "well nigh render war impossible between the two countries," and ushered in "an era of peace, good-will, and good-fellowship between these kindred nations."[76] The *Monetary Times* believed the treaty represented "a distinct step in the upward march of our western civilization."[77] The Ottawa *Evening Journal* used almost the same language, calling the treaty "a new era in civilisation, an epoch in history, a gigantic assertion of international common sense and humanity," and "a great stride ... towards the millennium."[78] The *Mail and Empire* also used the missionary rhetoric of Anglo-Saxonism, calling the arbitration treaty "one of the great movements set up in the history of the English-speaking people."[79] Finally, the *Canadian Magazine* published a cartoon entitled "What We Hope to See." In it, John Bull and Columbia drive a horse-drawn sleigh toward a sign indicating "To National and Commercial Advantage." The sleigh pulls behind it a sled carrying a young boy labelled "Canada." The scene conjures up a romance between John Bull and "Miss Columbia" as the "Young Canuck" says, "Here's hoping they may go on forever and never fall out."[80] The cartoon differed from most renderings of Anglo-American friendship, depicting a "courtship" between Great Britain and America, rather than "brotherhood" between John Bull and Uncle Sam. Yet the kinship of the two nations is still implied. The "Young Canuck" trailing behind the two adults also implies that Canada is an offspring of the two nations. Indeed, many English Canadians saw "British America" as a living link between the two Anglo-Saxon powers, and a still-young child in the Anglo-Saxon family.

Not all Canadians revelled in the Venezuelan settlement, however. Writing in *Canadian Magazine*, George Tate Blackstock, Q.C., severely criticized what he saw as British betrayal of Canadian interests. He lambasted Britain's "placid acquiescence" and the "habitual ignorance and indifference which Englishmen generally display in dealing with the American section of the Empire." Though Blackstock viewed Canadians as "Britons in America," he felt that this position left Canada in a hopelessly inferior position, caught between the machinations of the two great powers. The "American Briton," Blackstock believed, was subjected to "daily, if not hourly, humiliation" by British "weakness and pusillanimity." "[T]here is no claim too extravagant for the United States to champion, no proceeding too high-handed for her to defend, while, on the other hand, there is scarcely any imposition or indignity which England will not in the end condone," Blackstock stated. "Such a position is absolutely intolerable." The British deluded themselves in believing that the United States reciprocated "their idyllic and altruistic aspirations for the harmony and union of the two peoples." Indeed, the situation was the exact opposite: "England has no such deadly, jealous and persistent foe as the United States." After further avowals of American hostility and British acquiescence, Blackstock concluded by asserting the need for Imperial Federation to give the colonies a voice in the formulation of policy. "[I]f he had had a Canadian statesman of average patriotism and information at his elbow," Blackstock wrote, "Lord Salisbury could [n]ever have fallen into such an error."[81] Clearly the recent Anglo-American rapprochement had not dampened the burning Loyalism and anti-Americanism held in many English-Canadian quarters. Blackstock's article contained no small measure of a nascent Canadian nationalism, defining Canadians not as British but as "American Britons," and viewing Canadian interests as distinct from those of the Mother Country. Moreover, Blackstock did not rejoice in American power as being of benefit to all Anglo-Saxons, but viewed it as a direct threat to Canada's position on the continent. Blackstock's position was unusual, as he viewed the rapprochement as being of detriment to Canada, instead of its placing the Dominion in a more secure position.

Blackstock's damning article elicited a reply from John Charlton, an American-born Liberal Member of Parliament and wealthy Ontario lumberman who advocated closer Canadian-American commercial ties (see next chapter). In his reply, also entitled "Canada and the Venezuelan Settlement," Charlton repeated a number of themes that had been heard in Canada since January 1896. Charlton argued that "concessions, and even sacrifices, may be made" in order to bring about "harmony and union and a measurable unity of action among the various English-speaking commonwealths of the world." An Anglo-American war, Charlton stated, would have been "a measureless disaster ... a blow to civilization and human progress, a blow to human liberty, a crime black and direful." Charlton welcomed American hegemony in the hemisphere as the "guardian of the rights of the infant Republics of America." Most significantly, Charlton viewed Canada as sharing in America's rise to world-power status, and of being able to play a significant part in fostering friendly Anglo-American relations. Far from being a threat to Canada, American military power "may be made, in the good days to come when Anglo-Saxon unity and concert of action is secured, an auxiliary to our own." Within such an Anglo-Saxon family, Canada was unique among nations in the role it could play: "Our own influence upon the future relations of the various Anglo-Saxon commonwealths of the world can be made very potent, for nearly all the collisions and fractions that arise between Great Britain and the United States are of Canadian origin, and their evil influence can be minimized, if not entirely removed, by the exercise of forbearance and friendliness of feeling upon our own part." Charlton's entreaty might be likened to the opening of the medical profession's Hippocratic Oath: "First do no harm." Just as Canadians and Americans had viewed Canada as the potential battlefield in any Anglo-American conflict, so Charlton viewed Canada as the field where Anglo-American harmony could be cultivated. Charlton repeated his entreaty to Canadians in the concluding line to his article: "Let us pray that Canada will interpose no captious and unnecessary obstacles to the realization of a state of concord, peace, and good will among all the Anglo-Saxon States, and especially between the two great representative nations of that race."

Certainly neither Blackstock's indictment of the British nor Charlton's toadying to the Americans could be considered typical opinions of their day. Yet both writers incorporated old, familiar themes of Canadian ideas of nationhood. Blackstock's advocacy of imperial federation built upon related ideas of imperialism and anti-Americanism, while Charlton drew upon an Anglo-Saxon rhetoric that had long been established throughout the English-speaking world. Viewed separately, Blackstock's and Charlton's articles appear at odds not only with each other, but with much of English-Canadian opinion at the turn of the century. Certainly the coming of the South African war would make both men's opinions seem out of touch with the norm. Yet taken together, Blackstock's and Charlton's articles presented a growing conception of Canada and Canadian identity, previously espoused by members of the Canada First movement and the French-Canadian nationalist Henri Bourassa. Both men affirmed the need for a "Canadian voice" in world and continental affairs, and advocated Canada taking a greater responsibility for its own destiny. Blackstock saw Canada as achieving such a voice through an imperial framework, while Charlton conceived of an Anglo-Saxon framework. Moreover, despite the apparent contrast between Blackstock and Charlton's views, the two ideas of imperial federation and Anglo-Saxon unity were far from contradictory or mutually exclusive. After all, Imperial Federation implied union of all the Anglo-Saxon nations of the world save one. The incorporation of the United States into such a union appeared as a logical, final step.

Indeed, this appeared to be the position taken by the editor of *Canadian Magazine*, John A. Cooper. Writing in August, 1897, Cooper declared Canada as part of "The New Empire." Queen Victoria's

Diamond Jubilee in June, the attendant Colonial Conference, and the new Laurier government's proposal for preferential trade with Great Britain led Cooper to characterize Canada as "ten times as British to-day as she was a year ago." Such sentiment throughout the empire would forge closer links between the dominions and the mother country in terms of trade, defence, and representation. Yet Cooper apparently viewed such a closer federation of the empire as a preliminary first step only. "If this great combination of English-speaking nations can be made a financial and material success," the editor wrote, "there is no reason why the lost tribes should not return. The United States would find, perhaps, that their well-being, moral, intellectual and material, would be best promoted by a reunion of the Anglo-Saxon races. Such a union would be productive not only of great benefit to all concerned, but of the best interests of civilization, progress and development. Such a union would mean that Christianity and Liberty would rule the world."[82] Despite the varied racial makeup of the British Empire, Cooper, like many other English Canadians, really only considered the self-governing Anglo-Saxon dominions for any scheme of federation. The empire was, then, a "great combination of English-speaking nations." John Ferguson repeated this view in *Canadian Magazine* in his September 1896 article "Imperial Federation." A close union between Britain and the colonies would benefit all concerned in matters of trade and defence. "Bound together by the strong bonds of common origin and interests," Ferguson wrote, "the world would not again see a great schism of the Anglo-Saxon race, as was beheld when the United States declared for independence."

CONCLUSION

During the Venezuela crisis the United States asserted hegemony over the western hemisphere and explicitly included Canada within its purview. While the initial reaction to President Cleveland's December 18 message to Congress prompted traditional responses in both English Canada and the United States, the acquiescence of Great Britain in the face of a renewed Transvaal crisis and German belligerence significantly altered English-speaking North Americans' perceptions. Drawing upon common Anglo-Saxon rhetoric, with its emphasis upon kinship ties, Darwinian notions of racial competition, and a common civilizing mission, Americans and English Canadians adapted their views of each other and their continent to the new international status quo. Americans welcomed Canadians as fellow Anglo-Saxons, capable of self-government, and different from semi-civilized Latin Americans who must necessarily live under the protective wing of the Monroe Doctrine. Americans stressed Canadian autonomy from Great Britain, regarding the dominion as a virtually independent power and not "unnaturally" connected to a distant European power. English Canadians, while initially threatened by American jingoism, ultimately welcomed America's rise to great power status. As an Anglo-Saxon nation, the United States constituted a natural ally of Great Britain and the other Anglo-Saxon dominions. Moreover, as a nation of "American Britons" itself, Canada occupied a unique position among nations in fostering friendly relations between the two great branches of the English-speaking race. If Canada could act as an Anglo-Saxon "linch-pin" it could serve the progress of civilization and help usher in a new era.

Anglo-Saxonism was the language of the Anglo-American rapprochement; however, Anglo-Saxon rhetoric was not a determining factor in the establishment of the rapprochement. Anglo-Saxonism, although a powerful ideology, could not force nations to work against their perceived political and economic self-interest. A striking example of the limits of Anglo-Saxonism during the Venezuela crisis was found in Thomas Bayard, American Ambassador to Great Britain. Bayard, a former Secretary of State, was a prominent Anglo-Saxonist who advocated closer relations between the United States and Great Britain. Bayard arguably laid the groundwork for British protestations against an Anglo-Saxon war with offers of friendship. Prominent British church leaders, politicians, and members of the royal family may have especially utilized such language because the American ambassador himself did. They would understandably expect their Anglo-Saxon rhetoric to secure an appreciative reception in the United States and even be reciprocated. In reality, Bayard's Anglo-Saxonism alienated many Americans, including Secretary of State Richard Olney, and may have actually provoked the crisis.

Bayard was America's first ambassador to the Court of St. James, the former position of minister being elevated just before Bayard's confirmation. His biographer calls Bayard an "Ambassador of Goodwill" with an "instinctive feeling of friendship for England."[83] A former Third Assistant Secretary of State under Bayard wrote congratulations to the new ambassador, stating, "There are few ... who now realize the extent to which the two great English-speaking nations of the world are indebted to you for their present amicable relations."[84] Bayard himself would later humbly note that people called him "the Ambassador of good feelings rather than of diplomacy."[85] This was a curious compliment to give a former Secretary of State and a person occupying one of the nation's most important diplomatic posts. Yet upon first setting foot in England, Bayard set out to foster friendly Anglo-American relations through the use of Anglo-Saxon rhetoric, while downplaying anything that might cause a rupture. In his first speech as ambassador on British soil, Bayard declared it his duty to "bring together into harmony the interests of the two great branches of the English-speaking race."[86] At the unveiling of the Lowell memorial at Westminster, Bayard said, "It is a fine strong saying that 'blood is thicker than water,' and every day proves how the ties of a common origin and ancestry are stronger than written treaties, and inborn sympathies of race, in the end, can silence international discords and jealousies."[87] Bayard may have seen himself as fostering better relations between members of the same family, yet such an attitude was problematic when held by someone expected to serve American interests.

By 1895 many Americans were questioning the ambassador's anglophilism. While Bayard's rhetoric endeared him to the British, it angered many traditional anglophobes in the United States. Just as the two governments were exchanging missives concerning Venezuela, Bayard gave a speech at Edinburgh University praising Britain as a free-trade nation in contrast to the United States with its petty protectionism. Only days before Cleveland's explosive message on Venezuela, Republicans seized upon Bayard's comments in order to embarrass the Cleveland administration. In the House of Representatives Samuel McCall of Massachusetts submitted a resolution asking the president to give information concerning Bayard's speeches, and to inform Congress whether he had taken any steps to "recall or censure" Bayard. Nelson Dingley of Maine went a step further and called Bayard's speech an "impeachable offense," which led William Barrett, also of Massachusetts, to submit a resolution directing the Committee on Foreign Affairs to investigate Bayard's remarks and report whether impeachment should be considered. The Washington *Post* called for Bayard's resignation, saying, "If not, he should be recalled. If not, he should be impeached." With a major Anglo-American crisis brewing, the American ambassador to Great Britain had lost the confidence of large number of Americans.

From the beginning, Bayard's Anglo-Saxonism had coloured his view of the Venezuela situation. Reflecting his own feelings, he downplayed the affair as nothing worth causing an Anglo-American dispute. At the end of 1893 Bayard had written to Olney's predecessor, Walter Gresham, expressing his misgivings about the United States backing Venezuela's claims against Great Britain. He pointed to the instability of Latin American governments and the irrational hostility of some Americans toward the British. Moreover, Bayard said, it was unrealistic to believe that the United States might successfully extend American republicanism to Latin America: "We cannot give to the heterogeneous population of Mexico, Central America, and South America, the racial qualities, traditions, and education that are the prime bases of a republican state."[88] When the crisis came to a head in 1895, Bayard's view of the situation differed significantly from that of President Cleveland and Secretary of State Olney. When Bayard forwarded to the State Department Salisbury's didactic missive in which he dismissed the Monroe Doctrine and refused arbitration, Bayard characterized it as "in good temper and moderate in tone." "*Our* difficulty," he continued, "is the wholly unreliable character of the Venezuelan Rulers and her people." Finally, Bayard offered a lecture of his own on the nature of the problem. "I believe," he wrote, "that your interposition in this boundary dispute will check efficiently the tendency to 'land-grabbing' in South America, which is rather an Anglo-Saxon disposition *everywhere*. Arbitration is a most wise and honorable resort, but it must be conducted and executed in a wise and honorable spirit."[89] The British, according to the ambassador, were guilty of nothing that the United States had not done at some point in its history. Bayard was shocked at Cleveland's message to Congress, writing to a friend that he viewed "too much at stake even in the remote risk of a collision between the nations who are the main guardians under God of the world's civilization." Bayard, then, became willing to promote any action that would settle the dispute, even if it meant a sacrifice of American interests. He strongly supported Salisbury's suggestion for an international conference on the Monroe Doctrine, while Olney strongly opposed it. Time and again Olney expressed his firm disagreement with Bayard's proffered opinions. Finally, because he could not get rid of Bayard, Olney simply bypassed him by using Henry White as his personal agent in England.[90]

One of Bayard's longtime friends was Goldwin Smith, who in writing of his friendship with the American statesman referred to Bayard as "a sound free-trader."[91] Like many other Anglo-Saxon advocates in the late nineteenth century, Bayard and Smith linked the ideas of Anglo-Saxon unity and free trade in almost Darwinian terms. If Anglo-Saxon unity were the natural order of things, then trade barriers created obstacles to Nature's plan. Bayard found himself in trouble with American politicians because of comments he made critical of American protectionism. On March 20, 1896, the House of Representatives censured Bayard with a vote of 182 to 72.[92] Although Bayard received the censure ostensibly for criticizing American domestic policy, Olney's words make clear that the Secretary of State and others faulted the American ambassador for his too-vigorous advocacy of Anglo-American friendship. As the censure came right on the heels of the Venezuela crisis, the vote appeared to indicate American displeasure with Bayard's sacrificing American interests at the altar of Anglo-Saxon unity. Anglo-Saxonism, as Bayard may have discovered, had limits: it could not forge an entente that sacrificed American interests – or Canadian interests, depending upon the point of view. John Charlton, an Anglo-Saxonist and possibly the greatest turn-of-the-century advocate of reciprocity, would soon discover the same thing.

2 John Charlton and the Limits of Anglo-Saxonism: The Failure of Reciprocity and the Anglo-American Joint High Commission

> The commercial idea, prompted by gain, the national idea, strengthened by patriotic sentiment – these forces have vigorous play between two nations of the same race, and their opposition has created the perplexing resultant which now exists.
>
> John W. Russell, "Our Trade Relations with Canada,"
> *North American Review* June 1897.

> Reciprocity in adjectives, but no reciprocity in trade;
> rhetorical good-will, but tariff war all along the boundary.
>
> J.S. Willison in the Toronto *Globe*, 24 February 1899.

Like Thomas Bayard in the United States, many English Canadians associated the ideas of continental free trade and Canadian-American racial affinity. In the *Handbook of Commercial Union* published by the Toronto Commercial Union Club in 1888, a number of writers utilized Anglo-Saxon rhetoric to advocate Unrestricted Reciprocity.[1] In his "Introduction" and series of "Letters," former Oxford don and Canadian controversialist Goldwin Smith laced his writing with racial arguments that would be echoed a few years later in his landmark *Canada and the Canadian Question*. "Unifying forces of various kinds are constantly, and with ever-increasing energy, drawing together the two portions of the Anglo-Saxon race upon this continent," Smith wrote.[2] "It is my avowed conviction that the union of the English-speaking race upon this continent will someday come to pass," he asserted in one place, while in another he wrote, "The two families of the English-speaking race on this continent will some day be one people."[3] Employing kinship rhetoric Smith called Canadians and Americans "kindred" and identical "in blood."[4] For Smith, the questions of North American geographic, racial, and economic affinity were inextricably intertwined.

Although Smith clearly advocated Commercial Union as a precursor to continental Anglo-Saxon union, other English-Canadian free traders also pointed to the natural affinity between Canadians and Americans. In doing so they echoed Smith in lamenting the "schism in the Anglo-Saxon race," noted the essential kinship of Canadians and Americans, and presented Canada as a link between the two great Anglo-Saxon powers, the United States and Great Britain. In presenting his resolution on Commercial Union to the House of Commons in March 1888, Sir Richard Cartwright pointed to the "dangerous isolation" of the British Empire, and the great advantage of an alliance between "her and our kinsmen and friends on the other side of the border."[5] Commercial Union would not benefit Canada only, but "render a most important service to the whole empire by aiding to re-knit together those two great divisions of our race."[6] Moreover, the increasing number of Canadians living in the United States served to draw the two nations together. "To-day, Sir," Cartwright stated, "the United States, in the most emphatic possible manner, are becoming literally flesh of our flesh and blood of our blood."[7] Canadians, Cartwright said, faced a choice. The Dominion could continue to be "a sort of hostage to the United States for the good behaviour of England, or … a link of union and concord between the two great English races."[8] Commercial Union, Cartwright concluded, would be "best for us, best for the whole Empire, best for our kinsmen and neighbours on the other side of the line."[9]

Other Commercial Unionists took up the standard of racial affinity in advocating freer trade relations. In writing about mining interests, T.D. Ledyard pointed to the lunacy of erecting hostile tariffs between "the inhabitants of this great continent, who are of the same race, the same language, the same religion, and who have the same interests."[10] S.H. Janes, a Toronto real estate broker, echoed Ledyard by calling continental free trade, "a destiny that … is clearly indicated by geography, race, language, similarity of institutions, and the sacredness of religion."[11] Another Canadian writer spoke of Americans as "our own flesh and blood, speaking the same language … and with the same ideas of liberty and freedom."[12] The Attorney-General of Nova Scotia, J.W. Longley, called Americans Canada's "English-speaking brethren on this continent" and spoke of the shared "glory of the race in the development of North America."[13] Like Smith and Cartwright, these writers also found it impossible to separate the ideas of racial and economic affinity. If a map of North America, one of which was included in the *Handbook*, indicated the natural geographic and trading relationship between Canada and the United States, then common sense indicated the natural kinship between the Anglo-Saxon peoples of the continent.

Finally, one last advocate of Commercial Union also utilized racial rhetoric. The *Handbook* reprinted the House of Commons speech of John Charlton, a Liberal MP from Norfolk, as he replied to Conservative accusations of disloyalty:

I believe it is a matter of interest to the whole Anglo-Saxon race, to every English-speaking man ... that friendly relations should exist between the two great branches of the Anglo-Saxon family. I believe that any policy that will draw closer the bonds that connect the United States and England, that will increase the cordiality existing between those two great powers, that will have a tendency to bring those two powers to act in concert and in alliance, is a policy that should receive the commendation and the support of every man, not only in Canada, but in every English-speaking country in the world.[14]

Like Goldwin Smith and the other Commercial Unionists, Charlton employed Anglo-Saxon rhetoric to argue in favour of closer Canadian-American trade relations. As a wealthy Ontario lumberman whose business consisted of exporting sawlogs to the United States, Charlton clearly acted out of economic self-interest. Yet Charlton's ideas concerning free trade rested on a firm ideological foundation that consisted of a vehement belief in Anglo-Saxon affinity, superiority, and mission. As an English-speaking North American at the end of the nineteenth century, Charlton's beliefs simply reflected the ideas of his times. Beginning with the Commercial Union debate and continuing for the next fifteen years, Charlton emerged as arguably the foremost advocate of Canadian-American reciprocity in North America.

NORTH AMERICAN TRADE POLICY

Charlton's use of Anglo-Saxon rhetoric to serve his own business interests illustrated the limits of Anglo-Saxonism. Although his advocacy of closer relations among the Anglo-Saxon nations appeared to come at a propitious moment as it coincided with the Anglo-American rapprochement, his promotion of reciprocity was doomed to failure. The McKinley tariff of 1890, the Wilson-Gorman tariff of 1894, and the Dingley tariff of 1897 gave periodic proof of entrenched American protectionism. Moreover, despite the espousal of reciprocity by the Canadian Liberals in their platform as stated at the Ottawa convention in 1893 (the so-called Ottawa Program), the protectionist wing gradually eclipsed the free trade wing led by men like Charlton. Indeed, Liberal leaders like Wilfrid Laurier and Richard Cartwright viewed reciprocity as a political weapon with which to attack the protectionist National Policy of the Conservatives. This had led the Liberals to adopt Commercial Union briefly in the late 1880s, only retreating from the position after the Liberal defeat of 1891. Just as Commercial Union proved untenable to the Canadian electorate who viewed it as a threat to Canadian autonomy, a national dialogue about reciprocity could not take place without references to Canada's Loyalist heritage, American expansionism, and the integrity of the British Empire. "All kinds of seemingly extraneous issues are injected into the stream of discussion," the historian W.R. Graham wrote, "until cold considerations of economics are lost in the welter of words – loyalty, king, empire, nationhood."[15]

Indeed, the Commercial Union debate illustrated the limits of Anglo-Saxon rhetoric when discussing an issue that went to the heart of Canadian nationhood and the country's economic well-being. From the beginning, the movement's proponents had used Anglo-Saxonism as their chief rhetorical tool. Chief among the movement's advocates was Goldwin Smith, former Oxford don, founder of the Commercial Union Club of Canada, and devout Anglo-Saxonist. Smith, an anti-imperialist, viewed Canada's connection to a distant colonial power as unnatural and believed Canada's ultimate destiny was to unite with the United States. "People have been made to see," Smith wrote to a friend in 1884, "that a man may look forward to the union of the whole English-speaking race on this continent."[16] For Smith, Commercial Union would inevitably lead to Political Union and thus heal, in one of his favourite turns of phrase, the "schism in the Anglo-Saxon race."[17] Smith's greatest work on the subject was his widely read *Canada and the Canadian Question*, which was a scathing indictment of Confederation. The geographical and racial affinity of North America made the union of Canada on an east-west axis an abomination. Moreover, North America was destined to be an Anglo-Saxon continent, and Canadian-American union would ensure the "racial" absorption of Quebec.[18] For Smith, Commercial Union mainly served the ultimate goal of the complete union of the continent.

In his idealized advocacy of Commercial Union, Smith differed significantly from other supporters, such as Erastus Wiman, Richard Cartwright, and John Charlton. While all three used Anglo-Saxon rhetoric, they also had self-serving interests in Commercial Union. Wiman, a Canadian-born New York millionaire, had significant holdings in Canadian iron ore and American railway lines that he hoped would benefit from abolition of American mineral duties and integration of the North American transportation system.[19] Charlton, an American-born Ontario millionaire, would have benefited immensely from the removal of the American tariff on lumber. Cartwright, on the other hand, had long been a vigorous crusader against the tariff wall of the National Policy, which he viewed as profiting only a handful of manufacturers. Equally, if not more, important, free trade offered

Cartwright and his party a weapon with which to attack the Conservatives. The retirement of Liberal leader William Blake in the spring of 1887 had left the Liberal party in disarray and seemingly condemned it to the position of a perennial opposition party. Cartwright and the new party leader, Wilfrid Laurier, agreed on adopting Commercial Union as the new Liberal party standard, with Laurier cunningly letting his chief Ontario lieutenant lead the charge.[20] The new policy provoked not only attacks from the Conservatives, but also grave doubts within the Liberal ranks. Moreover, the Imperial Government, in the person of Colonial Secretary Joseph Chamberlain, spoke out against the policy, warning Canadians that Commercial Union meant the end of Canadian political independence and "political separation from Great Britain."[21] In 1888 the Liberal party began a slow retreat from Commercial Union, beginning a decade-long process of adopting an increasingly protectionist party platform; the 1888 Liberal party caucus adopted unrestricted policy as a less provocative policy. Laurier turned to Liberal backbencher John Charlton to test first-hand American opinion on reciprocity.

Charlton's Washington trips served his party leader's interests as much as they did his own. Such symbiotic self-interest reflected the nature of nineteenth-century Canadian party politics. As John English has pointed out, Charlton was one of many Canadian politicians who entered public life in order to press their own financial objectives. Along with Charlton such men were involved in businesses subject to government regulation and viewed their roles as necessary for the development of the young nation. Arguably, such economic self-interest served as the primary motive for men like Charlton to enter politics in the first place. Yet this self-interest also served the political development of an immature nation – it was a "Conjunction of Interests," as Ben Forster notes.[22] Far from being blind to Charlton's self-interest, Laurier carefully exploited it for his own political aims. The Charlton-Laurier relationship revealed Laurier as a shrewd political manipulator.[23]

Laurier's very success as a party leader depended upon his ability to balance the disparate regional interests of the Liberal party. With the political integration of the country still incomplete, Laurier necessarily pandered to regional and provincial interests to maintain party cohesion. His first cabinet in 1896 included three provincial premiers, notably the former Nova Scotian secessionist W.S. Fielding and Ontario nationalist Oliver Mowat.[24] Regional interests also forced Laurier to balance different attitudes toward free trade. From the time of his ascent to party leader in 1887, Laurier displayed a willingness to allow fellow Liberals to press extreme positions for the sake of political gain while he stayed safely above the fray. In 1887 Laurier agreed that the

Liberal party must adopt Commercial Union as the Liberals' "new departure," and watched from the wings as Richard Cartwright risked his political career as the movement's primary advocate. As the party turned away from Commercial Union toward unrestricted reciprocity, Cartwright "became the scapegoat and the sacrificial victim," while Laurier emerged with his party leadership enhanced.[25] After its 1891 defeat and the 1893 Liberal party convention, the party retreated further from the position of unrestricted reciprocity. By the 1896 election, with a healthy economy and a growing manufacturing sector, protectionists like Mowat held considerable power within the national party. Still, continuing support for free trade in regions of primary production, such as the prairies and rural Ontario, forced Laurier to pander to free trade interests. Laurier could balance these competing interests by giving Mowat a cabinet seat while sending Charlton on fruitless missions to Washington. While a one-time free trade Liberal like Richard Cartwright adapted to the changing political climate, Charlton maintained stubborn adherence to an increasingly isolated position.

W.R. Graham makes plain that "to a very large extent the temporary insertion of unrestricted reciprocity into the creed of Canadian liberalism resulted from the dictates of expediency." Moreover, he makes a point of differentiating the motives of John Charlton from those of Cartwright and Laurier:

A man like John Charlton, with his extensive lumber trade, was heart and soul a commercial unionist, partly because, as his diary makes clear, he effected a not unnatural identification of his own interests with those of the country as a whole. Not so with Laurier and Cartwright. Unlike Charlton, their personal affairs did not particularly predispose them to the support of free trade with the United States. To them it was primarily the one visible 'new departure' which had to be made if the party was to be rescued from imminent disintegration.[26]

This distinction between Charlton's interests and those of the party leaders would increase over time, and ultimately lead to Charlton's near-complete break with the Liberals. Moreover, this characterization of Charlton as a self-interested lumber baron, whose bungling advocacy of free lumber caused his party leaders no end of trouble, is a common one among Canadian historians.[27] Certainly Charlton acted out of self-interest in promoting Canadian-American free trade, and as Graham notes, identified his interests with those of Canada. Yet Charlton's interests were not limited solely to lumber. Charlton absorbed the arguments of men like Josiah Strong and Goldwin Smith, and in doing so, became one of the foremost proponents of friendly relations among the Anglo-Saxon nations. He infused his rhetoric with Strong's Protestant missionary zeal, and Smith's racial conception of North America. Moreover, Charlton aligned his interests not just with Canada alone, but with all of North America and Anglo-Saxon civilization. Since the progress of Anglo-Saxon civilization meant the progress of the world, Charlton felt that he held the destiny of the world in his hands. To dismiss Charlton as merely a self-interested lumberman would be to define the man as a two-dimensional caricature.

In his quest to secure freer Canadian-American trade relations, Charlton worked tirelessly to advocate reciprocity in North America. He published articles in major periodicals such as *Forum* and *North American Review*, addressed audiences in cities across the continent, and used his position as a longtime Canadian Member of Parliament and influential businessman to gain entry into the corridors of power in the American capital. For this reason, Laurier picked Charlton to be the Liberal party's "unofficial envoy" to the Americans. Over the span of a decade beginning in 1892, Charlton visited Washington at Laurier's request in order to sound out the Americans on the possibility of establishing reciprocity. Laurier sought to use Charlton's information to attack the Conservative tariff and illustrate that at least some measure of free trade could be gained from the Americans. After the Liberal victory in 1896, Laurier sent Charlton to Washington more to placate the free trade wing of the Liberal party, of which Charlton was a leader, than to secure any real advantages from the protectionist McKinley administration. Charlton's diplomacy, reaching its high point with his being named a delegate for the Joint High Commission of 1898–99, illustrated another key avenue by which Charlton sought to advocate reciprocity and foster friendly Anglo-Saxon relations. The unofficial nature of his diplomacy invited the abuse of his Tory opponents, his Liberal peers, and future historians. As an unofficial representative of Canada's prime minister, Charlton travelled to Washington as a private citizen, at his own expense, and without credentials. He displayed an amazing degree of naiveté and ingenuousness for someone who had been in Canadian politics for over two decades. Time and again he would say too much, give an inopportune interview, or publish an inappropriate article. Yet he was less a victim of his own self-interest than he was of the nature of his unofficial diplomacy.

For Charlton, then, reciprocity encapsulated his wishes for better relations among the English-speaking peoples of the continent. Instead of relying solely upon cold facts and figures to argue his point, Charlton utilized the more dramatic rhetoric of Anglo-Saxonism. In doing so he resembled public men in both Canada and the United States who drew upon the common language of race, knowing that their words would be instantly recognizable to and accepted by a wide audience. Yet just as Anglo-Saxon rhetoric failed to convince Canadians of the need for Commercial Union, so, too, it fell on largely deaf ears in the American capital. Anglo-Saxonism could not compete with a nation's perceived economic welfare. Nor could racial ideology force nations into agreement. For many English-speaking North Americans the Anglo-American Joint High Commission of 1898–99 represented a sterling opportunity to dispose of all the onerous obstacles blocking Anglo-Saxon harmony. Not only might old problems like the Bering Seals dispute finally be settled, but a measure of reciprocity might be negotiated. Despite such hopes, however, the Commission ended in failure, foundering upon the disputed Alaskan boundary. Moreover, few were overly displeased to see the Commission adjourn without an agreement in February 1899. Many people in both countries felt that no settlement was better than a bad settlement that bargained away national interests. Few invoked Anglo-Saxonism to mourn the Commission's indefinite adjournment. Although Charlton's diplomacy bore no fruit, his work and writings reflected a fundamental cornerstone of North American ideology at the turn of the century, and deserve further comment.

JOHN CHARLTON'S ANGLO-SAXONISM

In February 1894 John Charlton travelled to Washington to argue for lumber to be removed from the duty list under the pending Wilson-Gorman tariff bill. Alone in his hotel room and far from home, Charlton noted in his diary feeling "lonesome and blue." To alleviate his depression Charlton read the New Testament and "a couple of chapters of Strong's New Era." In 1893 the Reverend Josiah Strong published *The New Era: or, The Coming Kingdom*, eight years after his best-selling *Our Country: Its Possible Future and Present Crisis*.[28] Strong's books are widely seen as having helped formulate a rationale for American expansionism at the end of the nineteenth century.[29] The cornerstone of Strong's thinking was Anglo-Saxon superiority and mission, which brought Strong, as Richard Hofstadter says, "to the highest pitch of enthusiasm."[30] As an American nationalist, Strong also believed in American exceptionalism, and placed America's unique identity and mission within a clear continental framework. "There can be no reasonable doubt," Strong wrote in *Our Country*, "that North America is to be the great home of the Anglo-Saxon, the principal seat of his power, the center of his life and influence. Not only does it constitute seven-elevenths of his possessions, but his empire is unsevered, while the remaining four-elevenths are fragmentary and scattered over the earth."[31] Strong's view reflected not only pride in America's growing wealth and power, but older ideas about the reforming influence of the New World. "[O]n this continent," he wrote, "God is training the Anglo-Saxon race for its mission ... preparing in our civilization the die with which to stamp the nations."[32] For Strong, the limitless resources of North America made the continent the crucible of the race.

Strong repeated many of his themes about Anglo-Saxon superiority in *The New Era*. A strong believer in Anglo-Saxonism, Charlton must have read Chapter IV of Strong's book, "The Contributions Made by the Anglo-Saxon." After asserting the superiority of Anglo-Saxon religious life, language, and political institutions, Strong considered the great advantages of North America. "Surely this majestic continent with its unequaled resources is worthy and destined to be the home of this majestic race," Strong wrote. North America was destined to be "the great centre of Anglo-Saxondom." Finally, while sitting alone in his hotel room, preparing to act as liaison between Canada and the United States, Charlton may have read Strong's hopes, written on the eve of the Anglo-American rapprochement: "It is devoutly to be hoped that the various branches of the Anglo-Saxon race will sustain such relations to each other in the future that their overwhelming superiority of power will be able to compel the world's peace and deliver the nations from the vampire of militarism."[33] Strong might have been addressing Charlton directly, imploring the devout Presbyterian to foster friendly relations among the Anglo-Saxon nations for the sake of civilization. With the New Testament in one hand and Strong's *New Era* in the other, Charlton sat in his Washington hotel room and girded himself for the work ahead.

John Charlton was born in Garbuttsville, New York, in 1829.[34] His English-born father moved the family to a farm near Ayr, Upper Canada, in 1849. Four years later Charlton became partners in a general store in Lynedoch and soon began dealing in timber. From the age of about twenty-five until his death in 1910, Charlton made his home in Lyndedoch and his living in timber, expanding operations into northern Michigan and upstate New York. Charlton and his business interests prospered. In an 1896 diary entry Charlton estimated that his share of J. & T. Charlton, in which he shared interest with his brother Thomas, came to $325,000 for the American-based operations and $138,000 for the Canadian side. Adding to this his "individual account" of $366,000, Charlton was just shy of being a turn-of-the-century millionaire.[35] In 1899 he formed a new partnership with a Michigan lumberman to log Crown limits in northern Ontario, and within two years Charlton could note that the company already had net assets of $250,000.[36] The profits made on buying logging rights and selling the lumber regularly came to six figures. Charlton seemed to work unceasingly, travelling frequently between his home in Lynedoch and his American operations in Tonawanda, New York. Adding to this his visits to American lumber centres in Buffalo, Cleveland, and Detroit, Charlton seemed to have spent half his life on trains. The result of this lifestyle proved nearly tragic. In December 1895 a porter of the New York Central Railway ran into Charlton while he was alighting from a train, knocking him into a passing freight train.[37] Barely escaping death, Charlton was incapacitated for six weeks with severe injuries, including a fractured femur, and remained thereafter dependent upon a cane.

In their entry for Charlton in the *Dictionary of Canadian Biography*, Thomas Ferns and Robert Craig Brown rightly note that Charlton's career reflected the fact that "Politics in 19th-century Canada was about business and religion."[38] A strict believer in Sabbath observance, he forbade Sunday labour in his lumber camps and was elected vice-president of the Lord's Day Alliance in 1888.[39] He taught Bible class at his local Presbyterian church, and commented on the content and quality of the reverend's sermon in his diary each Sunday. In 1893 Charlton travelled to New York as one of the Canadian delegates to the National Conference of Evangelical Churches on Foreign Missions, where he happened to meet President Grover Cleveland.[40] The Presbyterian MP's political career reflected his faith. On numerous occasions Charlton introduced seduction bills that sought to raise the age of consent for girls and punish men who seduced women through promises of marriage. Receiving little support and numerous taunts, a watered-down version of the bill, known as the Charlton Seduction Act, passed the House in 1886.[41] Charlton's strong Protestantism also led him in 1889 to join only twelve other MPs to call for disallowance of the Jesuits' Estates Act, the Quebec law that compensated church authorities for confiscated Jesuits' estates as far back as the British conquest. Charlton thus became one of the Noble Thirteen or the Devil's Dozen.[42] This public break with the Liberal leadership would seemingly haunt Charlton's relationship with Laurier. At the end of 1897 a frustrated Charlton noted: "I think my position on the Jesuit Estates Bill [sic] has been laid up against me by the French Catholic Liberal leader."[43]

Charlton's description of Laurier as "the French Catholic" party leader reflected yet another component of Charlton's character. Like many English Canadians at the turn of the century, Charlton firmly believed in the superiority of Anglo-Saxons and of their God-given mandate to control the North American continent. Such beliefs influenced his stance on the Jesuits' Estates Bill in 1889,[44] and led him to call for a British garrison to be stationed in Quebec during the South

African War.[45] Moreover, Anglo-Saxonism strongly influenced his thoughts on Canadian-American relations. In 1897 Charlton, writing in *Canadian Magazine* on "American Trade Relations," stated: "It is desirable in the interests of the entire race, and desirable in the interests of humanity at large, that cordial relations should exist between the two great branches of the Anglo-Saxon people." Canadian Liberals, he continued, "hope to make the policy of the Dominion instrumental in promoting Anglo-Saxon peace and good will."[46] In 1898, Charlton praised the work of the Joint High Commission, of which he was a member, in its efforts to "remove the causes of friction and ill will that have existed between the two Anglo-Saxon commonwealths upon this continent."[47] Charlton expressed these beliefs in his interviews with American public men as well. When two members of the Senate's Ways and Means Committee agreed with Charlton's views on free lumber, but apologized that "political reasons" kept them from acting upon their beliefs, Charlton lectured them: "I urged that there were political considerations of a higher character than those that influenced them – the future relations for the two Anglo-Saxon states on this continent, and these were considerations of more importance than the mercenary selfish struggles of greedy interests to get the advantage of each other."[48]

For Charlton, then, Canadian-American relations meant the relations of "the two Anglo-Saxon states on this continent." Moreover, while discussing reciprocity in Washington, Charlton often argued that "close commercial relations would draw the two peoples nearer together and might ultimately lead to political union."[49] In part Charlton sought to counter the American argument that high tariff barriers would force Canada into the arms of the United States. Instead, Charlton cleverly turned the argument on its head and argued that reciprocity would lead to more "intimate" relations. As he told President Cleveland in 1893, Canada "could not be starved into annexation ... and that before the two countries were ready to unite there would need to be a period of greater social and business intimacy."[50]

In expressing his view of the fundamental unity of the continent, Charlton drew upon the work of North American controversialist Goldwin Smith, especially Smith's *Canada and the Canadian Question*. In 1898 Charlton wrote:

The geographical relations of the territories of the United States and Canada are of such a nature as to invite freedom of commercial intercourse. These countries are naturally drawn to each other by community of race, and similarity in their laws and institutions. Possessing a coterminous boundary, extending from ocean to ocean, and having common interests, it is only in their political autonomy that environment and natural conditions permit distinct and separate existence. Natural intimacy of association, if artificial barriers were withdrawn, would be greater between such groups of provinces and of States as the maritime provinces of Canada and the seaboard States of the Union ... than would be the intimacy of association and commercial transactions between many of the groups of States in the American Union.[51]

Charlton wrote again about the "geographical affinities" and "ties of race" in his entry for *Canada: An Encyclopedia of the Country*, "Canadian Trade Relations with the United States." The editor of the encyclopedia, J.C. Hopkins, felt obliged to note that Charlton's article presented the "Continental school of fiscal thought," calling it "controversial" but "none the less valuable to the student of Canadian political conditions."[52] Charlton's business, dependent upon exporting the natural resources of Ontario due south to the manufacturers of Michigan, Ohio, and New York, aptly reflected the "Continental school of fiscal thought." And Charlton himself, a Canadian who had been born in the United States, reflected the "natural affinities" of the two countries. Like many English-speaking men at the turn of the century, Charlton believed in Anglo-Saxon unity, and viewed friendly Canadian-American relations as essential to its achievement. In 1897 he wrote admiringly to Goldwin Smith, another man perfectly at home in any of the Anglo-Saxon nations: "I desire to express to you my high sense of the services you have performed for our common race, and my appreciation of the far-reaching prescience which enables you to gauge correctly the infinite importance of securing harmonious relation between all the Anglo-Saxon Commonwealths of the world."[53] Charlton, too, hoped to render services for the "common race," and he clearly viewed his trips to Washington to advocate freer Canadian-American trade through the prism of Anglo-Saxonism.

CHARLTON AND LIBERAL PARTY TRADE POLICY

Charlton apparently undertook his first trips to Washington in order to speak against the proposed McKinley tariff. In April 1890, and again in July, Charlton made the acquaintance of various senators and representatives, including the chairman of the Senate's Ways and Means Committee, future president, and author of the protectionist legislation, William McKinley. Passage of the McKinley tariff in 1890 introduced the highest American duties on Canadian natural products until that time, and led to Prime Minister John A. Macdonald's rejection of reciprocity in the 1891 election. After the Liberal defeat in that election, Laurier asked Charlton to "proceed at once to Washington

as the envoy of the Liberal party of Canada to establish an understanding as to what policy upon the question of reciprocity we can
take common ground with the Americans on." Charlton seemed quite
excited by the prospect, and heartily endorsed both the approach to
the Americans and the idea of reciprocity.

Our leaders have at least come to the conclusion that if the Liberal party of
Canada has the sympathy of American public men, as it undoubtedly has, it
is time we had frequent communication with each other and understand each
other more fully. Heretofore each side has been working in the dark as to the
views and desires of the other and we may just as well understand what are
the exact details of a commercial policy that can be made common ground
and then stake out unhesitatingly and boldly on that line arrived by official
assurances from American authorities that our labors will not be pointless if
we can carry the country.[54]

Over the next few years Charlton made several trips to Washington at
Laurier's request, meeting with American politicians and making the
argument for reciprocity. During his February 1894 visit he pressed
the Americans strongly and successfully for Canadian lumber to be
removed from the duty list under the pending Wilson-Gorman tariff bill.
    Charlton's Washington visits did not come without a political price
for the Lynedoch lumberman. The Tory press often reported that
Charlton travelled to the American capital to advocate Canadian
annexation, or to prevent Canadian export duties that might harm
Charlton's business. In the House of Commons Conservative Members
of Parliament denounced Charlton as a "Yankee traitor," and compared him to a rogues' gallery of famous turncoats including Guy
Fawkes, Benedict Arnold, and Judas Iscariot. Charlton often stood to
defend himself against such attacks, yet he did so without any support
from his fellow Liberals, let alone from his party leader. Indeed, when
the Conservatives were able to draw Laurier into the debate, the party
leader made a great effort to characterize Charlton's views as his "private opinion" and not "the opinion of the party." These scenes typified
the relationship between Charlton and Laurier. The Liberal leader used
the lumberman for his own political ends, while distancing himself
from the resulting criticism.
    The prospect of a Liberal victory in the 1896 election provided
Charlton with a number of possibilities. Having served in the House
for twenty-four years, Charlton thought it time to receive the recognition due to him. Such recognition would normally take the form of
a Cabinet position. Yet on April 17, two months before the election,
Charlton met with Laurier to discuss a position for Charlton if the

Liberals won. As Charlton would make clear in the years to come, he believed that he had exchanged the promise of a portfolio in favour of Laurier making him Canadian Commissioner to Washington.[55] Based on Charlton's later comments, the position was to be modelled on George Brown's temporary appointment to Washington in 1874, also to negotiate a reciprocity treaty. One wonders at the progression of the Charlton-Laurier conversation. Who suggested the idea of a Canadian Commissioner? Did Charlton really turn down the offer of a Cabinet position at the vague promise of the Commissioner's position? After all, only a handful of Canadian Commissioners had ever been credentialed by the British government. Did Laurier make the offer in order to keep Charlton out of the Cabinet? Laurier did not like Charlton and resented his previous positions on the Jesuits' Estates Bill and French Canadians generally. His sincerity appears even more dubious considering the Liberals' further retreat on reciprocity after the election. Moreover, the appointment of the "Yankee traitor" certainly would have attracted the disfavour of many Liberals as well as that of the Conservatives. No matter what the answer, Charlton accepted the "promise," and perhaps did so because he believed it held greater potential for him than any low-ranking Cabinet post.

Only three Canadians had ever visited Washington as temporary Commissioners with special missions: Prime Minister John A. Macdonald in 1871, "Liberal elder statesman" and owner of the Toronto *Globe* George Brown in 1874,[56] and Finance Minister and future party leader Sir Charles Tupper in 1887. Charlton's appointment as Commissioner would have been a historic act and would have catapulted him to the highest ranks of Canadian politics. Other, more personal considerations may also have weighed in favour of his decision. Charlton had suffered years of abuse for his American origins and his unofficial visits to Washington. His appointment as Commissioner would have silenced many of his critics and even justified his past actions. Finally, returning to Washington as the official representative might have fulfilled Charlton's notion of his personal mission. As Commissioner, Charlton would have embodied the link between his native and adopted homes, the two Anglo-Saxon nations of the continent.

In addition to his responsibilities as member of the Joint High Commission of 1898–99, Charlton continued his unofficial visits to Washington. Although Charlton now represented the head of the Canadian government, his position as unofficial diplomat remained largely unchanged. He still lacked credentials and visited the American capital on his own time and money. Despite his membership in the ruling party, and his acting on orders from the Prime Minister himself, Charlton still spoke to the Americans as a private citizen. With the Liberals in power, though, one thing appeared to have changed: Charlton now had even greater potential for embarrassing Laurier and the Liberal party. This he proceeded to do on a number of occasions. Instead of being impressed with the new gravity of his situation, Charlton seemed to feel that Laurier's promise actually gave him freer rein to express his views. In doing so Charlton drew down on himself the displeasure of Laurier and Liberal leaders. The combination of Liberal party criticism and Laurier's broken promises fuelled Charlton's resentment. Within a few years this resulted in Charlton's near-complete break with the Liberal party. The Liberal victory, Laurier's dissembling, and Charlton's increasing bitterness only made his position as unofficial diplomat more untenable.

With a fierce presidential campaign underway in the United States, pitting the free-trade silverite and populist William Jennings Bryan against the protectionist William McKinley, little note was taken of the Canadian election results. Most newspapers simply reiterated their old position regarding Canadian–American trade. In a July 3, 1896, editorial entitled "Trade Relations with Canada," the New York *Tribune*, a staunch McKinley organ owned by Republican insider Whitelaw Reid, made clear that the new Canadian administration had little to hope for from Washington:

The ultimate union of all the English-speaking part of the continent by the free consent of its inhabitants is not impracticable. It is not too much to say that it is inevitable. And nothing will more facilitate its coming than for this country to rescind the special privileges that make continued separation financially possible and even profitable to Canada. Once let our Northern neighbors be fully convinced that they can expect none of the advantages of the American Union so long as they remain outside of that Union, the sentiment for Continental Union will be immeasurably stimulated.[57]

The *Tribune* article illustrated that Political Union sentiment still found a following in the United States. Moreover, it reflected the view that a high tariff against Canadian products would force Canadians into a "union of all the English-speaking part of the continent." Just as Charlton and other English Canadians used racial rhetoric to advocate free trade, many Americans employed the same rhetoric to advocate restricted trade. As has been stated before, this very flexibility of Anglo-Saxon rhetoric constituted one of its strengths. Yet it also revealed the fundamental limits of Anglo-Saxonism as an argument for reciprocity.

Although the Liberals won the 1896 election on the promise of reciprocity, Ontario protectionists led by Oliver Mowat had already gained the upper hand within the party. Moreover, the November election of the protectionist McKinley administration made reciprocity a politically untenable position. Approaching the Americans about reciprocity in any official manner would only have led to an embarrassing rebuff. Instead, Laurier once again asked Charlton to visit Washington unofficially to take the pulse of Congressional opinion on the eve of the presidential inauguration. Upon arriving in the American capital Charlton gave an interview to the Associated Press that received wide attention. The New York *Tribune* placed the interview on the front page with a lengthy title: "Canada for Freer Trade: Reciprocity a Prominent Feature in the Liberal Party's Programme: An Attempt to Obtain a Treaty with this Country to be Made in the Near Future – Important Concessions which Premier Laurier is Prepared to Offer – An Interesting Talk with Mr. Charlton." The article characterized Charlton as a long-time Liberal Member of the House of Commons, and as speaking on behalf of both Canada and Prime Minister Laurier. "Canada, Mr. Charlton said, will unquestionably attempt in the near future to obtain a treaty of reciprocity in trade with the United States," the article stated. Moreover, Canada was willing to compromise – "to meet the United States in the middle of the stream" – on other issues, such as the fisheries dispute, in order to bring about such a treaty. "Mr. Laurier and his Government will be actuated," the paper continued, "not only by a desire to establish the relations of the United States and Canada on a mutually advantageous and friendly basis, but also by the hope that such an arrangement will prove conducive to the peace and welfare of the two great Anglo-Saxon nations of the world." As he had done frequently before, Charlton used the rhetoric of Anglo-Saxonism in order to advocate reciprocity. The article concluded by stressing one of Charlton's points. "One statement which Mr. Charlton emphasized seems to possess significance," the article stated. "He represents Canada as now standing at the parting of the ways," with the Dominion prepared to move toward closer relations with either the United States or the British Empire."[58] Such remarks by the "member from Michigan" were not calculated to find favour with many English Canadians, especially the Tories. Yet they represented Charlton's continuing effort to persuade his audience that more intimate commerce would create more intimate relations between the two North American neighbours.

No matter how Charlton may have represented himself to journalists, it was reported that Charlton visited Washington for official purposes. Laurier immediately wrote an urgent letter to Charlton in which he repeatedly impressed upon the Liberal MP the private nature of his mission:

There is a report current in all the newspapers that you have been sent to Washington on an official mission. I would depend on you to contradict this report yourself. In the correspondence exchanged between us, you remember that you told me that it was absolutely useless to send anybody on an official mission to Washington until the new Administration had been installed in office. This seemed to me perfectly reasonable and my colleagues also shared in the same opinion, but while it was unadvisable [sic] to send a Commission to Washington, it is quite proper that as many prominent Canadians as possible should visit Washington and become in touch with the leaders of the Republic, and in that connection, it is therefore quite advisable that you should go, but I wish you would be careful to let it be known that you come simply as a citizen of Canada, and in no other capacity. I wish also that you would utilize your stay there to obtain information and for nothing else.[59]

Laurier made it clear that Charlton visited Washington as only another "prominent citizen." Moreover, Laurier spread responsibility for his reprimand of Charlton among the Liberal leadership, indicating the agreement of "my colleagues." Finally, Laurier instructed Charlton to limit the scope of his actions, ordering him to "obtain information and nothing else." Laurier himself must have known that Charlton visited the American capital as more than just "a citizen of Canada." Laurier may have written the letter in order to avoid responsibility for any of Charlton's words or actions. Yet the message of the letter may also be viewed as that of a more politically astute party leader attempting to impress upon his unofficial envoy the great sensitivity of his mission. Laurier also displayed great sensitivity to the timing of Charlton's visit. Sending a Canadian representative to Washington only weeks before the inauguration of a new president might sour relations with the new administration. Despite his sincere desire for friendly Canadian-American relations, Charlton's continuing failure to understand the risks of his mission actually placed those relations in jeopardy.

Charlton made two more trips to Washington in 1897, in April and July, both of which resulted only in frustration. Once in Washington, Charlton ran headlong into a wall of protectionism. Upon his inauguration, President McKinley called a special session of Congress that enacted the highest tariffs in U.S. history under the Dingley bill. Charlton now began to alter his views toward reciprocity. At the end of the April trip he wrote to Laurier a lengthy summary of his mission, ending it with uncharacteristic informality. Referring to the Dingley bill, Charlton declared, "[I]f the policy that has been entered upon is continued we may just as well tell the Yankee to go to hades and we will go to England."[60] Indeed, the Liberals had already indicated their intention to "go to England" by means of a preferential tariff for Great Britain. Frustrated by the American tariffs, the Liberals sought to fulfill their campaign promise for free trade in the only direction possible.

Charlton shared this frustration. During his July trip he wrote in his diary: "I am discouraged about the prospects for Reciprocity and begin to suspect that it is the settled purpose of this Administration to give us no treaty arrangements in that direction."[61] The American politicians Charlton met told him that Canada "had nothing to hope for from this Administration – that the Republicans scoffed at the idea of retaliation and calculated to show us no favors." As a possible indication of the Republicans' attitude, Charlton arrived at the White House to keep a ten a.m. appointment with the President, only to be kept waiting until three in the afternoon. To Charlton's plea for trade negotiations, McKinley replied only that "he would bear the matter in mind." Charlton returned to his hotel in a black mood. "I have done my best to advance the interests of Canada at Washington," he wrote, "and do not see that I can do any more and I will leave for home tonight ... I shall advise that we pursue the matter no further and refrain from attempting to send a Commission and that we make no further advances for more liberal trade relations during the life of this administration."[62]

Charlton, however, spoke more out of frustration than from a desire to see Canadian-American communication on trade stopped. In September, he wrote to Laurier calling the Republicans "ultra-protectionist." Yet Charlton also suggested that the government send "a duly recognized and fully authorized Canadian Representative to Washington" in order to negotiate a trade agreement "through the medium of the British Embassy." Perhaps frustrated by the lack of results of his unofficial diplomacy, Charlton urged the sending of a credentialed representative. Although never referring directly to himself, Charlton left little doubt as to the best man for the job: "An intimate knowledge of all facts pertaining to the lumber question would be an indispensable qualification on the part of the Canadian Representative chosen to present the case at Washington, and this qualification should if possible be combined with a fair degree of knowledge as to American legislative methods, and acquaintance with leading public men."[63] Charlton's suggestion to send an official Canadian representative appears less an awareness of the limits of unofficial diplomacy, than a less-than-subtle hint for Laurier to name Charlton as Canadian Commissioner.

Despite Charlton's advocacy, powerful forces worked against reciprocity during 1897. Growing protectionsim on both sides of the border threatened to start a Canadian-American trade war. Moreover, Queen Victoria's Diamond Jubilee celebration in London that June resulted in an outpouring of imperial sentiment in English Canada. Reacting to Canada's preferential tariff, Laurier was feted in London and Canada was serenaded by the Empire's unofficial poet laureate

Rudyard Kipling in his "Our Lady of the Snows." Added to other imperial undertakings in Canada, such as the imperial cable and the fast Atlantic steamship service, even the most devout of American reciprocity advocates regarded free trade's future with skepticism. Among these was the weekly journal the *Nation*, which had referred to McKinley's call for a higher tariff and the resulting Dingley bill the "Twin 'Brothers of Satan.'"[64] By that summer, the journal noted that American trade policy and Canadian imperial sentiment worked to keep Canada and the United States apart.[65] "Mr. Goldwin Smith points to the map, and conclusively demonstrates the folly of separating Canada from the United States," the journal stated. "Separation, however, has become our settled policy."[66] In a letter to the editor Smith replied, disagreeing with the journal's belief that the Dingley tariff and "Jubilee fever" would decide the destinies of the continent. Greater forces, he said, were at work: "Already ... the two sections of our race on this continent are rapidly fusing. Hardly anything now divides them but the political and fiscal line."[67] Smith's refrain was an old one, and his arguments had already been widely absorbed by the frustrated advocates of reciprocity. Despite the despairing tone of Charlton and the *Nation*, reciprocity would receive a fillip the following year as one of the most important issues facing the Anglo-American Joint High Commission.

THE ANGLO-AMERICAN JOINT HIGH COMMISSION

In November 1897, Laurier and Fisheries Minister Sir Louis Davies travelled to Washington to discuss a means of settling outstanding Canadian-American issues.[68] They agreed to an American suggestion to establish an Anglo-American Joint High Commission to meet in 1898. From the outset, Canadians and Americans expressed high hopes for the Commission. In the *Review of Reviews*, Albert Shaw gave great prominence to an article by J.W. Longley, the longtime Attorney-General for Nova Scotia. Longley stated his belief in Canada's mission to foster friendly relations among English-speaking nations:

However much nations of other race and blood may quarrel ... every possible reason exists for amity and friendly alliance between all the members of the great English-speaking world. If Sir Wilfrid Laurier, acting for and on behalf of the Dominion of Canada, can assist to bring about a termination of the causes of misunderstanding and irritation between Canada and the United States, he has gone a long way to remove all causes which militate against friendly relations between Great Britain and the United States. No higher mission could present itself to a colonial statesman.[69]

Once again a leading Canadian had enunciated his belief in Canada as an Anglo-Saxon linch-pin, ideally positioned to help bring about peace between the United States and Great Britain.

Although the Spanish-American War delayed the sitting of the Commission, Canadians and Americans viewed the war and the resulting Anglo-American entente as providing a favourable atmosphere in which to settle outstanding disputes. When it was announced in May 1898 that the Commission would meet in Quebec that August, North American journals welcomed its propitious timing. A Toronto *Globe* cartoon of May 26 entitled "An Opportune Moment" depicted Uncle Sam and John Bull shaking hands in a blacksmith's workshop. The two Canadian "Helpers" in the background, Sir Louis Davies and Sir Richard Cartwright, implored the two gentlemen to "Strike while the iron is hot!"[70] The New York *Tribune* also commented on the effect the war had on delaying the potential settling of Canadian-American disputes:

But no doubt the war has expedited the settlement. Its rude shocks have demolished the artificial and deceptive barriers the twin nations have raised between themselves, leaving both revealed in elemental qualities of brotherhood. It is seen more clearly than ever, and perhaps more clearly than it could ever otherwise have been seen, that the Great Republic and the Great Dominion are one in ruling race, in spirit, in ambition and in self-interest, at least to an extent, that makes the points of difference seem petty and contemptible.[71]

Once again, the events of the Anglo-American rapprochement led to the adoption of Anglo-Saxon rhetoric when discussing Canadian-American relations. While the *Tribune* had previously reacted to Canadian entreaties with hostility, now the paper discussed the countries' "elemental qualities of brotherhood," and their being "one in ruling race." The protectionist journal even sounded a bit like Goldwin Smith as it decried the "artificial and deceptive barriers" between the North American neighbours. The war, the Anglo-American entente, and the Joint High Commission promised to usher in a corresponding Canadian-American rapprochement.

In the months before the Commissioners met in Quebec, the North American press remained cautiously optimistic about its possible outcomes. While declaring their hopes for the settlement of outstanding Canadian-American disputes, Canadian and American journals made clear that neither side would sacrifice their national interest. The Halifax *Herald* saw the Commission's meeting as "evidence of the friendly feeling between Great Britain and the United States," but cautioned against giving the meeting "any broader significance."[72] The *New York Times* came out strongly in favour of reciprocity. Far from

AN OPPORTUNE MOMENT.

The Canadian "Helpers" – Now, come along, gentlemen; "Strike while the iron is hot!"

The work of clearing up numerous long-standing controversies between this country and Canada is now taken up again under more favorable circumstances, and it is hoped that a common ground of understanding will be reached ... Sir Louis Davies and Sir Richard Cartwright will probably be the Canadian representatives. – Washington Despatch.

Although the Spanish-American War had delayed reconvening the Joint High Commission, the new Anglo-American goodwill seemed to make settlement of outstanding Canadian-American differences more lakely. The *Globe* depicted John Bull and Uncle Sam shaking hands while the Canadian "helpers" – Sir Richard Cartwright and Sir Louis Davies – toiled in the background. On the wall are indications of Anglo-American goodwill, including Chamberlain's speech on "Anglo-Saxon Unity." (Toronto *Globe*, 26 May 1898) seeing protectionism as forcing Canada into the arms of the United States, the paper viewed reciprocity with Canada as establishing a larger Anglo-Saxon entente on the continent. Reciprocity would be "a very practical contribution to the understanding which we all hope is to be brought about between the two great branches of the English-speaking race." If "freedom of exchange" could be established with Canada, "we should have the whole continent of North America from the Gulf to the arctic regions brought under the unchecked domination of the principal ruling race." Canada and the United States would then be "one people, acknowledging the same standard of national life, pursuing the same essential ends in the same spirit of ordered energy and freedom."[73] Like Goldwin Smith, Thomas Bayard, and John Charlton, the prominent American journal welded together the ideas of racial and economic affinity. Tearing down economic barriers meant tearing down barriers between members of the same racial family. Yet the paper also realized the obstacles in the path of economic and racial unity, stating that "as to reciprocity the outlook is not regarded as promising."[74]

English Canada also expressed a cautionary tone. As Blackstock had suggested after the Venezuela crisis, Canadians viewed any Anglo-American discussion of Canadian affairs with some skepticism, fearing that Canadian interests would be sacrificed at the altar of Anglo-American goodwill. The earlier expressions of cordiality immediately following the Spanish-American War and the initial announcement of the Commission became noticeably muted as the meeting in Quebec approached. The Montreal *Daily Witness* printed a cartoon of Uncle Sam and Laurier as children each holding a piece of candy. "Say, Wilfy," Uncle Sam says, "you give me two bites of yours and I'll give you one bite of mine." A thoughtful Laurier replies, "Aren't you a little bit greedy, Sammy?"[75] The Toronto *Globe* stated that the conference would not be a "sentimental meeting," but a "business meeting to settle certain business questions." "There is no reason why any Canadian right or interest should be sacrificed on a basis of 'treaty-at-any-price,'" an editorial declared. The paper warned the British representative that any concessions should result in obtaining not "amity or comity," but "advantages that will make for the strength and prosperity of Canada." "We are doing very well," the paper concluded: "Time is on our side in considering the commercial relations between the United States and Canada."[76]

While the English-Canadian press voiced caution over the upcoming conference, advocates of reciprocity sought to appeal directly to American public opinion by using Anglo-Saxon rhetoric. One of these advocates was Edward Farrer, Toronto *Globe* journalist and Liberal party operator, who had supported Commercial Union in the late 1880s.

Laurier had often utilized Farrer, a frequent visitor to Washington and one-time employee of the State Department, as an unofficial party spokesman much as he had John Charlton. In 1896 Farrer had advocated reciprocity to the House of Representatives' Ways and Means Committee, stating that "closer commercial intercourse" between the two nations would help settle other outstanding questions, like the fisheries problem.[77] On the eve of the Quebec Conference, the *Forum* published an article by Farrer entitled "The Anglo-American Commission." Though essentially an outline of the various topics before the Commission, Farrer couched his discussion in racial language. In the hundred years since the American Revolution, Farrer wrote, the "English of Boston have become a mighty nation, the larger half of the English-speaking race." While England desired American friendship, "owing to the friction continually rising between these powerful kinsmen and her present North American colonies, it is not always easy to maintain peace." Still, Farrer did not advocate "peace-at-any-price" with the Americans, but instead appealed to his neighbours south of the line using racial rhetoric. "Of all people Americans have the best right to know how hateful coercion is to men of English blood," Farrer stated: "It has never been applied successfully to an English-speaking community, nor, for the matter of that, to any community worth having."[78] Like Goldwin Smith, Farrer presented the American Revolution as a "schism" in the Anglo-Saxon race that had not altered the fundamental spirit of the English-speaking peoples. Farrer hoped that the three nations' common heritage would provide common ground for successful negotiations.

John Charlton also offered his view of the Commission, although with some added controversy. Charlton had been named as one of the four Canadian Commissioners, along with Prime Minister Laurier, Minister of Fisheries Sir Louis Davies, and Minister of Trade Sir Richard Cartwright, in June 1898. (This does not include Newfoundland Premier Sir James Winter or the British representative Lord Herschell.) Although Laurier had failed to honour his pledge to name Charlton as sole Commissioner in Washington charged with negotiating reciprocity, Charlton expressed dutiful gratitude to Laurier, writing to his party leader, "I thank you warmly for the honor conferred upon me – one more congenial to my desires than even a cabinet position."[79] As the only Canadian Commissioner without a portfolio, Charlton's name appears odd when placed beside the other Canadian members, and Canadian historians often add an explanatory note on Charlton. Laurier's biographer Joseph Schull explains that Charlton was included "because he was a large dealer in lumber with interests on both sides of the line, and lumbering was one of the problems."[80] Such an explanation is accurate, but not sufficient, for it does not acknowledge Charlton's years of unofficial diplomacy. Laurier may have picked Charlton in partial fulfillment of his promise to him on the eve of the 1896 election. Yet Laurier also must have realized Charlton's value to the Commission owing to Charlton's numerous trips to Washington. Charlton had an intimate knowledge of Washington politics and politicians, and his frequent contributions to journals identified him as an expert on Canadian-American trade. For the Canadians in 1898, Charlton was too valuable a commodity to leave in Lynedoch. Finally, it seemed, all of Charlton's efforts were about to pay off.

Almost immediately after the announcement of the Canadian Commissioners, Charlton found himself in a disagreement with Laurier. The editor of the *North American Review* asked Charlton to write an article concerning the issues facing the Commission. Charlton, a previous contributor to the journal, believed that such an article would help influence American public opinion and wrote to Laurier for permission, stating: "A judicious article I imagine would prove advantageous by directing attention in the United States to the sincere desire of yourself and all the leaders of the Liberal party to secure an amiable, honorable, and strictly fair adjustment of all differences between the two countries. I will await an expression of your opinion upon the point."[81] Laurier disagreed. In a firmly worded reply Laurier said, "I am strongly of the opinion that an article written under your signature, at the present time, would do no good, but, on the contrary, might do a great deal of harm." Laurier agreed to the possible advantages in directing public opinion, but felt that the Commissioners should not take part. "[M]embers of the Commission," Laurier continued, "should keep apart from appearing, at this moment, to have any participation in the direction of public opinion."[82] This seemed like an old disagreement between Charlton and Laurier. Charlton sought to influence favourably Canadian-American relations through any medium available, while Laurier sought to impress upon Charlton the value of reticence. Having seen the results of Charlton's previous public relations, including Tory attacks in the press and the House of Commons, Laurier's concerns appeared justified. However sincere, Charlton's words and actions seemed destined to be magnified and distorted. Laurier sought to avoid damaging the Canadian position with the Americans before the Commission even had a chance to meet.

Charlton's reply to Laurier's concerns illustrated he had learned a thing or two about evasive replies from the Liberal leader. Charlton gave indication that he had already written the article, and upon receiving Laurier's letter, "at once gave directions to withhold the article." Yet Charlton notes in his diary that he only began work on the article that very day. Moreover, Charlton did not completely comply with Laurier's request. Charlton told Laurier that he had given the journal's editor permission to publish the article anonymously, "over the sig[nature] of Canadian Onlooker, or Canadian Liberal."[83] Such an arrangement acknowledged Laurier's concern that "an article written under your signature" would harm the Commission's work. Laurier conceded the point to Charlton, yet indicated some displeasure by making the point of his previous letter more explicit. Laurier wrote back to Charlton, "If your article is to appear anonymously, there can be no doubt, though I would have much preferred that the substance of it should have been reserved for our negotiations." However, he now gave Charlton a thinly veiled order: "Our programme now must be to convince the Commissioners that nothing can be published now that would influence public opinion so as to have it bear on your negotiations."[84] Charlton had finally won a round with his party leader by sticking to the letter and not the spirit of Laurier's words. Charlton's independent action did not ingratiate him with the Prime Minister.

Charlton's article "The Anglo-American Joint High Commission" appeared in the August 1898 issue of the *North American Review*, just as the Commission met for the first time in Quebec. Although Charlton published the article as "A Canadian Liberal," anyone familiar with Charlton's public utterances would have almost immediately recognized him as the author. Moreover, many of the elements of the August 1898 article were identical to those in an article Charlton had published over his own name in the same journal less than a year before. In October 1897 Charlton had written "Canada and the Dingley Bill" for the *North American Review*. In both articles Charlton drew heavily on Goldwin Smith, as he would for the encyclopedia entry published in 1898. In the first article he wrote at length about the "geographical, ethnological, and physical conditions" of Canada and the United States inviting "intimate commercial and business relations." In the second, Charlton discussed the nations being "naturally drawn to each other by community of race, and similarity in their laws and institutions." These conditions, Charlton wrote, contributed to a "natural intimacy of association." In both articles, when writing of the "geographical and trade affinities," Charlton dwelt on the natural connection between the various regions of Canada and those of the United States. The tables Charlton included appeared almost identical, displaying the imports, exports, and duties collected on trade from the United States, Great Britain, and "all other countries." Finally, and perhaps most characteristically, Charlton coupled his writing on trade relations with that on Anglo-Saxon unity. In the 1897 article Charlton had expressed a desire to promote "better relations between the two

great branches of the Anglo-Saxon family," as well as "the best interests of the Anglo-Saxon race upon the American continent." In 1898
Charlton discussed bringing "the two great Anglo-Saxon powers into
more harmonious relations" as well as removing the causes of friction
between "the two Anglo-Saxon commonwealths upon the continent."[85]
No informed reader on either side of the boundary could have doubted
the authorship of the 1898 article.

If Charlton could not promote himself by claiming authorship of
the article, he could do so by referring to himself indirectly. He wrote
that, "Leading members of the Liberal party have visited Washington
seeking in a proper and legitimate manner to pave the way to the
opening of negotiations." He also noted the friendly feeling toward
the United States held by the Canadian Commissioners, "whose utterances in favor of cordial relations and friendly intercourse have earned
for them in the past a storm of obloquy from the ultra-loyal Conservative element of Canada, by whom they have often been branded as
disloyal men and annexationists." Even when writing anonymously
Charlton could not help promoting and defending himself, characterizing his previous unofficial diplomacy as "proper and legitimate" and
Tory attacks on his patriotism as unfounded. Charlton may have sincerely sought to foster good Canadian-American relations through
publication of his article. Yet, as in the past, Charlton's sentiment led
him to statements that bordered on obsequiousness. Aside from his
profuse statements regarding Anglo-Saxon harmony, Charlton stated
that the Canadian government was prepared "to meet the United
States half way, more than half way if necessary." Laurier was absolutely correct to fear that such a statement by one of the Canadian
Commissioners would put Canada at an immediate disadvantage at
the negotiating table. Moreover, no Canadian politician at the turn of
the century could go hat-in-hand to the Americans without incurring
some sort of fallout, as Charlton himself knew from previous experience. Finally, Charlton must have included arguments and evidence in
the article that he would utilize in discussion with the American members of the Commission. Laurier had already expressed his displeasure
at this, stating that Charlton's comments "should have been reserved
for our negotiation" and "well to keep to ourselves, until the proper
moment came to make use of them."[86] Charlton had illustrated on a
number of occasions that, unlike his party leader, he did not fully
understand the political game. By writing the "anonymous" article,
Charlton had shown the Americans his hand and once again provoked
the displeasure of the Liberal leader.

Although there is little evidence that Anglo-Saxon rhetoric affected
the proceedings of the Commission itself, the conferences at Quebec

and Washington were publicly discussed in racial language. Indeed, as one of the American delegates later related, racial rhetoric laced discussion of the proceedings right from the outset. John Foster, a former secretary of state, recounted in his *Diplomatic Memoirs* the story of how Senator Fairbanks, the head of the American delegation, penned an address to be read at the opening reception for the commissioners held by the mayor of Quebec. As the address circulated among Fairbanks's fellow American commissioners, Foster related how "Quite a discussion arose over the phrase '*Anglo-Saxon* race' as descriptive of the people of the two nations."[87] Finally, the phrase was changed to "English-speaking race." Unfortunately, Foster did not elaborate and explain why the phrase sparked such a controversy among the American delegation, or how the commissioners settled upon the term "English-speaking." Perhaps the Americans believed the phrase "Anglo-Saxon" to be offensive to their French-Canadian hosts. The debate over the two terms indicated how Americans viewed Quebec's position within a larger Canada, and even within the North American continent. For many Americans, as the debate over the Venezuela crisis and reciprocity illustrated, North America was an Anglo-Saxon continent. French Canadians, American blacks, and ethnic immigrants were anomalous groups who would eventually be absorbed into racial uniformity. As so many writers throughout the English-speaking world had said time and again, nature itself dictated that Anglo-Saxons were destined to rule the continent, if not the world. Certainly this view was reflected by one of Foster's Canadian counterparts on the Commission, John Charlton.

Once the Commission commenced on August 23, American and Canadian journals expressed their hopes for peace and goodwill among the members of the Anglo-Saxon family, while cautioning against surrendering national rights. The Atlanta *Constitution* noted the international interest in the conference, due to "the intimate relations which exist at present between the two great branches of the Anglo-Saxon race."[88] The *New York Times* called for an easing of Canadian-American trade relations in order to aid "the growth and permanence of the friendly sentiment that now marks our relations with England," which the paper called "the natural ally of the American republic," speaking "the same tongue" and following "the same ideals."[89] In an August cartoon, the Toronto *Globe* depicted John Bull and Uncle Sam walking arm-in-arm toward "Peace and Goodwill" while Laurier carried a satchel labelled "Canada's Case."[90] In an August 19 editorial the same paper stated that "the gathering cannot fail to increase the fast growing sentiment in favor of closer relations between the two great branches of the Anglo-Saxon race." While the *Globe* believed it to be "of importance that the two great Anglo-Saxon powers are friends and approach the questions in a friendly way," the paper cautioned that "Canada does not intend to give up pelagic sealing to the United States as a gift to a friend."[91] A few days later the journal worried over a London *Times* editorial that marked the negotiations as vital to Anglo-American understanding, saying "there must be a very active tendency to conciliation among the commissioners." The Canadian paper bristled at the suggestion that any treaty at all should be accepted: "we see no reason for talking as if it were necessary to make any sacrifice in the interests of peace."[92] The Montreal *Daily Star* referred to the Canadian and American delegates as "Commissioners of Peace," who could establish concord not only between "two nations cherishing the same ideals," but could, if the United States and England desired, "impose peace upon a great section of the world."[93]

The Commission adjourned after only a few weeks with little progress made. At the American *Review of Reviews*, Albert Shaw had asked Canadian journalist Agnes Laut to follow the proceedings. In the October 1898 issue, Laut discussed the Commission's work in an article laced with Anglo-Saxon rhetoric. Moreover, she associated the conference's significance with a reunion of the Anglo-Saxon family. With friendly relations between the United States and Great Britain the moment was a propitious one to bring about a settlement of Canadian-American issues. "If ever a good understanding is to be established between the two great branches of the English-speaking race on this continent," Laut wrote, "no occasion could be more opportune than the present." Far from affecting merely Canadian-American relations only, Laut saw "dazzling possibilities" in the Quebec Conference. "Friendly relations between the United States and the Dominion," Laut continued, "would do more to bring about a world-wide Anglo-Saxon reunion than formal compact between the American republic and the British empire." Once again an English-Canadian writer, this time writing in a leading American journal, expressed an Anglo-Saxon version of the linch-pin theory, viewing friendly Canadian-American relations as key to friendly Anglo-American relations.

Laut even interpreted the site of the conference in the context of North America's Anglo-Saxon destiny. "It seems peculiarly fitting," she wrote, that a conference that "might pave the way for a wider reunion of the English-speaking race" should meet in Quebec, which was the scene of "two epoch-making events in new-world history." The conquest of 1759 "brought the northern half of America under Anglo-Saxon sway," while the 1866 Confederation Conference "welded the isolated possessions of British North America into a homogeneous whole." Now Quebec hosted an event that could shape the future of the entire world. "Results affecting the peace and progress of the whole world,"

Laut wrote, "may follow from the International Conference of 1898. It is, at least," she concluded, "certain to promote friendship between the two most enlightened nations of the age." In the end, Laut's article said little concrete about the Commission's actual proceedings or results, instead offering little more than Anglo-Saxon rhetoric. Apparently fellow-Anglo-Saxonist Shaw saw little wrong with this, referring to Laut's article as a "well-informed note as to what would seem to have been accomplished at the time of the adjournment," and calling her piece "the ablest and most intelligent statement of the matter that we have seen anywhere."[94] Certainly Shaw would praise Laut's work as he had personally asked her to write the article.[95] Yet Shaw's own writings reflected concurrence with Laut's point of view, and may have even been the reason he chose her in the first place.

Laut's ideas were echoed by another Canadian writer. Robert McConnell, the editor of the Halifax *Morning Chronicle,* published an article in the January 1899 issue of *Canadian Magazine* entitled "Commercial Relations between Canada and the United States." McConnell argued against the American protectionists who sought to starve Canada into political union. Instead, echoing the sentiments of John Charlton, McConnell argued that "freer trade relations would promote the friendly relations that should always exist between the two neighbouring peoples, united by the ties of kinship, language, literature and religion." McConnell stated that the American jingoism, as expressed by Cleveland's Venezuela message and the Dingley tariff, had only "stiffened the backs of the Canadian people" to resist American pressures and strengthened the ties of loyalty to the Mother Country. Though nationalist and imperialist in outlook, McConnell placed Canada's destiny firmly within an Anglo-Saxon framework that included the United States:

Without in any way seeking to disparage the United States as a great nation, and her people as worthy of the Anglo-Saxon stock from which they sprang, the Canadian people feel that theirs is a higher national and political destiny – to be one of the great family of Anglo-Saxon nations composing a world-wide British empire, whose mission is to civilize, enlighten and Christianize the people who come under her sway, and by the agency of free institutions and the influence of a world-wide, peace-producing and humanizing commerce, to raise strong barriers against the demon of war and promote peace and good-will among the nations. (Why should not the United States come into the Anglo-Saxon family of nations and have a share in such noble work?)

As McConnell penned his article the United States was debating whether or not to annex the Philippines. Presaging Rudyard Kipling's own

Anglo-Saxonist plea to "Take up the White Man's Burden," which would be published only weeks later, McConnell called upon America to "come into the Anglo-Saxon family of nations and have a share in such noble work." For McConnell, the very Anglo-Saxon nature of the United States and Canada allowed the two to co-exist in harmony, and co-operate in their common racial mission:

There is room enough and scope enough on this continent for the two Anglo-Saxon nations, Canada and the United States – daughters of a common mother, custodians of a common liberty – to work out their separate destinies without being jealous of each other or coveting each other's patrimony and birthright. They can maintain a friendly and honourable rivalry in the world of industry and commerce, and at the same time co-operate heartily in promoting the arts of peace and civilization, and the welfare of our common humanity the world over.[96]

No doubt McConnell and Laut hoped to influence the American commissioners through their Anglo-Saxon entreaties. By appealing to commonly held ideas about Anglo-Saxon kinship and mission, the English-Canadian writers utilized the racial rhetoric commonplace during the Anglo-American rapprochement. Moreover, with America's victory over Spain and the resulting debate over the future of the former Spanish colonies, the success of the Joint High Commission took on global, if not biblical, significance.

McConnell's article appeared just as Nelson Dingley died and the surviving commissioners met an impasse. Despite the high hopes for an amicable settlement of Canadian-American problems, the reconvening of the Commission at Washington was met only by rancour, bad weather, fire, illness, and death. Moreover, the pace of the Commission was terribly slow as the commissioners constantly took time from their negotiations to attend an interminable round of dinners and receptions. "Awful dinners rage for the Kanucks," Henry Adams wrote Elizabeth Cameron on November 28, 1898.[97] In his diary of the proceedings, Cartwright's cousin and private secretary F.C.T. O'Hara gave prominent place to the slew of receptions, including one where the Chinese Minister "did the cake walk with Miss Faulkner, daughter of the Senator of Virginia."[98] Charlton, too, complained of the festivities, his displeasure the result, perhaps, of his age, bad hip, and dour Presbyterianism. The Ontario lumberman especially did not like the time the receptions took from the course of the Commission, which he felt to be taking overly long. "The round of festivities in Washington interfered with the work of the Commission," Charlton wrote in his diary, "and we did not make the progress with our work that I desired."[99]

He was not alone in this feeling, as Henry Adams indicated to a correspondent: "Lord Herschell came over to complain of the slowness of his Kanuck commission, while Jeff Coolidge [an American commissioner] complains tearfully of Herschell's long speeches."[100] Moreover, the very public nature of the Commission made it the target of every American interest group, from Gloucester fishermen to newspapermen concerned over the price of wood pulp.[101]

By January 1899 the commissioners found themselves in the midst of great disorder, with many of the problems caused by forces beyond their control. Excerpts from O'Hara's diary read like a litany of Job's trials:

January 4: Nelson Dingley ... is lying critically ill from pneumonia and Mr. Foster ... is also seriously ill. The British party is anxious. An adjournment now would throw the whole thing over indefinitely. Pneumonia is rampant in Washington ... Many prominent people have died. Sir R[ichard] and I have been taking precautionary doses of quinine.

January 10: Sir Louis Davies returned from the Session to-day very much put out. He said they had a very testy meeting – the Americans having refused to agree to terms relative to the Canadian fisheries that they had the day before consented to. Lord Herschell got quite testy about it and had a warm argument with Senator Faulkner of the U.S.

January 13: Dingley died to-day.

January 19: All the attachés except the private secretaries left for Canada this morning. The future of the Commission seems rather hopeless.

January 21: The outlook is still very cloudy.

January 24: I asked Sir Louis to-day what progress the Commission was making. He merely shut his eyes, shook his head and said nothing.

January 29: Sir Louis is very pessimistic over the outcome of the Commission's work. The illness of Mr. Foster is very disturbing. The Commission seems to be in a mild state of panic.

February 10: R. Boudreau, the premier's Private Secretary, had a fire in his room to-day ... The Commission is now struggling with the Alaskan Boundary question. That seems to be the piece de resistance at present. From what I can learn the hopes of making a treaty are very discouraging.

February 11: This has been the coldest day ever recorded in Washington. It was 14 below zero.

February 12: Sir Richard under the weather from a bad cold. Snowing hard all day and greater storms predicted.

February 13: Terrible storms raging this morning ... From three to five feet this morning ... Mr. Pope as a joke telegraphed to Ottawa for snowshoes ... The outlook for the Commission seems very blue.

February 14: [T]he outlook is dark. Sir Louis Davies told me this morning that Lord Herschell, the chairman, was foaming with rage and it was dangerous to go near him. As for Sir Wilfrid, Sir Louis said he never heard him swear so much. As for Sir Richard, Sir Louis said, he was too deeply angered to even utter a word but his eyes glistened with wrath.

February 17: Sir Louis said that Sir Wilfrid was in a very gloomy frame of mind and Sir Louis would not be surprised if Sir Wilfrid would break off the negotiations in anger at any moment, "so incensed is he over the contemptible methods of the Americans." ... Lord Herschell's injuries are serious. He fractured a bone in his hip and will have to remain in bed for several weeks. This will be serious for the Commission. Sir Richard remarked, "This may be used as an excuse to leave the Commission open and adjourn."

February 20: Anxiety hangs over the Commission to-day. It seems to be doomed. Sir Wilfrid told me that all was over. The Commission adjourned to-day ...

March 1: Lord Herschell died this morning.[102]

Anglo-Saxon rhetoric could not predict the weather, prevent fires, cure pneumonia, or save Nelson Dingley and Lord Herschell. Neither could it prevent powerful commercial interests from bringing their influence to bear on the negotiations. Despite the accepted interpretation of events that the Joint High Commission failed largely because of the Alaska boundary question, O'Hara's diary notations indicated that a slew of serious problems still faced the conference at its adjournment. Moreover, the death of Nelson Dingley on January 13, and the departure of the Canadian attachés only a few days later, seemed to indicate the essential end of the Commission's work nearly a month before its official adjournment. Despite the public expressions wishing for an amicable settlement of over a dozen outstanding disputes, the Commission ended in disaster. As Henry Adams put it succinctly in a letter to a friend, "That Canadian Commission has been a terrible Hoodoo. It killed Dingley, broke down Foster, killed Herschell, and itself failed disastrously, leaving a legacy of serious trouble."[103]

Few North Americans were sad to see the Commission adjourn. Its failure signified to both Canadians and Americans that their delegates had stood by their national rights instead of accepting an unfair treaty. While Anglo-Saxon rhetoric did not disappear entirely, Canadian opinion especially emphasized Canada's rights and separate national destiny. "Let the United States people pursue their own course," the Montreal *Gazette* declared in an editorial, "and we will pursue ours. We are not dependent on their goodwill. Let us spend no more money on international junketings."[104] The Toronto *Globe* hoped that the Commission's adjournment would not endanger Anglo-American friendship. Despite the insurmountable obstacle of Alaska, the paper said, "we shall be good British neighbors to the United States." "One would despair of civilization," the *Globe* concluded in phrases reminiscent of the Venezuela crisis, "if over a few acres of territory in the far and sterile north the common blood of the English-speaking nations could grow hot with anger."[105] A number of leading Toronto men expressed their gratification to the *Globe* that the Canadian delegates had stood by Canada's national rights. Premier Hardy believed it to be "far better that the commission has adjourned than that the Canadian commissioners had yielded to demands such as those made by the American commissioners on the British Columbia boundary question." The Honourable George Ross said "Canada would not be justified in taking any concessions, except for a quid pro quo." Colonel Denison predictably took a strong nationalist position, saying that Canada "should not attempt to rely for her national progress on the favor of any foreign country ... I am glad that our representatives have stood out firmly in the interests of Canada." T.C. Irving, Manager of the Bradstreet Company, remarked that "Canada is now in a position to look after herself," while William Massey believed "we do not need to ask favors of any nation."[106] The *Mail and Empire* referred to "The Washington Fiasco" and commented on the "relief at the failure of the prolonged and hapless Washington negotiations."[107] Though the Conservative organ predictably attacked the government's handling of the negotiations, pleasure over the Commission's failure was repeated through much of Canada.

Still, some English Canadians greeted news of the Commission's failure with Anglo-Saxon rhetoric meant to dampen any lingering ill-feeling on the continent. J.S. Willison wondered why Americans did not reciprocate recent British gestures of goodwill. [108] "The enthusiasm for Anglo-Saxon union in the United States is official rather than popular," Willison wrote in a front-page, featured article. Great Britain only acted in the best interest of progress, working to "subdue and colonize the waste places of the earth in the interests of British trade and Anglo-Saxon civilization." All that British people desired, Willison wrote, evidently including Canadians, was "that Great Britain and the United States shall stand together for the spread of Anglo-Saxon civilization and the integrity of the English-speaking nations." Willison wondered why Americans felt menaced by England, and "why should not the glory and splendor of our common mother country and the strength and stability of her world-wide possessions touch the springs of sympathy and of kinship in the United States?" Even with the Anglo-American entente in place, American policy toward Canada simply did not match the republic's kind words: "Reciprocity in adjectives, but no reciprocity in trade; rhetorical good-will, but tariff war all along the boundary."[109]

The American press also met the news of the failed Commission with restrained Anglo-Saxonism. Predictably, American papers blamed the Canadians as forcefully as the Canadian press blamed the Americans.

"Canadian Demands to Subserve British Interests Were Not Met," the
New York Times declared in a headline the day after the adjournment.[110] "Canadians Claim United States Territory," the Chicago *Tribune* announced in their own headline over the Alaska boundary
impasse. Even allowing for future efforts to negotiate a settlement, the
paper claimed, "the outlook is not hopeful."[111] "Americans Disavow
Blame," the *Times* continued the following day, "Members of the Joint
High Commission Yielded Much to Canadians." The Dominion delegates were swayed by Canadian politics, the paper stated, hoping to
better the Liberal position by asserting their refusal to abandon Canadian rights. Yet holding out for better terms was futile. "It is said that
the American side has made its last concession," the *Times* concluded,
"and the Canadians cannot expect any better terms than they have now
refused."[112] The failure of the Commission was met by little surprise
and no disappointment. Canadians and Americans both defended their
own delegates and stood by their national rights.

Still, Anglo-Saxon rhetoric did help to temper any bitter feelings.
Once again Agnes Laut wrote an article for Albert Shaw at the *Review
of Reviews*. While outlining Canada's claims, Laut framed her discussion in Anglo-Saxon language as she had in her September article.
America's recent rise to imperial power indicated the "forward movement of Anglo-Saxondom," Laut stated. "In all quarters it is acknowledged that the settlement of those international difficulties which have
kept the two Anglo-Saxon races in quarrelsome mood," Laut wrote,
"would do more for world-wide civilization than the most daring
optimist ever planned." The recent conference symbolized more than
just mere haggling over trade and boundaries, for "the Dominion
became, as it were, the meeting-ground for the two great Anglo-Saxon
nations," while the negotiations became "part of the broader scheme
for an Anglo-Saxon brotherhood." Canada played an essential role
both in bringing the two great nations together, and in providing
potential obstacles to keep them apart. "The first requisite for the
realization of the lofty ideals," Laut determined, "is the removal of
every cause of friction between the republic and the empire – in other
words, the satisfactory settlement of all disputes over Canadian affairs."
Laut defended Canada's position at the conference as fair, but she also
assailed both the American and Canadian special interest groups that
prevented Anglo-Saxon harmony – the "haggling marketplace huck-
sters," "party heelers," and "sectional wirepullers." "Opposing the
cooperation of kindred races in national progress stand the sectional
interests in solid rank," Laut observed, individuals who would "see all
of Anglo-Saxondom sizzling in flames of war before they would compromise one jot for the sake of progress and civilization." As long as
these disputes remained unsettled, any number of them might later

arise to "fan all the old time bitterness between brother races." Rather than let this happen, Laut concluded, both nations should agree to refer the issues to arbitration.[113]

Shaw evidently agreed with his Canadian correspondent that the unsettled disputes should not prevent Anglo-American harmony. "Fortunately," he wrote in July 1899, "this Alaskan matter does not in the slightest degree endanger good relations between the United States and Great Britain. It is not worth the quarrel." Moreover, Shaw's journal reprinted several North American cartoons that reflected Shaw's old ideas about Anglo-American harmony and Canadian autonomy. One cartoon from the Minneapolis *Journal* depicted the British lion and American eagle pulling the "Anglo-American Moveable Boundary" on wheels along the Alaska frontier. "No need to row about a little matter of boundary," the lion stated. "No, indeed," agreed the eagle, "not when you have one on wheels like this." Another cartoon from the San Francisco *Post* showed Uncle Sam and John Bull shaking hands as they manned twin cannons at the ramparts; "The Real Peace Congress," the caption read. Finally a cartoon from the Montreal *Witness* depicted John Bull addressing Uncle Sam while a John Bull-esque "Canada" watched in the background. "My dear Samuel," John Bull said, "let me once more impress upon you that this boy of mine attained his majority long ago. Settle your disputes with him (*aside*), and from what I've seen he's pretty well able to look after his own interests."[114] As well as his correspondence with his British friend and employer William Stead, Shaw's use of a Canadian journalist and Canadian cartoons reflected the broad base of opinion in the North Atlantic triangle that viewed Canada as central to much-desired Anglo-American harmony. Just as Goldwin Smith could easily make a home and find an audience in England, America, or Canada, so, too, Shaw could draw upon the common intellectual resources of the English-speaking world. Furthermore, his message would be easily understood because Shaw expressed it using the common lexicon of the English-speaking world. The Anglo-Saxonism of Shaw and Laut could only help foster friendly relations between Canada and the United States. However, as the failure of reciprocity and the Joint High Commission indicated, Anglo-Saxon rhetoric could not force nations to act against their own perceived interests.

CONCLUSION

In May 1903 John Charlton wrote a letter to Goldwin Smith in which he discussed his work as a reciprocity advocate:

When the Joint High Commission was in session in Washington in '99 I became thoroughly convinced that it was in the highest degree important that American public men should have their attention directed to the actual state of the trade relations between the two countries, and with scant sympathy on the part of my colleagues I entered upon the work of addressing commercial bodies and furnishing papers to periodicals and magazines, and have prosecuted that propaganda up to the present time. The results have been more important than I could reasonably anticipate, and the sentiment in favor of Reciprocity between Canada and the United States is rapidly gaining headway.[115]

As writing his article as "A Canadian Liberal" indicated, Charlton undertook his propaganda campaign expressly against the wishes of his party leader. By the adjournment of the Joint High Commission in February 1899, Charlton had become almost completely isolated from his peers. While in Washington Charlton returned to his old residence at Hamilton House, where his neighbour was the ultra-protectionist Nelson Dingley, while the other Canadian commissioners stayed at the Shoreham Hotel.[116] Charlton held his fellow Canadians, Laurier, Davies and Cartwright – the Liberal party leadership – in disdain, questioning Davies's influence over Laurier, and disparaging Cartwright's abilities.[117] A row over an Ontario law preventing the export of Canadian sawlogs only compounded Charlton's ire and isolation,[118] while the outbreak of the South African War in October 1899 distracted the country and the Liberal leadership from any thought of reciprocity. Against Charlton's suggestion, Laurier called for an election in November 1900, allowing Charlton a chance to show his displeasure and embarrass Laurier. Charlton hatched a plan with the Ontario Conservatives that Charlton would stand as an independent Liberal candidate; to ensure his victory, Charlton would run unopposed as long as he agreed not to campaign for other Ontario Liberals. On the evening he announced his decision to run as an independent Liberal, Charlton gave a speech to his constituents in which he called for a garrison of British troops to be stationed in Quebec for the duration of the war. Saying that, "the safety of Canada lies in Anglo-Saxon hands," Charlton explained that he did not mean to disparage the French Canadians, but that "Forewarned is forearmed."[119] As planned, Charlton ran unopposed in his riding and secured re-election. Charlton's actions and comments did not endear him to Laurier.

Charlton continued the dispute with Laurier over the courting of American opinion. "My material and information was of a character to set aside various false impressions existing in the United States," Charlton wrote in his diary during the Joint High Commission, "and I was incensed at the decision of my colleagues that this information must not be published for the purpose of influencing American public opinion."[120] With the Joint High Commission indefinitely adjourned, and Charlton's influence within the Liberal party severely limited,

Charlton began a solitary campaign to tilt American opinion in favour of reciprocity. Believing American trade policy to be unfair toward Canada, Charlton continued to advocate some protection of the Canadian market while undertaking his propaganda campaign in the United States. The vast number of speeches made, interviews given, and articles written by Charlton over the next few years made him possibly the greatest advocate of reciprocity at the time. In 1901 he addressed the New England Free Trade League in Boston, the New York Chamber of Commerce and the Merchants' Exchange of Buffalo. Moreover, two important developments in the United States in 1901 indicated to Charlton that American opinion was ripe for a change. First, Charlton viewed the new American president, Theodore Roosevelt, who succeeded the assassinated McKinley, as more inclined toward reciprocity. Second, Charlton attended and addressed the inauguration of the annual National Reciprocity Convention held in Washington. Year after year these conventions would leave Charlton with the impression that a wide section of American opinion favoured reciprocity with Canada.

The next year found Charlton, now seventy-three years old, campaigning just as vigorously for reciprocity. In January he published an article in *Forum* entitled "Reciprocity with Canada." The article began with a typical Charlton argument: "Geographical and ethnic conditions have always suggested to the Canadian that broad and liberal trade relations with the United States would be natural and mutually advantageous." Charlton ended the article with an observation reminiscent of Josiah Strong. He pointed out that the population of North America had become 80,000,000 "English-speaking people." Moreover, he continued, the continent, "an area of 7,000,000 square miles, rich in all the resources that the most advanced form of civilization requires, is now the heritage of the American Anglo-Saxon."[121] Once again Charlton enunciated his view of North America, populated by an English-speaking population he labelled "the American Anglo-Saxon."

The following month Charlton introduced in the House of Commons a motion giving a forty percent rebate on duties to any nation admitting Canadian natural products free of duty. The motion was later withdrawn. In June Charlton addressed the Marquette Club in Chicago, and published articles in the New York *Independent* and the Ottawa *Events*.[122] Finally, in December, he spoke at the National Reciprocity Convention in Detroit. A few months later, in February 1903, Charlton published an article in *Outlook* magazine entitled, "The Growth of Reciprocity Sentiment." In the article Charlton claimed that "public sentiment in the United States is rapidly assuming a more liberal attitude towards the question of reciprocity." Once again he utilized Anglo-Saxon rhetoric, calling for free trade "between kindred States inhabited by the same race, and with practically the same institutions."[123] Charlton may have been correct in his evaluation of American opinion concerning reciprocity. In his first message to Congress in December 1901, President Roosevelt dwelled at length on reciprocity. While maintaining the need to protect American industries, Roosevelt stated, "the principle of Reciprocity must command our hearty support."[124] Within a year, the United States and Newfoundland had concluded a reciprocity treaty. The Bond-Hay Treaty allowed Newfoundland fish and fish products into the United States free of duty, while admitting for free American agricultural implements and machinery into the British colony. In the United States Senate, Henry Cabot Lodge led the protests against admitting Newfoundland fish free into the United States, arguing that it hurt New England fishermen. By 1904 the treaty had been abandoned.

Despite Charlton's rift with Laurier, the Liberal leader had again asked Charlton to visit Washington in 1902 and 1903 to test American opinion regarding reciprocity. Having lost valuable support among Ontario Liberals during the South African War, Laurier once again seemed to use Charlton to signal movement toward reciprocity to his rural Ontario constituency. Charlton visited Washington as an unofficial diplomat two final times in December 1902 and February 1903. On both occasions he found the Americans very receptive to reciprocity. "The result of my investigations is encouraging," Charlton wrote to Laurier from Washington. "The President and the Secretary of State promise their support of, and their best efforts to secure Reciprocity in natural products," Charlton told Laurier. "I have no hesitation in expressing the opinion that the Commission should be again convened."[125] The prospects for reciprocity, the possible reconvening of the Joint High Commission, and his rapport with President Roosevelt made Charlton's last trip to Washington as Liberal envoy one of his most enjoyable. As he bantered with the President, a decade of bitterness seemed to slip away. "I proposed to the President a moose hunt on our Upper Spanish limits," Charlton wrote, referring to limits he had purchased in northern Ontario. "He regretted that he could not leave the United States while President and I said that would prevent our enjoying the pleasure of his company at our camp for the next six years. With a hearty shake of the hand and mutual expression of good wishes we parted company and my own feelings were light and buoyant."[126] With his return to Washington to advocate reciprocity, and his pressing for reconvening the Commission, Charlton's diplomacy appeared to have come full circle. Despite his rift with Laurier, and his many disappointments, Charlton's ideas about the future of the continent remained consistent.

Still, events of 1903 indicated that Charlton's advocacy of closer relations between the United States and Canada could not contend with the realities of North American relations. During the year Charlton remained furiously active, travelling throughout the United States advocating reciprocity. He again addressed the Reciprocity Convention that November in Chicago and remained optimistic about the chances for establishing freer North American trade relations. He even wrote Laurier to suggest that a propaganda fund of about $10,000 be established "for promoting an active campaign." Once again, Charlton showed himself out of touch with Canadian opinion and blinded by his own self-interest. As Charlton discussed reciprocity at the Chicago convention, Canadians reeled at the results of the Alaska Boundary Tribunal. The single British representative had voted against the Canadian claim while the two outraged Canadian representatives had refused to endorse the award. Canadians saw themselves as pressed between a grasping and unfair United States and an acquiescent Britain, all too eager to betray Canada to gain American good will. Laurier felt equally stung by the award and sought to impress upon Charlton the scope of Canadian sentiment. "I do not think I would take the same sanguine views as you do about the prospect of reciprocity," Laurier wrote to Charlton. "The disappointment over the award of the Alaska boundary is very keen, and I certainly share it." Laurier concluded by stating, "it is clear to me that the time is not propitious for any propaganda in the direction that you suggest."[127] Laurier made it clear that the Alaska award had at least temporarily set aside any future approaches to the Americans over freer trade. Within a month Charlton fell gravely ill, preventing him from standing for his riding in the election the following year. Charlton's North Norfolk riding went Tory, and Charlton remained ill until his death in 1910.

"I have never been very anxious for popularity," John Charlton told the House of Commons in 1893, replying to Tory accusations concerning his trips to Washington. "My wish has been rather to leave a good name behind me. I do not want to leave behind me the name of traitor or the name of one given to chicanery or fraud."[128] Unfortunately for Charlton, he ended his days with his loyalty and good name questioned by Tories and Liberals alike. Ironically, his death corresponded with a shift in the Liberal party back in favour of reciprocity with the United States. Moreover, the good feeling between the two nations, the settlement of outstanding Canadian-American disputes,[129] and the active advocacy of President Taft made the moment seem propitious. Early 1911 found Canadian negotiators in Washington and a fierce debate raging in the House of Commons. In July Laurier dissolved Parliament and called an election on the subject of reciprocity.

The subsequent campaign revealed that little had changed since Charlton's advocacy of reciprocity. All of the old anti-American and Loyalist arguments were dusted off and given full rein, contributing to a Liberal defeat.[130] The enduring potency of Canadian suspicions of the United States indicated the difficulty Charlton had faced a decade earlier. Despite the Anglo-American rapprochement and the widespread use of Anglo-Saxon rhetoric, English Canadians could not relinquish the idea that reciprocity somehow equalled absorption. As Colonel Denison told a cheering audience in 1903, "Canada should avoid Reciprocity as she would the plague."[131]

3 "White Man's Burden": English-Canadian Anglo-Saxonism and the Spanish-American War

> If the Americans emancipated the down-trodden Cubans,
> they are bound to see that their liberty does not become
> a curse to them ... This is the work of the victorious
> people – not a simple or an easy one.
>
> *Canadian Churchman*, 25 August 1898.

> Take up the White Man's burden -
> Ye dare not stoop to less -
> Nor call too loud on Freedom
> To cloak your weariness.
>
> Rudyard Kipling, "The White Man's Burden"

INTRODUCTION

Racial ideas figured prominently in America's expansionist experiment in 1898. Walter LaFeber noted the "virulent strain of Anglo-Saxonism" that emerged among American intellectuals at the end of the century, including the "expansive expansionism."[1] Ernest May and Richard Hofstadter also noted the influence of intellectuals such as Fiske and Josiah Strong, with Hofstadter writing that the "Anglo-Saxon dogma became the chief element in American racism in the imperial era."[2] Other historians have explicitly explored the connection between race and American imperialism or expansionism, including the racial motives behind the Progressives' support of imperialism.[3] The United States did not go to war with Spain or annex the Philippines because of race, however. Advocates of the "large policy" were much more concerned with maintaining American dominance in the western hemisphere and finding overseas markets for American goods. Instead, Anglo-Saxonism and the accompanying Protestant missionary rhetoric provided, in the words of Lincoln Steffens, the "pious justification" for a departure in American policy.[4] Race served as the hand-maid to concerns over trade, territory, and American security.

The Spanish-American war also marked another step in Great Britain's abandonment of its "splendid isolation" in favour of rapprochement with the United States. British officials and public opinion were chiefly concerned with threats to England's overseas empire by the European powers and the maintenance of an open China. Yet as in the United States, "Anglo-Saxon race sentiment fostered vital public support for the growing international friendship."[5] The use of Anglo-Saxon rhetoric to foster friendly Anglo-American relations reached its high-water mark with Colonial Secretary Joseph Chamberlain's call for an "Anglo-Saxon alliance" only a month into the war. Moreover, racial rhetoric also figured prominently in British support for American retention of the Philippines after the war. Once again, the British were concerned with keeping the islands out of the hands of another European power, while establishing the United States as a new, friendly power in the Pacific. British preaching about a common Anglo-Saxon mission to civilize "lesser races" culminated in Rudyard Kipling publishing his poem "White Man's Burden" just as the United States Senate voted to annex the Philippines.

Much more elusive, however, is the question of English-Canadian opinion toward the war. The lack of direct Canadian-American relations in 1898 has apparently caused historians of Canadian external relations largely to ignore the war.[6] Others have discussed the war only in relation to the delayed Joint High Commission, the Rush-Bagot Agreement forbidding construction of warships on the Great Lakes, and the expulsion from Canada of two members of the Spanish Embassy in Washington.[7] While both Norman Penlington and Robert Craig Brown have noted the outpouring of friendly feeling by Canadians toward the United States, they have taken pains to characterize it as superficial and fleeting. Penlington states that "many Canadians could not forget the decades of hostility" while Brown writes, "Still, thoughtful people asked, how much of this Anglo-American friendship from which Canadians benefited was genuine and lasting?"[8] The most thorough study of Canadian opinion during the war is Graeme Mount's "Friendly Liberator or Predatory Aggressor? Some Canadian Impressions of the United States during the Spanish-American War." Mount concludes that, aside from "a sizable minority, most Canadians supported the United States' efforts against Spain," and he gives prominent place to Anglo-Saxonism.[9] Still, Mount offers only half the story, because he does not place English-Canadian opinion within a larger context. Before the war many English Canadians remained very skeptical of American motives in Cuba, reflecting, as Penlington and Brown emphasize, years of suspicion and antagonism. Moreover, the month preceding the war witnessed a Canadian-American dispute over a Liberal plan to build a railway from an American town in Alaska to the Canadian Yukon. Interference in the plan by the United States Senate smacked of the same type of American aggrandizement being displayed in Cuba. On the eve of war, even the Canadians most friendly to the United States remained noticeably cool toward their neighbours in the republic.

Only British expressions of sympathy altered English-Canadian opinion.[10] In March, Queen Victoria sent a letter to President McKinley indicating British support of the American course. In April, Britain stood opposed to possible intervention on behalf of Spain by the European powers. In May, Joseph Chamberlain called for an Anglo-American alliance. Liberal politicians and the British press matched official pro-American sentiment with gushing expressions of Anglo-American kinship and mission. Great Britain applauded Admiral Dewey's defeat of the Spanish navy at Manila Bay in May, annexation of the Hawaiian Islands in July, and the taking of the Philippines in August. From August 1898 until February 1899, British official and public opinion urged the United States to bear its share of Anglo-Saxon duty and retain the former Spanish colonies. Great Britain welcomed with open arms American hegemony in the western hemisphere and American power in the Pacific.

In the face of British sentiment, English Canadians were forced to alter their rather negative views of the United States. As during the Venezuela crisis, many Canadians accommodated their often anti-American views through the medium of Anglo-Saxon rhetoric. Many leading Canadians and much of the English-Canadian press came to view the war with Spain in racial terms, decrying the savagery of the "cruel" Spaniard. English Canadians also welcomed the new Anglo-Saxon understanding between the United States and Great Britain. Finally, far from worrying about American expansion in the western hemisphere and in the Pacific, Canadians largely echoed British sentiment and urged the United States to take up the "white man's burden." Canadians did more than just ape their British counterparts, however; they expressed a personal stake in the outcome of the war as part of a larger Anglo-Saxon brotherhood. During the war Canadians welcomed an Anglo-Saxon alliance that would pit the British Empire and America against the rest of the world, especially Russia. With the end of the war, much Canadian opinion focused on the common destiny of the entire English-speaking race, even postulating an Anglo-Saxon federation. Anglo-Saxon sympathy for the United States did not exclude Canadian nationalism or imperialism. Just as the great imperialist Joseph Chamberlain could call for an Anglo-Saxon alliance to serve British interests, so, too, many English Canadians preached an Anglo-Saxon patriotism that comfortably accommodated both Canadian nationalism and imperialism.

Canadian attitudes toward American imperialism revolved largely around the issue of security as Anglo-American friendship served Canada's security interests. By 1898, with Russia threatening British interests in Asia, Canadians, with some initial hesitation over the future of the Yukon, welcomed America's victory over Spain and its acquisition of former Spanish colonies. If American continental expansionism threatened Canada, American overseas expansion actually ensured Canada's security. With the British government working diligently to promote amicable Anglo-American relations, it became increasingly anachronistic for Canadian George Denison to equate British loyalty with anti-Americanism. With the rapprochement, many English Canadians became Atlanticists, seeking to establish a special place for Canada as a link between the United States and Great Britain. Historian Michael Fry notes this of the post–First World War era, yet his words apply equally to the turn of the century: "They were Atlanticists at the same time as being nationalists, anglophiles, and devotees of a maturing commonwealth relationship, because the vital consideration of Canadian and imperial policy seemed realistically to permit no other posture."[11] During 1898 many English Canadians used Anglo-Saxonism to reconcile these national, imperial, continental, and cultural outlooks.

PRE-WAR ENGLISH-CANADIAN OPINION

In the months before the outbreak of the Spanish-American War in April 1898, English-Canadian opinion remained wary of American intervention in Cuba. English-language newspapers, regardless of party affiliation, criticized American jingoism so reminiscent of the recent Venezuela scare. Editorials also suspected American commercial interests of desiring war profits. Finally, many English Canadians questioned America's right to interfere in internal Spanish affairs. Again, such misgivings echoed the Canadian critique of the Monroe Doctrine during the Venezuela crisis. If a self-interested and grasping America could rightfully intervene in Cuba, many Canadians seemed to ask, what would stop the powerful republic from turning its attention north? Many Canadian papers viewed Spanish Cuba as a fellow colony of a European monarchy, reflecting much of the rhetoric of the American press. Only with the later expressions of clear British sympathy did many journals alter their characterization of Cuba, while remaining skeptical of American outrage.

The two events that galvanized American opinion shortly before the war, the "De Lome Letter" and the "Maine" explosion, found a much cooler reception in Canada. On February 9, William Randolph Hearst's New York *Journal* printed the private correspondence of the Spanish minister to Washington, Dupuy de Lome. The "De Lome Letter," as it became infamously known, had been stolen from a Havana post office by Cuban insurgents months before and held for public release until an opportune moment. In the letter, de Lome called President McKinley "weak and a bidder for the admiration of the crowd, besides being a common politician who tries to leave a door open behind himself while keeping on good terms with the jingoes of his party." Moreover, the minister suggested having a prominent Spaniard sent to Washington "in order that I may make use of him to carry on a propaganda among the Senators and others in opposition to the junta."[12] The outcry was immediate, loud, and sustained. The State Department demanded de Lome's recall, only to find that the minister had already resigned. Americans chafed not only at the unkind portrait of their president by a foreigner, but by the suggestion of cunning Spanish manipulation of the American democratic process. In Canada, however, the Manitoba *Free Press* believed the minister's only crime to be, as the title of an editorial indicated, "The Crime of Being Found Out." "[I]n private correspondence to friends at home," the paper stated, de Lome "had a perfect right to express any opinion of the president he might happen to entertain." The *Free Press* praised de Lome's "self-respect and dignity" and criticized the Cuban insurgents for their crime. Not only had they stolen the letter, but in translating it the Cubans had "distorted its meaning to make the expressions as offensive as possible."[13] The *Mail and Empire*, though rarely in agreement with Clifford Sifton's journal, took a similar view, calling the scandal another victory for "American jingoes." The Toronto paper echoed the *Free Press* in underscoring the private nature of the letter, stolen by the Cuban junta with its headquarters in New York. For the Tory paper, the de Lome affair reflected typical American self-aggrandizement: "The eagle will, of course, clap his wings and scream, but whether, in view of all the circumstances he will, in doing so, make a very dignified appearance, is a question which we do not care to attempt to decide."[14] Doubtless the de Lome affair reminded Canadians of the American eagle's convulsion of only two years before.

Within a week of the de Lome affair, the American battleship "Maine" exploded in Havana harbour. As Walter Millis writes, "the match had at last been applied" to the powderkeg of American opinion. The "yellow" journals of Hearst and Pulitzer competed to keep the word "Maine" on every American's lips, while the navy immediately established a board of inquiry. Meanwhile, in his superior's absence, Acting Secretary of the Navy Theodore Roosevelt, with the advice of his good friend Senator Lodge, ordered the Pacific fleet under Admiral George Dewey to Hong Kong in preparation of a possible attack on the Spanish fleet at Manila. As with the de Lome affair, however, the Canadian press viewed the objectivity of the naval board with much skepticism while continuing to vent their mistrust of American motives. The Montreal *Gazette* believed the board would have "a natural, though perhaps unconscious leaning to the view most favorable to the skill, dutifulness and general fitness of the officers of the doomed vessel." The paper also viewed the current uproar in the United States as part of a broader, historic strategy to acquire Cuba.[15] The *Globe* considered the outcome of the board's inquiry predetermined, considering the number of interests concerned with shifting responsibility for the disaster away from themselves: "The United States naval authorities and their shipbuilders will, of course, be anxious that the disaster shall not be attributed to lack of discipline or faulty construction of the vessel, and general sympathy for the Cuban cause and the antipathy to Spain will all tend to the rendering of a verdict of guilty or to the confirming of suspicions which would be almost fatal to peace." The paper considered the outbreak of war nearly inevitable, especially when supported by those who grew rich not "by stopping the enemies' bullets, but in supplying bullets and other munitions of war."[16] The Toronto paper seemed to pre-date by sixty years Eisenhower's warning about the American "military-industrial complex."

Before the war much of English-Canadian opinion elaborated on the theme of American land-grabbing and the republic's inclination to intervene in others' internal affairs. This old Canadian irritant was exacerbated by the growing clash of Canadian and American interests in the Yukon. With the recent discovery of gold, thousands of prospectors poured into the Canadian territory, primarily through American-controlled port towns in the Alaskan panhandle. The undefined Alaskan boundary made the American-claimed towns a source of Canadian-American tension, and a source of anxiety for Canadians worried about the United States taking preemptive action to seize the disputed territory. In August 1897 a strange, anonymous letter circulated among top members of the Laurier cabinet. "An attempt is to be made to seize the Klondike by a big American Company," the letter warned, "The whole scheme will be unofficially supported with Government influence. Cannon are now on the way to Seattle accompanied by military experts." The letter made vague references to "The American Oligarchy ... private individuals who own the U.S. Government" and urged Canada to "fight for its independence." Though the letter appeared to have been written by a crank, Sir Richard Cartwright thought it important enough to show to the Attorney General, Oliver Mowat, and forward to Clifford Sifton, the Minister of Interior. "I send you this for what it is worth," Cartwright wrote to Sifton, "At the same time it might do no harm to cause some trusty person to make inquiries. Anything of this sort must come from the Yukon."[17] In early 1898 Sifton, alarmed by a concentration of American troops in Portland, Oregon, secretly dispatched fifty Northwest Mounted Police to the Yukon.[18] Despite the Anglo-American rapprochement, leading English Canadians still suspected that their interests might not coincide with those of their southern neighbours.

In response to the huge volume of traffic bound for the Yukon, the Liberal government made plans to build a route to the Yukon that required the use of the American town of Wrangel at the mouth of the Stickine River. While the government assumed that the Americans would give Canadian goods the bonding privilege based on the 1871 Washington Treaty (allowing goods to be transshipped through a foreign territory duty-free), the American Senate sought a *quid pro quo*. The Senate demanded that American miners be allowed to bring into the Yukon one-half ton of supplies duty-free, that American fishermen be allowed to purchase bait in Canadian ports, that Canada grant American railways charters to build in the Yukon territory, and that mining licences be given at points convenient to Americans. Meanwhile, the Laurier government had awarded the contract to build the railway portion of the route to Liberal party supporters without taking other bids, and had agreed to an enormous land-bonus for each mile of rail built. With the Laurier government seemingly trapped between their own questionable dealings and the American Senate, the Tory papers attacked. The *Mail and Empire* demanded that no more American miners be admitted into the Yukon, while the Ottawa *Evening Journal* called the American demands "Rather Bandit-Like."[19] Moreover, both papers carried strikingly similar cartoons of Uncle Sam pointing a revolver at Laurier. "Holding Him Up," the *Journal* cartoon was entitled, while within Laurier's grasp lay another pistol labelled "A Truly All-Canadian Route." In the *Mail and Empire* cartoon Uncle Sam's gun was labelled "U.S. Demands" while the caption also urged Laurier to "try another route."[20] While the cartoons were clearly politically motivated, Laurier was depicted as the victim of a hostile Uncle Sam, being urged to "fight back" with a route to the Yukon that would not rely on the United States. Uncle Sam was the villain, not the Liberal leader. Given the paper's strong partisan policy, such a depiction suggests that other attitudes transcended party politics.

Although he had initially supported the railway bill as an emergency measure designed to relieve suffering in the Yukon and help Canada monopolize Yukon trade, irate Tory backbenchers forced Sir Charles Tupper to attack the bill in the House of Commons. He called for the government to abandon the bill, yet like the Tory press, reserved his

WHAT WILL HE DO?

Hadn't he better drop them and try another route?

While Americans debated intervention in Cuba, Canadians bristled at apparent American interference in the Yukon. The United States Senate seemed to be "holding up" Laurier's plan for a route to the Klondike using the American port of Wrangel. Even a partisan paper like the *Mail and Empire* portrayed Uncle Sam, and not the Liberal leader, as the villain. (Toronto *Mail and Empire*, 8 March 1898)

JACK CANUCK   Drop that: "deal," Wilf; don't get into a "Wrangel," but grab your gun."

As the *Mail and Empire* had a few days before, the Ottawa *Evening Journal* portrayed the United States as a bandit, while urging Laurier to "grab your gun" – "a truly all Canadian route." (Ottawa *Evening Journal* 12 March 1898)

most heated remarks not for Laurier, but for the Americans. "[T]he dominion of Canada," Tupper told the House, "will never submit to any terms dictated to it which strike at the very root of the independence of the Government and of the Parliament of this country." Although Laurier and other leading Liberals defended the railway, they agreed with Tupper's defence of Canadian rights in the face of American intervention. "I agree with the hon. Leader of the Opposition that nothing should be given away of our national dignity," Laurier stated.[21] Sir Richard Cartwright said that while he had worked to "promote friendship and alliance between the English-speaking nations of the earth, ... under no conceivable circumstances would I as a Canadian representative submit for one moment that any foreign power should dictate to us where we should build railways or where we should not build railways."[22] The Liberal press defended the railway and lambasted the Opposition for advocating abandonment of the route and for not standing up to the United States. "We Stand On Our Rights," read the caption of a *Globe* cartoon depicting Laurier standing upon the granite-like "Treaty of Washington," while an angry Uncle Sam waved the "U.S. Senate Bill" of demands. "There is not a petty South American State that would allow itself to be held up in this manner," the paper stated, calling the Senate bill "international highway robbery."[23] The Liberal paper's description of the American actions as "robbery" with Canada being "held up" closely resembled the Tory press's characterization of Uncle Sam as a "bandit." Despite the clear political battle during the Yukon debate, Canadians united in their condemnation of American land-grabbing and unwarranted intervention in the domestic affairs of an independent state.

American demands upon Canada regarding the Yukon seemed to parallel the American demands upon Spain regarding Cuba. While not about to take the Tory side in the Yukon debate, Liberal papers echoed the Conservative organs in decrying American belligerence toward Spain. Moreover, many English-language papers rejected America's right to interfere in what was characterized as an internal Spanish affair. The Toronto *Globe*, Canada's leader in the use of Anglo-Saxon rhetoric to foster Anglo-American goodwill, lambasted "Our Belligerent Neighbors." The paper commented on the same day as the U.S. Senate's Yukon bill, "the general attitude of pugnacity formerly displayed toward the whole fighting world by our neighbors has been concentrated on Spain." The paper referred to Americans as "that volatile people" marked by "belligerent irritability," and "meddling" in others' disputes.[24] The *Free Press* affirmed Spain's right to "misgovern her own colony," and asked, "What right has the United States to interfere with the government of Cuba, any more than with the government of Canada or Siam?"[25]

No newspaper staked out the position of non-interference more strongly or continuously than the Halifax *Herald*. The paper especially bristled at the American claim to the right to intervene in the internal affairs of a European colony, while holding the Cuban "rebels" in disdain. The Americans, the *Herald* stated, mistakenly acted "under the assumption that if one nation thinks that another is not administering its affairs or the affairs of one of its colonies efficiently, then the first nation has a right to interfere by force, and to free the rebellious section or colony from the control of its rightful sovereign. No such right of foreign interference, however, is recognized by the nations of the world." The journal cited the American Civil War as a case in point, stating that the United States would not have tolerated any European interference. Such a "right of foreign interference," the paper repeated, "is without any justification."[26] The *Herald* maintained this position well into April, calling the Cuban insurgents "mere banditti, with no fixed territory, no organized government, preying upon the peaceful people of the country (the reconcentrados) and doing more harm to them than to the Spanish government." If the United States desired to interfere, the paper said, "they should assist Spain in putting down the rebellion, if indeed it be allowable to call such murderous guerrilla work a rebellion."[27] A few days later an editorial called the "alleged reasons" for American intervention "very weak and inconclusive," and called the Spanish "the very best friends of both the Cubans and the United States." Moreover, neither the United States nor the world in general had anything to gain from "the setting up of another Spanish-American republic of warring, murdering factions."[28] Only two days later another editorial largely repeated the same ideas, saying of the American claim to intervention, "A more preposterous and outrageously dishonest doctrine could not be imagined."[29]

The long history of troubled Canadian-American relations, and the dispute over the bonding privilege at Wrangel, must be taken into account when evaluating Canadian opinion on the eve of the war. Many English Canadians bristled at what seemed like another instance of America's "Monroe Doctrine" and "Manifest Destiny" run amok. Yet Graeme Mount is right when he concludes that most Canadians came to favour the war. What he fails to take into account was the developing British strategy of abandoning its "splendid isolation" in favour of an understanding with the United States. As the United States contemplated war with Spain, the British Empire faced threats from the French in both West Africa and the Nile River valley, the Russians in China, the Boers in South Africa, and a belligerent German Kaiser apparently ready to seize an advantage anywhere. In early March Queen Victoria sent a note to McKinley, delivered in person by British ambassador Sir Julian Pauncefote, praising the American president on the wise course he had pursued in the Cuban situation. Moreover, as the *Free Press* noted, the Queen's message conveyed British sympathy with America's position and intimated that, in case of war, "the United States might depend on something more than the moral support of Great Britain."[30] The Queen's message led to much discussion among the nations of the North Atlantic triangle of a possible Anglo-American alliance. Canadians could not ignore the tremendous outpouring of British sympathy for the United States. On the eve of war the British journal *The Speaker* talked of "a feeling of mutual friendship and confidence, founded upon the sense of kinship in blood, language and ideas."[31] A new poem by the British poet laureate Alfred Austin, entitled "America and England," also enjoyed wide circulation in North America. The poem included lines such as "Kinsmen, hail! We severed have been too long," and "Answer them, sons of the self-same race, And blood of the self-same clan." The poem clearly advocated an Anglo-American alliance, in order to combine the strengths of the two nations and face common enemies.

> A message to bond and thrall to wake,
>   For wherever we come, we twain,
> The throne of the tyrant shall rock and quake,
>   And his menace be void and vain,
> For you are lords of a strong young land,
>   And we are lords of the main.[32]

On the very eve of the Spanish-American War, Canadians were faced with the undeniable fact that the British empire, faced with threats on a number of fronts, was actively currying the favour of the United States.

As the Venezuela Crisis had done, the Spanish-American War marked another step in the development of the Anglo-American rapprochement, and English Canadians were obliged to modify their position. Once again, many English Canadians utilized Anglo-Saxon rhetoric to accommodate their views to the reality of international affairs. The *Free Press* noted the recent expressions of British friendship and, speaking for the Americans, stated that the Americans reciprocated. Americans, the paper declared, have an "affection for their kindred across the sea" and feel "that there is a bond between the two nations such as cannot exist between them and any other."[33] The Montreal *Gazette* found Spanish governance of its colonies "out of harmony with American and even with British ideas." While not advocating that England should take the American side in a quarrel with Spain, the journal noted that "the best people in both countries are conscious at all times of the kinship of race and speech, of letters of constitution, of love of justice and freedom, of lofty aspirations for human improvement and the ultimate reign of peace and truth, which knit the two nations into spiritual unity."[34] "HANDS ACROSS THE SEA" the *Herald* trumpeted, and quoted at length from a dispatch from the New York *Tribune*'s correspondent in England. The dispatch included exclamations of Anglo-American friendship from prominent British men such as Sir

Charles Dilke, Arthur Conan Doyle, and James Bryce. The solicitation of British opinion by an American journal, and reprinted in English-Canadian newspapers, closely paralleled the act of the New York *World* during the Venezuela Crisis. The American writer reported the British feeling "that American opinion is settling strongly in the direction of cordial co-operation and intimate association with England for the promotion of THE HIGHEST INTERESTS OF ANGLO-SAXON CIVILIZA-TION [original emphasis]."[35] The *Mail and Empire* believed that an Anglo-American understanding would be "a good thing for the Anglo-Saxon race, and for the English-speaking peoples," and referred to the United States and England as "two members of one family."[36]

Expressions of Anglo-American amity also found an outlet in editorial cartoons. Acknowledging the fact that the two songs used the same tune, the *Globe* depicted John Bull singing "America" and Uncle Sam singing "God Save the Queen," while a female figure labelled "Peace" played accompaniment. "Two Songs But One Tune," the caption read, "Long may the unison continue!"[37] The *Mail and Empire* reprinted a cartoon from the British journal *Punch* entitled "Blood Thicker than Water." In it, an American sailor and a British sailor shook hands in front of the Union Jack and Stars and Stripes, with the military theme of the cartoon reflecting the growing agitation for an Anglo-American alliance. British expressions of friendship on the eve of war had a profound effect on English-Canadian opinion, forcing many journals to make a quick about-face. In referring to British and American kinship and shared interests, the journals accommodated their positions using Anglo-Saxon rhetoric. As the cartoon of the British and American sailors indicates, Canadians came to view American power as a supplement, instead of a threat, to British power, and Anglo-American amity as the ultimate source of Canadian security.

Not every Anglo-Saxonist in Canada supported an Anglo-American entente on the eve of the Spanish-American War. Most important of these was Goldwin Smith, who decried America's embarkation upon an imperial experiment. For anti-imperialist Smith, an Anglo-American alliance in the name of empire was a distinct step backward. "I desire American friendship for our country," Smith wrote to a British friend, "but I do not desire an Anglo-Saxon conspiracy against other nations, because I believe it would bring on us the deserved enmity of the world and in the end lead to disaster." Moreover, Smith echoed the sentiments of many English Canadians when he took a dim view of the Cuban people. "A Cuban Republic," Smith stated, "with a population largely consisting of negroes and mulattoes ... would scarcely be a hopeful experiment."[38] In another letter he declared that a "Republic for the mongrel and half barbarian population of Cuba would be preposterous." As for the possibility of making Cuba part of the United States, Smith believed "No sensible American wants to annex Cuba which they all know will be a poisonous element in their politics."[39] Smith's use of racial rhetoric to condemn both the Anglo-American entente and the war with Spain reflected both his liberal sentiments and his ideas about North American political union. For Smith, Canadian-American racial affinity and geographic conjunction made North American union desirable. No such affinity existed between the United States and the peoples of Latin America or the Philippines. As Anglo-Saxons Canadians and Americans had an innate endowment for self-government. The "mongrel" and "half barbarian" population of Cuba, however, could never hope to be self-governing, nor could it be successfully added to the United States.

For Smith, the war also distracted Canadians and Americans from the issue of political union, and sent American attention careening off in a fatal direction. In March Smith turned down the offer of writing an article on the "Canadian Question" for the *North American Review.* "The public mind is now," he wrote to the journal's editor, "and is likely for some time to be, completely turned in another direction."[40] To John Foster he lamented that the "prospect of Continental Union is, I fear, for the present clouded. No wise Canadian would wish to embark with the United States on a career of tropical and barbarian 'expansion.'"[41] The quotation marks around the word "expansion" were significant. As will be seen later, Smith resented the application of the word to the acquisition of overseas territory. For Smith "expansion" meant adding contiguous territory – like Canada. In the end, the events of 1898 represented for Smith a complete contravention of his desire for Anglo-Saxon continental union and the end of British imperial power in the hemisphere.

WAR

Upon the outbreak of war in April 1898 much of the English-Canadian press still questioned American motives in Cuba. Americans were characterized as reckless and jingoistic, thoughtlessly rushing into war and, in the event of an American victory, taking upon themselves the difficult task of administering Cuba. The Montreal *Gazette* declared that, "A struggle with a civilized power was never entered on with less deliberation." The paper called the United States "reckless" lacking "logic" or any "regard for justice."[42] The Toronto *Globe* echoed Goldwin Smith's doubts concerning American administration of Cuba: "What benefit would the United States derive from the possession of ruined, wretched Cuba, with a population divorced by years of rapine and massacre from habits of industry, divided into sections which hate each other with vitriolic bitterness, largely composed of negro and mixed race?"[43] The Ottawa *Evening Journal* also noted the "mixed nature of the population" requiring a "strong hand" for their administration.[44]

The Halifax *Herald* remained the most critical of American actions, and embarked upon a campaign to characterize Cuba as an independent colony of Spain. Cuban rebellion, according to the journal, was baseless and American intervention unjustified. A May 5 editorial entitled "Autonomous Cuba" stated that the island "has unquestionably the means of self-government based upon popular election." All the Cuban government desired was "time and opportunity ... to administer Cuban affairs in the interest of the people." "It may still remain," the editorial concluded, "that the banditti insurgents should be dealt with as they have long deserved." The very next day a front page headline proclaimed "THE FIRST CONGRESS OF CUBA OPENED," while sub-headlines referred to the "Autonomist Representatives," and declared "SPAIN'S PROMISES FULFILLED." The fourth and final headline revealed the depth of the *Herald*'s anti-American feeling: "Home Rule Ample as That in the British Colonies Established in Cuba, Despite the Insincerity of United States."[45] Certainly very few Canadians would have compared Cuba to Canada. The *Herald* appeared to be intentionally disingenuous in order to characterize American intervention in the worst possible light. In other words, the United States and not Cuba was the real focus of the journal. While most English-language papers did not go to the same lengths as the *Herald*, Canadians' attitude toward their American neighbours on the eve of war remained distinctly chilly.

Within only a few days, however, it became clear that British authorities were sympathetic to the American cause, to the point of warning off the other European powers. Historian H.C. Allen refers to the British position as "benevolent neutrality."[46] British consuls took charge of American interests in Spain and its colonies, while in Hong Kong British aid in re-coaling allowed Admiral Dewey's victory at Manila Bay.[47] As the British journal *The Spectator* stated, "English sympathy is with our own flesh and blood." While selfish interests and jingoism might exist, the paper said that "no one shall persuade us that it is not in the cause of humanity and good government on the one side and of callous pride and savage ineptitude on the other."[48] Another British journal, the *Contemporary Review*, expressed a similar sentiment regarding the righteousness of the American cause: "The broad fact is that a great colony, in which large American interests are at stake, and which is itself the next neighbor of the United States, has been for generations abominably misgoverned, and has been for an intolerable period in revolt; that Spain has proved to be hopelessly unable to re-establish a stable and civilized government of affairs in the island; and that in her fruitless efforts she has for a long time past been guilty of revolting cruelty."[49] This single paragraph contained a number of elements that would be echoed by the Canadian press. Cuba's proximity to the United States, Spain's misgovernment, and the military's cruelty justified American intervention.

Once the war had begun, English Canadians could not fail to note the warmth of British feeling toward the United States. The *Globe* explained that while Great Britain did not want European interference in the western hemisphere, it could look on American authority over Cuba with "comparative indifference." The paper welcomed Anglo-American understanding during the crisis, happy that "people of the same tongue, the same traditions, and the same interests" looked to each other for support.[50] Indeed, British sympathy with the United States constituted news itself in the English-Canadian press. The very word "sympathy" would be repeated endlessly, indicating England's friendly attitude while maintaining technical neutrality. The *Free Press* noted "British sympathies" to be "completely with the United States."[51] In a front-page headline the Montreal *Star* proclaimed "SYMPATHY OF ANGLO-SAXONS," and in a sub-headline, "United States Warmly Supported in England."[52]

As with the Venezuela crisis, many English Canadians were forced to accommodate their negative view of the United States to the realities of British policy and Anglo-American relations. Journals that had questioned American motives in early April now began to preach the righteousness of the American cause. "A great, enlightened and progressive nation is about to grapple with a less enlightened, somewhat cruel-tempered ... people," the *Globe* stated, not long after condemning American jingoism and economic self-interest. "We who speak the English language," the paper continued, "under whatever flag, under whatever skies we dwell, cannot but believe the United States right in the grand point at issue, cannot but assent to the righteousness of the decision to use force to put an end to bloodshed and barbarity." All Anglo-Saxons, the paper seemed to say, were united in the cause of Cuba. "The cause of solidarity of the English-speaking nations," the paper concluded, "has received a definite and, we may hope, enormous impetus."[53]

British sympathy, then, quickly translated into Canadian sympathy. Many English-Canadian papers, previously critical of the United States, now accepted American intervention based upon the proximity of Cuba, Spanish cruelty, and the overall "righteousness" of the American cause. "On Which Side?" asked a *Globe* editorial, declaring that "hearts are not bound by neutrality declarations," and making the case for American intervention. "A civilized nation is justified in insisting that there shall be no nuisance maintained in its immediate neighborhood," the editorial stated, sounding very much like the later Roosevelt Corollary to the Monroe Doctrine. For those still unconvinced, the paper established a clear dichotomy between the United States and Spain and pressed Canadians to choose sides: "On the one side is the embodiment of wicked selfishness and corruption in the treatment of subject countries, snarling defiance over its sole remaining victim; on the other an English-speaking nation, possessing, it may be, some objectionable peculiarities, but thrilled with a generous impulse and bent upon lessening the sum of human misery. On which side Canada?"[54] In the *Globe*'s contrast between the two countries, America's greatest attribute seemed to be its status as "an English-speaking nation." The Montreal *Star* also preached the essential unity of Americans and "Britons," calling the two nations "one people." "Their blood, their traditions, their history in great part, their characteristic virtues, and their characteristic faults," the paper said of the Americans, "are all ours." Moreover, the United States shared in the superior English civilization, "civilization that the aliens do not love; a type characterized by civil and religious liberty, by enlightenment, progress and prosperity."[55] All English-speaking peoples, then, necessarily shared in the American cause. Finally, a *Globe* cartoon depicted "John Canuck" warmly clasping the hand of Uncle Sam as he departed for war, with a rifle labelled "Cuba Libre." In the background, a sign read "This Continent for Free Governments Only," while John Canuck said, "We have our own little border squabbles, Sam, and will attend to them in due course; but when it comes to fighting foreigners in a righteous cause you know where my heart is!"[56] For "citizens" of the same race, and speaking the same language, all others were "foreigners."

The term "righteous" received wide use throughout English Canada in describing the Spanish-American War, especially among the religious press. Journals essentially characterized the conflict as a holy war, a humanitarian crusade by the Americans against a despotic and cruel government. The Manitoba *Free Press* believed Americans fought for "the cause of humanity." "[W]e have faith in their Anglo-Saxon breed," the paper declared.[57] "SIC SEMPER TYRANNIS!" read the caption of a *Globe* cartoon, depicting a mighty American Columbia lifting little Spain out of Cuba on the tip of her sword.[58] The Halifax *Herald*, though still skeptical of American motives, reprinted a cartoon from the British journal *Puck* entitled "The Peace Maker." In it Uncle Sam prepared to separate warring Cuba and Spain, saying "in the cause of humanity it is my duty to separate them."[59] The *Canadian Churchman* described the state of Cuba as "lamentable and intolerable," saying of Spain, "ultimately they must be judged by the mind and voice of the civilized world of the nineteenth century."[60] The *Presbyterian Record* stated that "the cruelty of and oppression of Spain ... has driven her colonies to revolt," and blamed Spanish cruelty on two primary influences – the Inquisition and the bull fight.[61]

Writing in *Queen's Quarterly*, George Grant summed up much of English-Canadian opinion in the April issue, just before the outbreak of hostilities. He spoke of Great Britain as America's only "reliable ally in the hour of danger," predicting that any move by the European powers would result in a "permanent union of the English-speaking peoples." Considering the reports of Spanish brutality just off the Florida coast, Grant wondered at the restraint of "our cousins." "The British people in like circumstances would not have been so patient," Grant wrote. Like a number of other writers, Grant pointed out the racial problem of Cuba: "the blacks, half-breeds and whites, who are in arms against Spain testify to her unfitness to rule, but they themselves are equally unfit." Having freed the Cubans from Spain, then, the United States could not "wash her hands of all responsibility as regards their future." "In the hands of Britain it would soon be turned into a garden of the Lord," Grant stated, "but that is out of the question." The United States must take up the work that Great Britain could not, for both nations strove for "the welfare of humanity by the extension of liberty, the reign of law and the establishment of justice." Grant concluded that "the great forces all tend to reunite the English-speaking race."[62] For Grant, as for so many other English Canadians, the war with Spain had a clear advantage to Canada and the rest of the English-speaking world; namely, the Cuban situation fostered Anglo-American friendship and underscored the essential unity of the Anglo-Saxon people of the world. However, Grant did not believe that the United States and Great Britain needed to make their understanding official. "A formal alliance is not needed," Grant stated. "Their interest is the same, and so is their heart." Within a month, though, the word "alliance" would be on every tongue in the English-speaking world.

JOSEPH CHAMBERLAIN AND THE "ANGLO-SAXON ALLIANCE"

By early May, only two weeks into the war, an Anglo–American understanding had been firmly established. The rapid and seemingly effortless destruction of the Spanish fleet in Manila Bay only underscored the value of American friendship. The battle had catapulted the republic to the status of world power, and created a valuable British ally in the

CIVILIZATION'S ULTIMATUM.

UNCLE SAM – Now, see here, you bull-fighting barbarian – war or no war, you've got to git out of this continent bag and baggage right now, and if you ever show your ugly mug again I'll wipe you out of existence!

· Far from being threatened by an American war in the hemisphere, English Canadians supported American intervention in Cuba as defending Anglo-Saxon civilization. In this *Globe* cartoon, Uncle Sam delivers "Civilization's Ultimatum" to Spain, while John Bull, standing in Canada, voices his support (Toronto *Globe*, 9 April 1898)

Pacific. English Canadians also expressed their deep sympathy with the United States, based upon common ties of blood. The *Globe* described the victory as "The Anglo-Saxon Opportunity" in an editorial headline. The paper identified the old reasons behind "Canadian sympathy," including "blood is thicker than water" and "Our hearts are with the men who speak our tongue." "Anglo-Saxon unity would be a momentous development in the world's history," the paper stated. Moreover, American friendship remained vital to Great Britain in her "splendid isolation." Canada, the paper said, had a special role to play in indicating British sympathy to the Americans: "[T]he British soil nearest to them is Canada. The portion of the British Empire they know most about is Canada. The Britons with whose sentiments they will be in closest touch are Canadians. Let us, as Canadians, earnestly set ourselves to do our part in achieving this great result."[63] As it had so often before, the Toronto *Globe* interpreted Anglo-American friendship through the prism of racial affinity. Moreover, the journal gave Canada a special role in bringing about Anglo-Saxon unity. Such a view did not run counter to Canadian loyalty to Great Britain, but actually reinforced it. Instead of a Canadian nationalism that excluded the United States, the *Globe* asserted a Canadian nationalism that included America, Canada, and Great Britain under the umbrella of Anglo-Saxonism.

By early May, the twin ideas of "Anglo-Saxon unity" and "Anglo-Saxon alliance" had received wide attention. In the *North American Review* for that month, the Reverend Lyman Abbott published an article entitled "The Basis of an Anglo-American Understanding." The article constituted the strongest call yet from a prominent American for an Anglo-American alliance. Abbott broke little new ground in his article, reiterating the old ideas about Anglo-Saxon kinship, liberty, and Christianity:

[T]he United States is of kin to Great Britain. The two represent the same essential political ideals: they are both democratic; they both represent the same ethical ideals; they are Christian; and they both represent the same race leadership; they are Anglo-Saxon. In so far as their conjoint influence dominates the world, it will carry with it a tendency toward liberty in the political institutions organized, a tendency toward Christianity in the ethical spirit of society created, and a tendency toward that energy, that intelligence, and that thrift which are the characteristics of the Anglo-Saxon race in the life promoted. It is from the combination of these three elements of society – political liberty, Christian ethics, Anglo-Saxon energy – that what we call civilization proceeds.

A combination of the two countries, Abbott believed, would promote Christian civilization and political liberty throughout the world. Moreover, the alliance need not be limited to Great Britain and the United States only. "Such an alliance would include not only our own country and the British Isles," Abbott wrote, "but all the colonies and dependencies of Great Britain ... It would unite in the furtherance of a Christian civilization all the Anglo-Saxon peoples."[64]

Abbott's call for an Anglo-Saxon alliance was answered by one of the foremost imperialists of the day, British Colonial Secretary Joseph Chamberlain. A vocal and devout advocate of imperial federation,

Chamberlain had been instrumental in undermining the North American commercial union movement in the late 1880s. Yet Chamberlain was no champion of British isolation, and viewed an alliance with either the United States or Germany, or even both, as necessary for the security of the empire. Ultimately, though, Chamberlain's heart lay with the United States.[65] With an American wife, Chamberlain's trans-Atlantic marriage ranked second only, perhaps, to Lord Randolph Churchill's and represented a significant trend in the turn-of-the-century Atlantic community.[66]

Chamberlain's views illustrated that even the most fervent imperialist of the day could find common ground with the United States through the employment of Anglo-Saxonism. In a speech to his constituents in Birmingham on May 13, in an apparent answer to Lyman Abbott as well as in an attempt to break the Liberals' monopoly on the alliance issue, Chamberlain regretted the American war with Spain, but added, "even war itself would be cheaply purchased if, in a great and noble cause, the Stars and Stripes and the Union Jack should wave together over an Anglo-Saxon alliance." Noting the web of European alliances, Chamberlain stated that the British government had two duties. The first was "to draw all parts of the empire closer together – to infuse into them a spirit of united and of Imperial patriotism." The second duty was, Chamberlain said, "to establish and to maintain bonds of permanent amity with our kinsmen across the Atlantic. They are a powerful and a generous nation. They speak our language, they are bred of our race. Their laws, their literature, their standpoint upon every question are the same as ours; their feeling, their interest in the cause of humanity and the peaceful development of the world are identical with ours."[67]

The twin duties Chamberlain spoke of – one to the empire and one to Anglo-American harmony – were far from contradictory. With England menaced by combinations of European powers, imperial solidarity and Anglo-Saxon solidarity constituted the twin pillars of British security. Moreover, no one would accuse Chamberlain of betraying the idea of imperial patriotism by his call for an Anglo-American alliance. Chamberlain's speech illustrated that imperialism and Anglo-Saxonism comfortably co-existed even in the most devout imperialist.

Had Chamberlain's peers in the government or British editorial opinion condemned Chamberlain's speech as provocative or untimely, English-Canadian opinion likely would have echoed the sentiment. Yet the Birmingham speech received little but applause. Thanks once again to the New York *Journal*'s solicitation of opinion from leading Britons, Canadians and Americans could easily see that British opinion warmly received the call for an Anglo-Saxon alliance. The *Journal* included favourable comments from the Duke of Argyll, Herbert Spencer, Baron Russell (the Chief Justice of England), the Earl of Kimberly (House of Lords Liberal leader), the Duke of Westminster, the Marquis of Lorne (former governor-general of Canada and Queen Victoria's son-in-law), the Marquis of Ripon, and the Duke of Newcastle. The Duke of Fife called for complete understanding "between the two great peoples which have sprung from the Anglo-Saxon race," while Albert Shaw's old friend William Stead said, "Unity of the race is the dream of my life." British papers such as the *Times*, *Daily Chronicle*, and Yorkshire *Post*, also supported Chamberlain's speech. The *Standard* applauded the call for an Anglo-American alliance, noted British isolation in the face of European alliances, and noted the warm British feeling toward "the great kindred community on the other side of the Atlantic."[68] In supporting Chamberlain's speech British leaders and the press made full use of Anglo-Saxon rhetoric. Moreover, by voicing their support for an Anglo-Saxon alliance, these Britons essentially voiced their own call for an alliance of the English-speaking world.

Leading Canadians followed the British lead. In June Laurier, using language reminiscent of Anglo-Saxon rhetoric, told Whitelaw Reid that an Anglo-American alliance "must be the potent factor that has yet taken place in history in the advancement of civilization."[69] Even Colonel Denison expressed pleasure with the alliance talk, telling Lord Salisbury, "Anglo-American unity is a good thing to talk about just now, and following the English lead, our papers almost universally, as well as our public men in public utterances, are friendly to the United States."[70] While some British and English-Canadian journals regarded Chamberlain's speech as an "indiscretion" and "alarming,"[71] most welcomed the idea of an Anglo-Saxon alliance. The *Free Press* noted the Anglo-American "identity of interests," and said the "suggestion of an Anglo-American alliance is warmly applauded."[72] In an editorial entitled "British-Americanism" the Toronto *Globe* commented that "the permanent forces seem to be on the side of union," and that such an alliance "would help the progress of civilization."[73] As it had before, the *Globe* also took pains to give Canada a central role in fostering Anglo-American amity. In one cartoon John Canuck danced between Uncle Sam and John Bull under the banner "Alliance," while Chamberlain played a lute labelled "Anglo-Saxon Unity." "The Music of the Future!," the caption read, "And Jack Canuck's the connecting link!"[74] In another cartoon John Canuck watched as Uncle Sam and John Bull watered a small tree labelled "Anglo-Saxon Unity." "It Has Taken Deep Root!," the caption read.[75] The *Canadian Churchman* believed the time had come "to encourage unity of spirit and aim between peoples who are one in race, in language, and in institutions."[76]

"THE MUSIC OF THE FUTURE!"

CHAMBERLAIN STRIKES THE POPULAR CHORD.

Yes! And Jack Canuck's the connecting link!

The Toronto *Globe* welcomed Jospeh Chamberlain's May 13, 1898, speech to his
Birmingham constituents calling for an Anglo-Saxon alliance. While Chamberlain plays
a harp labelled "Anglo-Saxon Unity," Jack Canuck provides the "connecting link"
between Uncle Sam and John Bull. In the background, a Spaniard looks on with dismay.
(Toronto *Globe*, 17 May 1898)

Believing Chamberlain's speech to be "almost accepted as an unofficial
answer to Dr. Abbott's," the Montreal *Gazette* quoted at length from
Lyman Abbott's *North American Review* article, explaining the identity of interests between the two "Great Anglo-Saxon communities."[77]
Even the often anti-American Halifax *Herald* could not stem the tide
of opinion following Chamberlain's speech. In a cartoon entitled "The
Alliance Wheel," Uncle Sam and John Bull rode a tandem bicycle with
each wheel a hemisphere of the globe. "Now, Jonathan, steady," John
Bull cautioned his riding partner, "both together, and we'll control the
movement of this old wheel."[78] Only a month into the war, English-
Canadian opinion had altered significantly. The strength of feeling

IT HAS TAKEN DEEP ROOT!

The growing herb that will become a tree, so that the birds of Peace will come and lodge in the branches thereof.

With growing evidence of Anglo-American friendship during the Spanish-American War, many in Canada and the United States began to discuss Anglo-Saxon alliance and even eventual union. In this *Globe* cartoon, under the watchful eye of Jack Canuck, John Bull and Uncle Sam care for a tree labelled "Anglo-Saxon Unity." Leaves labelled "Emerson," "Shakespeare," and "Tennyson" indicate a common language and literature, while other leaves are labelled "Brotherhood," "Fellowship," and "Sympathy." The tree is threatened by pests "Fenians," "Jingoism," and "US Silver Bug." (Toronto *Globe*, 31 May 1898)

emanating from England, especially from a fervent imperialist and a member of the British Cabinet, forced Canadians to adapt their view of the United States. Moreover, just as Lyman Abbott and Joseph Chamberlain utilized Anglo-Saxon rhetoric .in their public appeals for Anglo-American alliance, English-Canadian journals echoed the rhetoric in welcoming the growth of English-speaking amity. Canadians adopted the British position of seeing American power as a guarantee of imperial security, and differentiated between American "intervention" in Cuba and American "aggression" in the Yukon.

In his speech calling for an Anglo-American alliance, Chamberlain stressed British isolation in the face of European combinations. Canadians

THE ALLIANCE WHEEL,

John Bull – "Now, Jonathan, steady, both together, and we'll control the movement of this old wheel."

The Halifax *Herald* was one of the most Loyalist and anti-American of English-language Canadian newspapers. With growing Anglo-American friendship, however, the paper welcomed Chamberlain's call for an Anglo-Saxon alliance, believing that together the United States and Great Britain would essentially control the world. (Halifax *Herald*, 20 May 1898) such as Richard Cartwright had previously cited British isolation in calling for Anglo-American amity and positing a special role for Canada in fostering that amity. Now in the aftermath of the Birmingham speech, English-Canadian journals gave a prominent place to British isolation in their discussion of an Anglo-American alliance. Moreover, the swift American victory at Manila Bay had underscored American power and the enormous potential benefit of American friendship, especially in the East. With an identity of Anglo-American interests, American power did not constitute a threat, but actually served to complement imperial, and thus Canadian, security. Days after Chamberlain's speech, the *Mail and Empire* noted that the Colonial Secretary's "outspoken declaration" was "at first glance somewhat questionable policy." Yet the Tory journal accepted Chamberlain's position because it constituted "a sharp warning to Europe." Pointing to Russia, France, Germany, and Austria, the *Mail and Empire* stated "they are coming to an understanding and shaping their policies to the one end of destroying Britain's position." The danger facing Britain justified the appeal "for support to the other great Anglo-Saxon nation, whose interests should lie in the same plane."[79] The *Monetary Times* also noted that "Russia, Austria and Germany are said to be drawing closer together," while "a conviction that their civilizing mission must draw the two branches of Anglo-Saxons together is uppermost in England and the United States." "The interests of the United States in China are identical with those of England," the journal declared, "and the possession of the Philippines will enable the Republic the better to bear her share in safeguarding those interests."[80]

Foremost among the nations apparently threatening British interests in the East was Russia. By building the Trans-Siberian Railway and demanding concessions from China, Russia appeared poised to emerge as the new power in the Far East. Canadians understood this. With the American victory in the Philippines and the Anglo-American rapprochement in place, English Canadians looked to the United States to counter the Russian threat and protect common Anglo-American interests. Moreover, English Canadians regarded the Far Eastern question in terms of race. In the June 1898 issue of *North American Review*, the Canadian Minister of Justice, David Mills, published an article entitled "Which Shall Dominate – Saxon or Slav?" Writing of America's future in international affairs, Mills asked, "Shall she unite with Russia, and endeavor to put an end to Anglo-Saxon leadership in the world, or shall she join with the British Empire in giving additional strength and assured permanency to that ascendancy?" For Mills the history of the world was marked by "a succession of distinct races," with each race representing "a distinct group of ideas which were essential to the progress of mankind." As other writers had noted, Anglo-Saxon civilization had been marked by progress, liberty, industry, and the rule of law. The spread of the British Empire had resulted in the spread of Anglo-Saxon values and civilization. Mills welcomed the United States as a fellow Anglo-Saxon nation in maintaining that civilization. "I embrace the United States as a part of the Anglo-Saxon community," Mills wrote, because "the present order of things rests upon Anglo-Saxon supremacy." Russia threatened British supremacy, and thus Anglo-Saxon civilization throughout the world. "The danger is a danger not to one state," Mills wrote, "but to the race to which we all belong."[81] For Mills, the events of the previous months had underscored the necessity of American friendship in maintaining British interests and imperial security. As English-Canadian writers had before, Mills called upon a higher patriotism – that of race – to bring the United States into the Anglo-Saxon fold.

A few months later, Archibald Colquhoun made a startlingly similar appeal in *Harper's* magazine. Indeed, some portions of the article seemed nearly identical to that of Mills. Mills had asked, "Shall she unite with Russia, and endeavor to put an end to Anglo-Saxon leadership in the world, or shall she join with the British Empire in giving additional strength and assured permanency to that ascendancy?" Colquhoun wrote: "The problem by which the United States is confronted ... is whether she will merge her forces with those of Russia, and thus put an end to Anglo-Saxon leadership in the development of the world, or co-operate with Britain in strengthening that ascendancy, so making it practically unassailable." Like Mills, Colquhoun also viewed human history as the result of "racial competition carried throughout countless ages." Mills had stated that the United States "has not, and cannot have, an independent existence." Colquhoun wrote that with America now established in Puerto Rico, Hawaii, and the Philippines, "she can no longer lead an independent existence." Like many other writers, Colquhoun noted the "bond of race, of language, of religion, and of government" between the United States and Britain, indicating a common destiny. "The danger threatening Britain is one threatening the Anglo-Saxon race," Colquhoun stated, while Mills had written, "The danger is a danger not to one state, but to the race to which we all belong."[82] Colquhoun may have, unthinkingly or otherwise, borrowed from Mills's article, yet the similarity of the articles should not mask the conformity of opinion. Written five months apart, one during the war and one after, the two articles represented a continuing feeling among English-speaking peoples that the Anglo-Saxon race had reached a crossroads in human history. Either the United States could join with Great Britain to uphold Anglo-Saxon civilization everywhere, or Anglo-Saxons would be superseded as the dominant race.

Not all the English-speaking world accepted the idea of an Anglo-Saxon union controlling the world's destiny. Like Goldwin Smith, many Americans were anti-imperial or anti-monarchical, and shuddered at the thought that the United States would support the British anachronism. In condemning the present path of the United States, many writers attacked the Anglo-Saxon rhetoric of those calling for an English-speaking union. John Clark Ridpath ridiculed the "oft-sung strain of common language, common race, and the common historical destiny of the English-speaking nations," and dismissed "all this 'English-speaking race' business."[83] The Irish nationalist Michael Davitt wrote a widely circulated article that argued, as many others did, that the United States could not be considered an Anglo-Saxon nation. Professor of Archaeology Charles Waldstein agreed with Davitt, pointing out the mixture of races in the United States. Yet he objected more strenuously to the employment of the term "Anglo-Saxon" because it indicated what he called "Ethnological Chauvinism ... that most baneful and pernicious of modern national diseases." Such "Pan-Anglo-Saxonism" Waldstein likened to anti-Semitism and other racial and religious prejudices.[84] Yet the professor merely replaced the racial idea of Anglo-Saxonism with the term "English-speaking Brotherhood," indicating "common language; common forms of government; common culture, including customs and institutions; a common history; a common religion ... and, finally, common interests." While many writers used the terms "Anglo-Saxon" and "English-speaking" interchangeably, Waldstein was one of the few who made a distinction between the racial and lingual concepts. Few writers, however, were professors of archaeology or ethnology.

In Great Britain, the *Saturday Review* maintained its opposition to any Anglo-American alliance with a mix of anti-Americanism and defence of imperial isolation. Writing in the *Nineteenth Century* Frederick Greenwood also attacked the use of Anglo-Saxon rhetoric in appealing for such a union. "If at bottom it really meant partnership in armed defence, it could have no other origin to be sound," he wrote. "Say that it sprang from the consideration that 'blood is thicker than water,'" Greenwood continued, "and if you really think that you give expression to a stronger or trustier motive than mutual need you may depend upon it that you are mistaken." As proof, he cited the "unspeakable slaughter" of the American Civil War.[85] Still, the progress of the Spanish-American War witnessed only continued expressions of goodwill from British writers. Goldwin Smith's friend James Bryce wrote an article entitled "The Essential Unity of Britain and America," and gave prominent place to Canada. Bryce noted that "intensified race consciousness" had "deepened the sense of solidarity in the scattered members of the race, and drawn Englishmen nearer and nearer to the great branch in the United States, now larger than their own, as well as the smaller branches in Canada and Australia." For anti-imperialist Bryce, Anglo-Saxonism, not imperialism, drew together the various parts of the empire. Moreover, the same racial affinity drew all the English-speaking world together, regardless of nationality. Once again, Anglo-Saxonism was offered as a higher patriotic concept. Bryce also explicitly hoped that the United States would spread its influence over Latin America, "reclaiming those regions from misgovernment or barbarism by an infiltration of the surplus population of North America." As a self-governing Anglo-Saxon nation, Canada need not cause a dispute between the United States and Canada. Indeed, after a recent trip to Canada, Bryce believed that the friendly spirit between Americans and Britons "is now the prevailing spirit among Canadians also."[86] Bryce would soon accept membership in the newly created Anglo-American Friendship League. His friend Smith declined to join.[87]

Continued British expressions of friendship and the call for an Anglo-Saxon partnership stimulated similar appeals in Canada.[88] During the war such expressions had taken the form of calls for an Anglo-Saxon alliance to protect common Anglo-American interests around the globe. The arrival at the Philippines in August of a large German naval squadron, with the apparent mission to pick up any leftover scraps, only heightened the spectre of a European menace. With the end of the war, American occupation of the Philippines and annexation of Hawaii, the attention of the English-speaking world focused on America's possible colonial future. Writers called not for a defensive alliance against Russia or the European concert, but for an Anglo-Saxon alliance to spread civilization, Christianity, and freedom to the far corners of the world. Working together, Anglo-Saxons would become the "ruling race," able to bring peace and progress to the globe. American and British writers took up the question with relish. Writing in the *Arena*, Frank Anderson contended that, "The irresistible weight of Great Britain and the United States allied would settle every quarrel in the manner most to the interests of the Anglo-Saxon race until at last the end would be a world governed by that race, speaking the English tongue, moulded on our institutions, and federated into one great earth-embracing commonwealth."[89] Writing in the *Nineteenth Century*, Edward Dicey declared that "With us of the Anglo-Saxon race ... it is our mission, our manifest destiny to rule the world."[90] In the United States, B.O. Flowers called for a federation of all Anglo-Saxon nations to "secure for civilization, progress, and humanity the authority which the English-speaking races should exert."[91] With the end of the century approaching, such calls for an English-speaking union took on a millennial tone. British and American writers looked forward not just to an Anglo-American alliance in defence of common interests, but to a world dominated by the ruling race.

At the end of the war, English-Canadian opinion echoed the sentiments heard throughout the North Atlantic community. Additionally, running through much of the Canadian comment was a strong religious, missionary strain. Looking to the Philippines, the *Mail and Empire* believed that "under the Stars and Stripes commerce and Christianity will advance where disorder and crime have for years existed unchecked and unpunished." Sounding like its British and American counterparts the paper added, "The domination of the Anglo-Saxon race is being further assured."[92] The Toronto *Globe* printed a cartoon of Uncle Sam and John Bull entitled "Let the Good Work Go On!" In the background a Spaniard lay on the ground under the description "Spanish Tyranny!" including "Misrule, Extortion, Outrage, Starvation," while a still-healthy Turk stood behind John Bull. "Now, John," Uncle Sam said to his British cousin, "it's your turn to clean out that eastern savage just as I did the western tyrant; and you can count on my moral support just as I counted on yours!"[93] The Halifax *Herald* printed a feature article by R.R. McLeod entitled "Universal Empire for Anglo Saxon Stock." McLeod believed that the "emancipation of down-trodden millions" indicated "some divine far-reaching purpose in our history." McLeod added, "The large lines of God under-running human affairs are surely to be seen in the evolution of this fine Anglo-Saxon stock."[94] Anglo-Saxons were a chosen people with a common, God-given mission in the world. Far from seeing America's ascent to world power status as a threat, English Canadians shared in the American victory as of benefit for the entire English-speaking world. The *Mail and Empire* summed up Anglo-Saxon interests nicely by calling them "commerce and Christianity."

The September *Methodist Magazine* summarized a number of points concerning an Anglo-Saxon alliance. The journal predicted that the next great conflict would be between the Saxon and the Slavic races, and stated that in such a conflict, "the forces by land and sea of the great republic of the west would find their place side by side with those of the Mother Country." Yet such an alliance would be not merely defensive, or a "jingo alliance" to dominate the world. "The ideal of the Anglo-Saxon alliance," the journal continued, "would be to "establish a supreme force that will make for righteousness, for law and order and liberty, for the 'open door' in commerce and the open Bible in religion throughout the world."[95] The "open door in commerce and the open Bible in religion" sounded very much like the *Mail and Empire*'s "commerce and Christianity." While much of the English-speaking world failed to realize that most Filipinos were already Christianized, even those in Canada who understood this still viewed the islands as fertile ground for missionary work. After all, Anglo-Saxon influence in the Philippines meant Protestantism, not Roman Catholicism. In the same September issue of *Methodist Magazine* appeared the call of an American bishop for the immediate occupation of the Philippines by American churches. "We should go there to Christianize them," Bishop Thoburn urged, "to elevate them in the scale of civilization and to fit them for a place among the Christian nations of the earth."[96] With the American victory in the war began a new debate about America's role in the world. Should the United States retain the Philippines and become a colonial power? Even before the war ended, English Canadians pressed for American retention of the islands as a field for missionary endeavour.

"WHITE MAN'S BURDEN"

Months before Kipling printed his plea for the United States to take up the "white man's burden," English Canadians utilized Anglo-Saxon rhetoric to urge the United States to retain the Philippines. Essentially, American occupation of the Philippines would serve British interests in the East, and counter the German and Russian threat. Yet just as Kipling's poem did not address matters of international diplomacy and strategy, English-Canadian opinion cloaked a desire to serve imperial interests in the "pious justification" of racial rhetoric. Americans, it was believed, would bring civilization, progress, and Protestant Christianity to a semi-barbarous people. The Protestantism of English Canada displayed itself in the pages of journals like *Queen's Quarterly* and *Canadian Magazine*, while the religious press voiced strong opinions about the character of Filipinos, Spanish Catholic rule, and the potential for missionary work. As fellow Anglo-Saxons English Canadians expressed a personal stake in the question of the Philippines, and a shared mission with the United States. Although the idea of an Anglo-Saxon mission had already become part of the lexicon of the English-speaking race, Kipling's poem helped entrench the doctrine through the introduction of a new catch-phrase. Just as journalists and politicians had continually repeated the same words – words such as "kin," "blood," and "civilization" – to express clearly a popular idea to a large audience, now Kipling's phrase would drop from every tongue and flow from every pen.

Even before the end of the war the British hoped that the United States would retain the Philippines. In July 1898 the American Ambassador John Hay cabled the State Department that the "British Government prefer to have us retain Philippine Islands, or failing that, insist on option in case of future sale."[97] While official British opinion clearly wanted to prevent the Philippines falling into the hands of a hostile power, the British public expressed the same hope in racial terms. "It would be a relief if another English-speaking power would take up the task," the *Spectator* stated, because the "weary titan" needed an ally. The journal concluded that "the only ally whose aspirations, ideas and language are like his own is the great American people."[98]

The English-Canadian press agreed. "Should the United States decide on the expansive policy," *Queen's Quarterly* stated in July, "the world will no doubt benefit."[99] German actions around the Philippines only heightened the sense of danger. Though Dewey had defeated the Spanish navy at Manila in late May, American troops did not arrive for several weeks. In the meantime, a large German fleet, with vessels outnumbering the Americans', arrived in the bay along with other smaller flotillas from three other neutral powers including Great Britain. The Germans evidently hoped that a large presence would buttress any German claims to the Philippines in the case of American abandonment. The German presence, however, alarmed both the British and Americans. A series of incidents found the British admiral, a good friend of Dewey's, taking the American side against the Germans. On August 13 the British admiral, wanting a better view of the American bombardment of the city, moved his ships so that they came between the German and American fleets, giving rise to a legend of significant British aid in the face of a German threat.[100]

For English Canadians, the American capture of Manila obligated the United States to remain in the Philippines for the sake of civilization and fair government. With the subsequent end of the war, some Canadians also urged American retention of Cuba, despite pre-war fears of American aggrandizement. "The United States has contracted a responsibility for the good of the government of the islands by arming the rebel forces," the *Monetary Times* believed, "forces which, in the interest of civilization, she must direct and guide, and if they refuse direction and guidance she must control."[101]

The *Times* echoed much of the pre-war doubts concerning the Filipinos' and Cubans' suitability for self-government. As non-Anglo-Saxons, they required an Anglo-Saxon power to "control" them. The *Canadian Churchman* agreed: "If the Americans emancipated the down-trodden Cubans, they are bound to see that their liberty does not become a curse to them." The *Churchman* declared it the American "duty not to let go of the incipient republics, if that is to be their destiny, until they have been got into some kind of shape and order." Presaging Kipling's warning about the "burden" of imperialism, the journal added, "This is the work of the victorious people – not a simple or an easy one. All just and true men will watch the doing of it with sympathy, interest and good-will, and also with boundless patience."[102] The Toronto *Globe* printed a cartoon of an exhausted Uncle Sam pushing a child-like "Cuba" on a bicycle, with wheels labelled "Self-Government" and "Native institutions." The dark-skinned child's feet do not reach the pedals. "A Long, Hot and Unexpected Job," the caption read, while Uncle Sam complained in American-ese, "Gee whiz! Ef I had s'posed I'd a-had to hold this thing up till he growed big enough to work the pedals for hisself, I'd a-kep' out of it altogether, you bet!"[103] Other journals likened American responsibility in the former Spanish colonies to British duty in the empire. "If they decide to go into the higher politics," the Montreal *Star* stated, "civilization and the advancement of liberty will undoubtedly be the better for it. They can do in other corners of the world what Britain has done in Egypt. They may thus fulfill their destiny."[104] While the United States might have freed the Cubans and Filipinos from Spanish rule, the native populations needed some guiding hand to steer them toward self-government. According to English Canadians, the British had already shown themselves adept at such work, and few doubted the capabilities of the Anglo-Saxon republic. Indeed, such work was the "destiny" of the United States.

However, as the debate over American expansionism wore on through autumn and early winter, many English-speaking North Americans spoke out against American imperialism. In the United States these detractors included former president Grover Cleveland, Andrew Carnegie, Carl Schurz, Stanford President David Starr Jordan, and William Jennings Bryan. While most Republicans followed the lead of the "large policy" advocated by Lodge and Roosevelt, Republican Speaker of the House Thomas Reed opposed American expansion. Anti-Imperialist Leagues sprang up in American cities that fall. The anti-imperialists argued that American expansion ran counter to American ideals embodied in the words of the Founding Fathers and Lincoln's Gettysburg address.[105] Americans could not rule other peoples without their consent. Or, as Bryan said, paraphrasing the Great Emancipator, "this nation cannot endure half republic and half colony – half free and half vassal."[106] Anti-imperialists also utilized racial rhetoric. Noting that the Philippines contained "a large mass of more or less barbarous Asiatics," Carl Schurz believed expansion would mean "the moral ruin of the Anglo-Saxon republic."[107] Andrew Carnegie, desiring to preserve "the English-speaking race," feared Americans settling among the Filipinos, "alien races, ignorant of our language and institutions."[108]

In Canada, Goldwin Smith struck up a correspondence with the anti-imperialist and anglophobic Congressman from New York, W. Bourke

Cockran, and complained about the misuse of the term "expansion."
"It seems to me that you allow your opponents an undue advantage
in permitting to use the term 'expansion' as they do," Smith wrote.
"Expansion means extension without breach of continuity ... Louisiana
was expansion. Canada would be expansion. The Phillippines [sic]
clearly are not." Smith made a clear distinction between expansion
within the continental United States, whether actual or hypothetical,
and the acquisition of an overseas empire. Calling imperialism "expansion" seemed to dilute the enormity of the new American policy.
Indeed, Smith suggested that Cockran make clear the distinction and
resurrect "expansion" on the continent as an anti-imperialist argument. "Might not you find in expansion proper a counter charm to
imperialism?" Smith wrote, "'A hair' of a much better dog than that
which has bitten your people!" While an unusual argument among
anti-imperialists, Smith's concern over expansion clearly reflected his
continuing advocacy of continental union. Smith worried about the
effect of an American imperial policy, warning Cockran, "if your
people continue their present debauch, government of the people, for
the people and by the people *will* perish from your part of the earth."[109]

Smith also exchanged correspondence with the anti-imperialist Carl
Schurz along the same theme. "Imperialism will be the death of Continental Union," Smith wrote from the Grange. "No Canadian, however desirous of incorporation with the American Commonwealth, would
desire incorporation with a Negro and Malay Empire." Once again
Smith expressed grave concerns over the racial make-up of America's
new overseas territories. His concerns were so great that even after
advocating continental union for decades, Smith wrote to Schurz that
as a Canadian, "I should vote against Union with an American Empire."
Smith suggested to Schurz a counter-argument to the imperialists: "The
incorporation of Canada with the United States would surely be of all
'expansions' not only the most natural but the best."[110] Schurz wrote
back immediately, calling Smith's argument "a very weighty one," yet
noting that any such proposition should originate "from your side of
the line, not from ours. Can you not find an opportunity for launching
it in a manner to attract general attention in the United States?" Schurz
asked.[111] Smith's attempt to counter overseas expansion with continental expansion appeared intellectually sound, yet carried little weight
with most Americans. Given the aftermath of the Venezuela Crisis and
the Anglo-American rapprochement, few turned to Canada as a field
for expansion. Anglo-Saxonism had helped to differentiate an English-
speaking, self-governing Canada from the "uncivilized" peoples of
Latin America and the Philippines. Continental union would rear its head
once more during the South African War, yet it originated not in Canada,
but among anglophobic Americans.

Yet the English-speaking world continued to support American expansion using racial rhetoric. Writing in the *Fortnightly Review*, British author William Laird Clowes called American expansionism the "Inheritance of the Race," the word "inheritance" indicating both entitlement and the British legacy. Underscoring the affinities of Great Britain and the United States, "the two great kindred countries," Clowes believed that "there is no question that Americans are as capable as any other person of their race of becoming successful managers of colonies which are mainly peopled by inferior stocks." Clowes pointed to the successful education of freed American slaves after the Civil War who "were so ignorant that, alone, they could not govern." Great Britain and the United States must work together because, Clowes wrote, "the future of civilization depends upon our race."[112] Writing in the *Atlantic Monthly*, Horace Fisher called for government of the former Spanish colonies "for the benefit of the inhabitants until we are satisfied of their willingness and ability to maintain in a reasonable degree peace and order, law and justice." Far from preaching government "of, by, and for the people," Fisher wrote that "the grand central Anglo-Saxon idea in the founding of states," was that "government is organized according to the condition of the people to be governed."[113]

English-Canadian writers also called for Americans to fulfill their duty to "civilize" and "Christianize" the "lower" races. In *Queen's Quarterly* George Grant called America's war in Cuba "an act of philanthropy very needful." With the war over, Americans "have discovered that they will have to remain there to save the Cubans from themselves, an act of philanthropy still more urgent." Grant called the inhabitants of the former Spanish colonies "quite unfit for self-government," and believed the United States "must not abandon them to self-government," a fate Grant presented as no better than Spanish rule. The *Presbyterian Record* believed America had a duty to undo the abuses of Spanish rule and to civilize and Christianize the natives. "A more degraded race could hardly be conceived," the journal said of the various indigenous tribes; "they wander through the forests in a state bordering closely on absolute nudity, and live on whatever they can pick from the trees or dig out of the ground." The *Record* reserved its greatest outrage for the Catholicism of the Philippines. "There is not a Protestant minister in the islands," the journal stated, adding ominously, "Were one to attempt to work in the provinces he would be likely to encounter conditions not conducive to longevity." Native villages were dominated by the "padre, or village friar," who "becomes a demigod." "In spite of their vows of poverty and chastity two or three of these orders of friars constitute the wealthiest, as well as the most shameless, class in the islands." The *Record* claimed that lascivious friars had become responsible for the "extensive half-caste population which almost invariably springs up in their vicinity," exploiting their holy office for "the ruin of the simple and superstitious native women and girls." Finally, the journal reported that any official who tried to investigate the situation "has met a sudden and mysterious death," and concluded that "it would be a happy day ... should some civilized power take possession" of the Philippines.[114]

In early February 1899 the Filipinos rose in revolt against the American occupation under the leadership of Emilio Aguinaldo. British journals maintained the need for American control of the islands in the face of native inability to self-govern.[115] The Anglican *Guardian* regretted the American need to crush the rebellion, but concluded it necessary "because the alternative is to give over their conquests to the rule of a half-caste populace."[116] English-Canadian journals may have smirked at the stumbling of the American giant, but they, too, continued to preach of America's imperial duty. The Toronto *Globe* poked fun of the American plight in a cartoon called "Philanthropy Up to Date," depicting an Uncle Sam presenting "The Blessing of Liberty and Good Government" to a rebelling Filipino at the point of a bayonet. "Consarn yer picter," Sam cried, "I'll larn you that 'Government derives its just powers from the consent of the governed,' whether they like it or not!"[117] Months later, however, an editorial about American occupation of the Philippines in the *Globe* stated: "We firmly believe that this is the best thing that could happen to the inhabitants, but the difficulty is that they cannot be made to see it in that light." The paper believed that "every Canadian" who thought the matter out "must wish that the Americans may be enabled to pacify the inhabitants of the Philippines at an early day and extend to them that safety for their bodies and their possessions which is the first requisite of civilization."[118] As the *Globe* cartoon showed, Canadians may have been tempted to gloat over America's troubles in their new colonies, yet as American retention of the Philippines still served imperial interests, English-Canadian journals reiterated old ideas about America's duty to the lower races. With Aguinaldo's revolt, America's duty was to "pacify and civilize."

In stating their support for American suppression of the Filipino revolt, other papers cited the intimate relations between Great Britain and the United States and the British support of American retention of the Philippines. The Manitoba *Free Press* decried the "reckless fanaticism of the Malay," and felt certain that the United States would conquer the insurgents, "no one knowing the race from which they have sprung may doubt." The journal also noted the continuing friendship of Great Britain during America's time of need, with England having essentially said to the European powers, "Hands off; these be my kin." "Blood is thicker than water," the *Free Press* concluded, "and the bonds of a common race, tongue and religion are strong ties in time of stress."[119] Two days later in an editorial entitled "Shoulder to Shoulder," the same paper noted the growing realization of "the duty of the two branches of the race working in harmony and unity of aim."[120] English-Canadian journals did more than express sympathy with America's plight in the Philippines. Through the unity of the Anglo-Saxon race many Canadians shared in the American imperial experience. Yet as experienced imperialists themselves, English Canadians often expressed a cautionary tone, characterizing the Philippine rebellion as the burden of Anglo-Saxon duty. The Montreal *Star* noted that "our neighbours seem to fail to appreciate the added risks and responsibilities attendant upon the possession of colonies over sea."[121] In other words, Aguinaldo's rebellion did not constitute a people fighting against a foreign, occupying power, but merely one of the "risks and responsibilities" of imperialism.

Rudyard Kipling published his poem "White Man's Burden" nearly simultaneously in the London *Times* and the February issue of *McClure's* magazine. The poem's appearance coincided with Aguinaldo's rebellion on February 3 and the Senate's ratification of the Treaty of Paris on February 6, giving the United States the former Spanish colonies of Guam, Puerto Rico, and the Philippines, the last for a sum of $20 million. For those who read the poem in early 1899, Kipling only repackaged ideas that had been circulating throughout the English-speaking world for nearly a year. Yet he addressed these issues in such a way as to make them a creed for Anglo-Saxon imperialism. For Kipling, the "White Man's burden" meant serving the needs of ungrateful, lesser races – "Your new-caught sullen peoples, Half devil and half child." The poet characterized suppressing rebellions as "savage wars of peace" for the sake of civilization and progress: "Fill full the mouth of Famine, And bid the sickness cease." Kipling also infused a missionary spirit into this burden: "The cry of hosts ye humour (Ah, slowly!) toward the light – 'Why brought ye us from bondage, Our beloved Egyptian night?'" With the Senate's ratification of the peace treaty delayed for nearly two months, Kipling addressed the anti-imperialists who declared imperialism as contrary the American doctrine of government by the consent of the governed:

Take up the White Man's burden -
    Ye dare not stoop to less -
Nor call too loud on Freedom
    To cloak your weariness.[122]

Kipling also likened America's new burden as the responsibility of a mature nation, replacing "childish days" with the search for "manhood." Again, the idea of bringing civilization, progress, and Christianity, to "silent sullen peoples" was not new, nor was the concept of American maturity or "manhood." Yet by encapsulating all of these ideas in a few memorable lines, Kipling forever altered the language of Anglo-Saxon imperialism.

Kipling's entreaty for the United States to "Take up the White Man's burden" could also be seen as a plea from the British empire for the republic to shoulder its fair share of international responsibilities. The unofficial laureate of the empire wrote in the vein of an experienced imperialist. Indeed, the words of his poem might have been spoken by a "weary Titan," made a little cynical after centuries of shouldering the burden alone. The imperial responsibility was a "burden," a "heavy harness," full not of glory, but the "toil of serf and sweeper – The tale of common things." Finally, Kipling spoke not of an American or British duty, but of the burden of "the White Man." Like many English Canadians, Kipling's Anglo-Saxonism included the United States. Like fellow British imperialist Chamberlain, Kipling was married to an American woman and had lived in Vermont for several years. His writing penetrated deeply into American thought, with thirty-five United States editions of his works published by 1898. The same month "White Man's Burden" appeared Kipling lay ill in a New York hotel, as crowds waited and prayed outside.[123] Even anglophobes Roosevelt and Lodge could not help appreciating Kipling's sentiment. Roosevelt sent Lodge an advance copy of the poem, calling it "rather poor poetry, but good sense from the expansion standpoint."[124] Lodge replied that he liked it, and considered it "better poetry than you say."[125] With this poem, Kipling added another Anglo-Saxonist work to his repertoire and solidified his place as the Anglo-Saxon poet laureate. Anderson cites French author Victor Bérard's "grudging tribute" to Kipling's influence: "wherever penetrated the works of Rudyard Kipling – that is to say, among the one hundred or one hundred twenty millions of Anglo-Saxons scattered throughout the world – a mighty stream arose which swept away everything."[126]

Kipling's phrase certainly touched a nerve in English Canada. Not only did English-Canadian writers incorporate the "song" or "sermon," as it was variously called, into their Anglo-Saxon rhetoric, but they offered their own interpretations. After the poem appeared in *McClure's*, an editorial in the Montreal *Gazette* commented on what constituted the "white man's burden." It is, the paper stated, "the civilization of the uncivilized; the instruction of the ignorant; the taming of the savage; the controlling of the lawless; the substitution of a life of peace, industry, competency for a life of strife, indolence, and frequent famines."[127] The editor of *Canadian Magazine* declared that Kipling "has given the Anglo-Saxon race a new song." "It is a wonderful sermon," the journal concluded, "and will tend to impress upon the two great English peoples the size and importance of the task they have undertaken in acquiring control over great nations of uneducated people."[128] In *Queen's Quarterly* George Grant, writing of the American war in the Philippines, wrote that "the bearer of the white man's burden" had to compel the Filipinos "to live in ungrateful peace and prosperity by enforcing law and order and infringing upon unsanitary liberty and indolence." Grant did not speak ironically when he spoke of the "unsanitary liberty" of the Filipinos. He went on to call the Declaration of Independence an "unfortunate document" that American anti-imperialists continually cited as part of their critique. "It's quite untrue that all men are created equal," Grant wrote, "that they are endowed with unalienable rights, such as life, liberty and the pursuit of happiness, that governments are created to secure and preserve those rights, and that they derive their just powers from the consent of the governed ... So far as these rights and privileges have yet been secured, instead of belonging to man by nature, they are slowly and arduously acquired by him, and to be retained and improved demand constant effort through an indefinite future." Grant offered an unambiguous and unapologetic defence of imperialism. In doing so, he presented a view of self-government not as a natural right, but as a privilege to be earned. The debate concerning colonial expansion, whether American or British, Grant said, should not concern "the inherent rights of inferior races to govern themselves. Government, in the civilized sense," Grant concluded, "they cannot give themselves."[129]

While Grant and *Queen's Quarterly* represented Presbyterian thought in English Canada, the religious press also adopted Kipling's attitude, if not always his actual words. As with other English-language periodicals, *Methodist Magazine* took a benign view of American suppression of the Philippines. Under the banner "The White Man's burden," the journal argued that the war against the Filipinos "seems the only alternative, unless the insurgents recognize the hopelessness of the conflict and throw themselves on the generosity of their conquerors." In the meantime, their guerrilla war placed them "outside the pale of civilization." The journal also noted the heavy burden the United States carried in Puerto Rico and Cuba where "the supple natives ... have already grown restive." "A strong hand," the magazine stated, "a hand of iron in a glove of silk – is needed for the management of both islands." Despite any mistakes made by the United States in governing its new colonies, *Methodist Magazine* concluded, "a brighter day for the Pearl of the Antilles has dawned."[130] Months later, with the Philippine rebellion dragging on, the journal praised the "unfailing valour" of the American troops. The rebels, the journal maintained, represented only a small, "desperate faction." The vast majority of the people of the islands were "eager to welcome the even-handed justice they may expect from the United States."

The journal of the Canadian Church of England, the *Churchman*, took a similar view: "We must confess ourselves among the number of those who rejoice to hear of the successes of the American arms in the Philippines," a March editorial stated, "and who regret that a lack of intelligence on the part of a portion of the inhabitants should lead them to resist the measures which are calculated to lead to their own ultimate benefit." Americans also had a duty to the islands "to hold them and civilize them," the journal declared. The *Churchman*'s reasoning reflected a concern with the racial difference between Anglo-Saxons, Spaniards, and the "lesser races":

We have the deepest sympathy with the work of the Americans on two quite clear grounds. In the first place, on account of the various peoples and tribes which are found in those Asiatic islands. There seemed no prospect of the Spaniards bringing them into a civilized condition. Whether that was the fault of their race, or of their religion, or of their government, we need not enquire. Now white men, especially men of our own race, have a very remarkable faculty of extending civilization and of making other peoples capable of being treated as civilized human beings.

The *Churchman*'s "deepest sympathy" with the Americans seemed derived from their common race, which made their fellow Anglo-Saxons especially capable of "extending civilization." The "White Man's burden" meant "making other peoples capable of being treated as civilized beings." Conversely, one assumes, until that point the "other peoples" would not be treated as civilized human beings. Finally, the Anglican journal noted the essential unity of British and American work in the civilizing field: "Americans and British are engaged in the same work," the journal stated. "They are meaning to do that work in the same spirit, and largely by the same methods. It is a great thing that they should work side by side, and shoulder to shoulder."[131] English-Canadian journals appeared particularly pleased that the Anglo-Saxon world seemed united in their civilizing mission. As a part of that world, English Canadians took a personal pride in both the American military victories, and the missionary work of peacetime. The "weary titan" could no longer maintain her "splendid isolation," and Canadians welcomed their kin in helping shoulder the "White Man's burden."

CONCLUSION

Kipling's poem was not the cause of the United States Senate's ratification of the Treaty of Paris, nor is it responsible for the United States embarking generally upon the imperial course. Anglo-Saxonism did not lead English Canadians to support the American cause against Spain, nor to call for American retention of the Philippines. Indeed, in March 1898 many Canadians recoiled at the faintest whiff of American intervention. With the Venezuela crisis still a recent memory, and a bitter dispute ongoing over control of Yukon trade, American belligerence toward Spain seemed to many Canadians part of a larger pattern of hemispherical aggrandizement that might ultimately include Canada. A war with Spain over a colony resting within America's sphere of influence would set a dangerous precedent. Anglo-Saxonism could not overcome old Canadian concerns about maintaining Canadian independence and protecting Canadian national rights in the face of the grasping American republic. Only Great Britain's policy of abandoning its isolation in favour of an Anglo-American understanding altered Canadian opinion. Using the prism of Anglo-Saxonism, Canadians adopted the British view of Anglo-American amity as serving imperial security. One or two expressions of British good will might have gone unheeded in Canada, but the tremendous outpouring from both official and unofficial sources could not go unnoticed. From the Queen herself to Chamberlain, with his call for an Anglo-Saxon alliance, British authorities looked upon America's ascent to world power status as a buttress to imperial security. Canadians took note of this, and, as Colonel Denison noted, followed "the English lead." Conscious both of British opinion and the concern over imperial security that lay behind it, many English Canadians echoed their British counterparts in calling for Anglo-American harmony, and even union. Canadians did not merely ape the British, however, but viewed American actions and victories as their own, sharing in the American war and annexation of Spanish colonies as fellow Anglo-Saxons.

Kipling's "White Man's burden," then, belonged not only to the United States, but to all Anglo-Saxons, Canadians included. Moreover, the field for Anglo-Saxon endeavour was not limited solely to Cuba or the Philippines, but wherever "lesser races" lived in darkness. "He endeavors to impress the Anglo-Saxons with a sense of their responsibilities," the editor of *Canadian Magazine* wrote of Kipling. The "new races" of Africa, Asia, and Central America must be "brought under Anglo-Saxon rule" and Anglo-Saxons must do "the work which the white races must do in civilizing the uncivilized."[132] Between March 1898 and March 1899 the tone and scope of Canadian opinion had changed dramatically. Not only did Canadians embrace the war with Spain as serving the interests of all Anglo-Saxon civilization, now they preached about a continuing global mission for the entire race. If Americans had to bear their share of "burden," certainly Canadians were not exempt.

The Canadian religious press had done much in characterizing the war with Spain as a religious mission, a "holy war" against the forces of darkness and ignorance. The Protestant press also became the greatest apologists for the Americans in their war against Aguinaldo and his Philippine insurgents. The annexation of Catholic Spain's former colonies represented a giant stride forward for the Protestant church, and opened vast new fields for missionary work. Moreover, with the end of the century near, the rhetoric of the religious press took on a fervent quality. "The missionary spirit is universal," declared the Reverend Burwash, Chancellor of Victoria University. "Now it is recognized as the onward movement of light and truth, bringing higher civilization and better life ... Is it too much to expect that this movement will result in the next century in the evangelization of the world?"[133] Just as Josiah Strong had urged Anglo-Saxons to spread their religion throughout the world in the wake of the Spanish-American War, English Canadians took up the cry with relish.

With the various emphases on war and mission, security and racial duty, no wonder that the English-speaking world often fused racial, religious, and military rhetoric. Indeed, the religious press often failed to distinguish between missionary work and war-making. Writers presented the material world as a dualistic reflection of the spiritual world, a fight between good and evil. A British Methodist minister declared that "the nations of the world may be divided into two groups – those that are growing and those that are decaying; those that are becoming stronger every day, and those who are sinking into hopeless decrepitude. Open your eyes, survey the civilized world, and you will see that the Protestant nations are all prospering, and that the Roman Catholic nations are all withering away." The writer openly equated Methodist mission with war, and urged his readers to give money to the twentieth-century Fund so that the church might "carry the war into the enemy's country." The money represented merely "a sign that the Holy War is to be waged more fiercely than ever." "When our American kinsmen proclaimed war against the hateful clerical despotism of Spain, their first practical essential act was to vote an immense sum of money to military and naval preparations," he reminded his audience. The Methodist church must do no less. "We must no longer stand upon the defensive – a base and fatal attitude. We must become the attacking force ... It means war to the knife with everything and everybody that opposes Christ. It means a universal conscription in the military service of God and Humanity." The forces of good must mobilize against the forces of evil, every Methodist "regiment and company" must "Follow thy Captain to war."[134] With the dawn of the new century, English-Canadian Protestants were asked to carry on a war to the death with darkness and barbarism.

The Spanish-American War and the Philippines debate necessarily left an indelible imprint upon English-Canadian thought. Canadians had not merely watched the Americans from the sidelines, but had taken a personal interest in the outcome. They had adopted the rhetoric of the war and made it their own. The war had served as a sort of schoolroom, indoctrinating English Canadians in the Anglo-Saxonist language of imperialism: "mission," "civilization," "barbarism," "progress," "cruelty," "backwardness," "liberty," and "white man's burden." As Americans continued to "fight the good fight" against Filipino rebels, Canada would be faced with its own "pious war" and, taking the lessons learned from the American struggle, would follow their "Captain" into battle.

4 The Crest and Decline of North American Anglo-Saxonism: The South African War, the Alaska *Modus Vivendi*, and the Abrogation of the Clayton-Bulwer Treaty

> The relations between Canada and England always tend
> to bring on friction between us and both of them.
>   Theodore Roosevelt to General James H. Wilson, 12 July 1899[1]

> When a new-found friend asks to be allowed to put a pistol
> to your head as a proof of reconciliation, the man or nation
> that allows it has no brains worth blowing out.
>   Major-general T. Bland Strange, Canadian militia, March 1899

INTRODUCTION

One month before the outbreak of war in South Africa, the African explorer Sir Henry Morton Stanley published an article in the American journal *Outlook* entitled "Anglo-Saxon Responsibilities." Stanley had been born in Wales as John Rowlands, hired on to an American merchant ship at fifteen, jumped ship in New Orleans, renamed himself, and fought on both sides of the American Civil War. As a reporter in 1872 he had gained fame as the man who tracked down another African explorer, David Livingstone. Stanley went on to make a name for himself as an explorer of the "dark continent" and a brutal Congo agent of Belgium's colonizing King Leopold II.[2] In his *Outlook* article Stanley reaffirmed the ideas of Kipling's poem "White Man's Burden" and advocated close Anglo-American cooperation in the good work to be done. "The Americans are [Englishmen's] kinsmen," Stanley declared, "chips of the old block." Far from being a "burden," imperial responsibilities rested lightly on Britannia's shoulders, "because," as Stanley wrote, "as a race we are fitter for these responsibilities than any other." Referring to the English-speaking dominions, Stanley noted that "All our colonies manage themselves fairly well." Trouble, though, seemed to be brewing in South Africa, due to the "narrow anti-liberty policy of president Kruger, the unceasing complaints of the overtaxed, disfranchised and despised Uitlander, and the corruption, wastefulness, and extravagance of the Transvaal Government, the cost of which means more taxation and oppression of the 'aliens.'" Stanley noted that Great Britain looked on benevolently as the United States continued to work with its "supplicants ... for their own welfare, progress, and interest." "And it may be that we shall both be called to do the same again," Stanley concluded, "but our duty will be smoother and easier if we know that we have each other's sympathy."[3] The British Empire's war in South Africa would sorely try American sympathy.

Stanley's British rhetoric on the eve of the Boer War echoed American rhetoric on the eve of the Spanish-American War. Yet just as the United States went to war over issues of trade and hegemony, so, too, Great Britain went to war over gold, diamonds, and the need to keep Germany out of the Cape. English Canadians did not merely follow the mother country's lead, but largely expressed great enthusiasm for Canadian participation. Canadian historians have explored the reasons behind this outpouring of imperial fervour at the turn of the century. Norman Penlington concluded that the Alaska boundary dispute with the United States was the "underlying issue that brought Canada into the South African War."[4] Most historians have found that anti-Americanism alone could not explain Canadian imperialism, and have instead sought to dissect the nature of English Canada's imperial fervour. Carl Berger characterized Canadian imperialism as a form of nationalism, giving English Canadians a "sense of power." Robert Page has investigated imperialism as "the embodiment of many of the ideals of the age," and looked at the literary, educational, economic, and religious sources of Canadian imperialism. Carman Miller has presented English-Canadian zeal for the Boer War as a combination of several factors, including Canadian Loyalism, nationalism, militarism, and the Social Gospel.[5]

What many historians have failed to note was the positive example provided to Canadians by the events of the previous year. After following the Spanish-American and Philippines Wars with rapt attention, Canadians naturally adopted much of the rhetoric heard on both sides of the line over the previous two years. While many in the Dominion might have been fascinated with American military exploits or concerned with the balance of power in Asia, English Canadians made a seamless transition into the new crisis by using the same lexicon of Anglo-Saxon superiority. In 1900 E.B. Biggar explained the reasons why Canadians should be interested in the war. He described the Boers as a cruel, narrow, and repressive people who sought to exclude English-speaking colonists from the apparatus of self-government. The Boers, Biggar wrote, were "as ignorant of the outside world as the Hudson Bay Indians."[6] Like Stanley's article, Biggar utilized the same rhetoric heard during and after the Spanish-American War. Indeed, he might have been an American journalist describing Spanish rule in Cuba only a year before. While Canadians may have been motivated by the desire for adventure, the love of the Mother Country, or the desire to safeguard the "halfway house" to India and the antipodes,[7] many used Anglo-Saxon rhetoric to justify Canadian involvement. Much of the rhetoric focused on the Boers as a cruel, barbarous, religiously narrow people completely unfamiliar with the concept of political liberty. Moreover, English Canadians employed such rhetoric fully conscious of the heritage of the Spanish-American War. Both wars were seen as part of a single crusade to relieve suffering and bring liberty and justice to the far reaches of the globe.

The South African War also marked another step in the Anglo-American rapprochement. Despite much sympathy for the Boers as a morally upright and downtrodden people fighting valiantly against a giant distant empire, and distant cousins of America's Puritan forefathers, official American opinion adopted the same "benevolent neutrality" that Great Britain had maintained eighteen months earlier. Indeed, Great Britain's friendship during the American crisis weighed heavily in America's sympathy during the South African War. Although Americans reciprocated the use of sentimental rhetoric during the war, British victory in the Cape served America's new global interests. Historians have also noted that Anglo-Saxonism and Social Darwinism played a part in shaping American opinion during the war.[8] As one historian has written, Americans thought "justice lay with the Boers, but the locomotive of history was owned by the British."[9]

The war in South Africa continued to delay the reconvening of the Joint High Commission, which had adjourned in February 1899 without settling the Alaska boundary question. Rising tensions in the disputed area made some sort of quick settlement in the interests of all three governments. Moreover, with a new overseas empire in both the Pacific and Atlantic oceans, America pressed ahead for the construction of an isthmian canal. The 1850 Clayton-Bulwer treaty required the joint Anglo-American construction and ownership of any Central American canal. With the British empire mired in a costly war in the Cape, the United States desperately wanted the British government to agree to an abrogation of the treaty, allowing the United States to build a canal on its own. The twin Anglo-American issues of Alaska and the canal initially placed Canada in a highly advantageous position. The

Canadian government believed that the United States would be forced to compromise on Alaska in order to receive Great Britain's approval for abrogation of the treaty. The Laurier administration pressed this view throughout 1899, blocking plans for settling Alaska that had been agreed upon by both the American State Department and British Foreign Office. The beginning of the South African war actually seemed to bolster Canada's claims, as the British Government welcomed strong Canadian support. Yet British reverses in the Cape and growing American impatience over the delayed canal impressed upon the British government the need for American sympathy. The British agreed to abrogate the Clayton-Bulwer treaty without a quid pro quo on Alaska. Canada had lost its strongest bargaining chip, and the Liberal government was forced to retreat from its previously intense rhetoric.

While Anglo-Saxonism might have created an identity of outlook regarding the common mission of the English-speaking peoples, the on-going dispute over the Alaska boundary once again revealed the limits of such ideological rhetoric. Like the debate over reciprocity, Alaska underscored national questions of trade, territory, and power. The years of the South African war, then, witnessed the crest and decline of North American Anglo-Saxonism. Canadians and Americans both utilized the "rhetoric of righteousness" when discussing the Philippines and South Africa, but concerning Alaska, old animosities came to the surface.

CANADIAN ANGLO-SAXONISM AND THE LEGACY OF THE "SPLENDID LITTLE WAR"

Not all English Canadians favoured Canadian participation in the Boer War. Carman Miller has studied opposition to the war among farmers, radical labour, Protestant clergy, and "stout anglophobic Canadians."[10] Perhaps foremost among those English-speaking Canadians opposed to the war was Goldwin Smith. Not only did Smith contribute a weekly column to his paper, *The Farmers' Weekly Sun*, but he actively sought to influence American attitudes toward the Boers. In Canada, Smith's opposition seems to have been largely ignored, with his secretary Arnold Haultain noting that "nobody replies to it or takes note of it ... He has not for many years said anything which he has not already said a dozen times."[11] Smith complained to W. Bourke Cockran, a pro-Boer, anglophobic, continental unionist Democratic Congressman, that "Toronto is the centre of Jingoism and almost its circumference."[12] Smith suggested to Cockran paying "some tribute to the Boers who have fallen fighting heroically not in their own cause alone but in that of humanity."[13] When the Boer envoys visited Cockran in Washington, the Congressman read to them letters of sympathy from Smith.[14] Smith also sought to influence the platform of the 1900 Democratic Convention. Writing to Cockran not long after the June 1900 Republican Convention, Smith explained the planks he would like to have included. These included a "declaration in favour of genuine expansion, that is to say the free and peaceful Union of this Continent, in opposition to the subjugation of distant countries and alien races," and a "refusal to be drawn into complicity with the predatory powers of Europe in the extinction of independence and the oppression of the weaker communities and races."[15] Smith must have been happy, then, with the result of the Democrats' Kansas City convention. The platform condemned the acquisition of an overseas empire, whose people could not be made citizens "without endangering our civilization," yet advocated "territorial expansion when it takes in desirable territory which can be erected into States of the Union, and whose people are willing and fit to become American citizens." The Democrats also stated that "we view with indignation the purpose of England to overwhelm with force the South African Republics" and "extend our sympathies to the heroic burghers in their unequal struggle to maintain their liberty and independence."[16] The Democratic platform reflected the division of American opinion over the South African War. The very overwhelming support for the war in English Canada may have turned Smith toward other fields in which to extend his influence.

While English-Canadian support for the war had many different motivations, writers continued the practice of the previous year of positing a foreign race's "cruelty" or "barbarism" against Anglo-Saxon "civilization." Moreover, writers often compared the South African and Spanish-American Wars. "The United States went to war with Spain to enforce internal reforms in Cuba," the Reverend J. Tallman Pitcher of Iroquois, Ontario, wrote, "and if that was a righteous war with a foreign power for internal reforms, Britain's action might be classed in the same category."[17] "The Spanish-American war," wrote John A. Ewan, editor of *Canadian Magazine*, and "the South African war ... are curiously connected."[18] Dr. Withrow of *Methodist Magazine*, writing under the headline of "The Cost of Liberty," noted that "the costly libation of human blood is being poured out both in the Philippines and in South Africa for the extension of constitutional liberty."[19] "The Americans are continuing to bear the white man's burden in the Philippines," Withrow continued. "The Tagalos, however, are not the fierce fighters that the Boers are, but will, like them, be compelled to yield to the onward march of civilization." The English-speaking peoples of the world were seen to be engaged in a single crusade of many fronts, their victories representing the "onward march of civilization."

Wilfrid Laurier stood in the vanguard of those characterizing the war as a holy crusade. As he told the House of Commons, "Great Britain stands in the defence of a holy cause, in the defence of holy justice, for the defence of the oppressed, for the enfranchisement of the down-trodden, and for the advancement of liberty, progress and civilization." As Blair Neatby has shown, Laurier's belief in Great Britain as the "bulwark of political liberty" constituted the root of his imperialism.[20] While clearly not an Anglo-Saxonist, as a small-*l* liberal politician in the Victorian English-speaking world, Laurier could hardly avoid utilizing the lexicon of Anglo-Saxon superiority.

Just as some Protestant clergy publicly opposed the war, others expressed some misgivings over the "bloodletting." As during the Spanish-American and Philippines Wars, the English-Canadian religious press offered "pious justification" for the South African war using the language of moral righteousness. *Methodist Magazine* published Kipling's poem "The Old King," a savage characterization of the Transvaal president, Paul Kruger, written from the point-of-view of a Uitlander.

> He shall take his tribute, toll of all our ware,
> He shall change our gold for arms – arms we may not bear;
> He shall break his Judges if they cross his word,
> He shall rule above the Law, calling on the Lord.

The poem continued with characterizations directed at the Boers generally as much as "Oom Paul" specifically.

> Sloven, sullen, savage, secret, uncontrolled -
> Laying on a new land evil of the old;
> Long-forgotten bondage, dwarfing heart and brain -
> All our fathers died to loose he shall bind again.

The same issue of the magazine elaborated on the "savage" nature of the Boer republics, speaking of the "crimes of the tyrannical oligarchy," and the "flagrant wrongs, tyrannies, and oppression of the South African Republic."[21] While the plight of Africans figured very little in the reasoning of many English Canadians, the magazine condemned the "oppression of the natives, and the gross injustice inflicted upon them by the Boers." The journal recounted the story of the Boer farmer who, lacking mules with which to plow his fields, "inspanned the black women of the estate." "Under British administration, South Africa," the magazine concluded, "from the Zambesi to the Cape, will enjoy a reign of peace, prosperity, and constitutional liberty akin to that of the Dominion of Canada."[22]

Canada's English press repeated largely the same justification of British intervention in South Africa as they had of American intervention in Cuba and the Philippines. As was the case in the American war, much of this justification centred on demonizing the enemy as cruel, backward, and unable to govern. In his article on the Transvaal the Reverend Pitcher summed up many of these ideas. The Boers, Pitcher wrote, had displayed "little capacity for self-rule," and, "in sullen aversion to change," were "morbid adherents of antiquated ways, neither willing to be led nor be driven in the path of progress." President Kruger, Pitcher concluded, "seeks to retard the growth of constitutional freedom and the spread of civilization."[23] Others of the religious press echoed the hopes of the Spanish-American War that the former Spanish territories would make for vast new fields of missionary work. "The redemption of Africa," proclaimed the *Presbyterian Record*, "and the transformation of its trackless wildernesses, vast forests, and great lakes, now the habitations of wild beasts, and, perhaps, of wilder men, is not a chimera. The time is surely coming," the journal concluded, when all of Africa would become "inhabited by a people whose God is the Lord."[24] The issue seemed to become distilled down to the question: Under whose control will Africa be most likely transformed into a garden of the Lord? Only Great Britain could bring the "wild men" of the dark continent into the light.

The use of righteous rhetoric helped dispel any lingering doubts over the morality of a war against admittedly virtuous, white Protestants. The transformation of George Grant from a pro-Boer to a pro-war position illustrated the way Anglo-Saxon rhetoric could accommodate one man's opinion to changing circumstances. Writing in July 1899, months before the outbreak of hostilities, Grant characterized the Boers in Anglo-Saxon terms. Grant called the Boers a "freedom-loving" people who had "conquered the cruel heathen." Nowhere else on earth could one find a country "more united and orderly and religious." For Grant, the lack of a Uitlander franchise was of no concern to any outside power. "The franchise is a matter internal to every independent country," Grant wrote, sounding like some of the Canadian press on the eve of the Spanish-American War, "and no outsider has a right to speak on the subject." Grant concluded by saying, "[M]y sympathies are with them."[25] By the time the next issue of the journal came out in October, war was imminent, and Grant had begun to alter his view. The editor began with a defence of "The Policy of Imperialism." "At bottom the Imperialistic instinct is the instinct of a nation to make provision for the expansion of its race," Grant reasoned. "The instinct, strong in every great nation, to extend its type of civilisation, the moral ideals and discipline which it represents over barbarous and rude communities where nothing valuable to humanity is displaced; to put order instead of disorder – what Kipling has called "taking up the white man's burden," this has its due place in the great movement of imperialism." Grant's imperial declaration served as preamble to his addressing "The Transvaal Question." Grant blamed the situation on "a certain number of the Boers hating civilisation ... because civilisation as represented by the British government interfered with their vices, their practice of enslaving the native, their disdain of arts and industries, [and] their nomadic and half savage habits." "Nowhere in the world do men of white race live under more unequal and oppressive laws," Grant declared. Time and again Grant depicted the Transvaal situation as a conflict of different "civilizations" – the advanced civilization of Great Britain, and the backward civilization of the Boers. Grant called the Transvaal a "half-civilized state saved probably from extinction at the hands of the Zulus by the intervention of Great Britain in 1875." In another place he called the Boers "half-civilized and wholly ignorant." By calling the Boers "half-civilized" Grant may have been making a distinction between the Protestant South African Dutch and the African natives. Still, Grant left no doubt that the superior civilization would triumph. Grant depicted the Great Trek as merely an attempt to escape civilization, while the influx of British settlers "threatened to absorb their peculiar type of civilization and to overthrow their supremacy." "Civilization has again overtaken them," Grant concluded.[26] The English-Canadian press presented the war as a dichotomy between the "civilization" of an Anglo-Saxon power and the barbarity of a "backward" race – the same way it had presented the Spanish-American War and the American annexation of the Philippines.

ANGLO-AMERICAN RELATIONS AND THE COMPARTMENTALIZATION OF CANADA

Despite widespread sympathy for the Boers among the American public, the United States reciprocated the British "benevolent neutrality" displayed during the Spanish-American War. By taking care of British interests in Pretoria during the war, American actions paralleled those of the British in Havana during the war with Spain.[27] Many historians have credited John Hay, the anglophile Secretary of State and former ambassador to Great Britain, with thwarting any pro-Boer sentiment among official opinion.[28] Howard K. Beale writes that Hay was "so passionately pro-British that he could not understand friendliness for the Boers except in terms of partisanship of some sort."[29] Ultimately, though, the United States supported Great Britain for the same reason the British had supported America a year earlier: both nations recognized their mutual interests in a world with shifting lines of power. Indeed, Hay took the lead in formulating America's new, outward-looking policy. Even before war broke out in South Africa, Hay began formulating his Open Door policy for China. In September 1899 Hay sent his first Open Door notes to Britain, Germany, Russia, Japan, Italy, and France. The note asked that no power within its own sphere of influence interfere with any treaty port or vested interest, or discriminate in favour of its own nationals in harbour dues or railroad concessions. Essentially, Hay asked, but did not demand, that Americans be given equal commercial opportunity in China. Great Britain welcomed Hay's policy which established Anglo-American solidarity in Asia. Indeed, the Republican administration had to fend off accusations of a secret Anglo-American alliance. Although no alliance existed, a clear mutual understanding had been established by the time the first British soldier set foot on the veldt. "Protection of the Open Door, security in terms of the Monroe Doctrine, racial considerations and British reliance on our good will," one historian has written, "were pressing enough for those with a comprehensive understanding of these considerations to commit the United States to a policy which seemed to deny the very essence of the American epoch."[30]

Such a swift reversal of decades of American policy forced a radical shift of opinion among many American policy makers. Foremost among these was Theodore Roosevelt. Having gained national fame at the head of his "Rough Riders" regiment during the Spanish-American War, Roosevelt had been elected governor of New York in 1898 and vice-president in 1900, and succeeded McKinley as president after his 1901 assassination. A leader of the expansionist school of American foreign policy, Roosevelt had long been an anglophobe because British power appeared anathema to American power. After 1898, however, Roosevelt understood that the reverse was now true. "I feel a keen remembrance of England's friendly attitude during the Spanish-American War," he wrote to the British journalist, John St. Loe Strachey.[31] "I used to be rather anti-British in feeling," Roosevelt wrote to another correspondent, "but England's attitude towards us in our war with Spain impressed me deeply and I have ever since kept it in lively and grateful remembrance."[32] An avid admirer of the Boers' fighting ability (here were true Rough Riders!), and of Dutch descent, Roosevelt nonetheless expressed the need for ultimate British victory. In accommodating his view to the altered international situation, Roosevelt drew upon Anglo-Saxon rhetoric to express support for England. "[F]undamentally

I feel that all the English-speaking peoples come much nearer to one another in political and social ideals," he wrote to a correspondent, "in their systems of government and of civic and domestic morality, than any of them do to any other peoples."[33] Roosevelt declared the need for Anglo-Saxon supremacy throughout the world, and believed that the English-speaking race needed to take strong measures to maintain its dominance. He viewed the assimilation of immigrants in the United States, the recent federation of Australia, and the South African war as positive examples of the race combating "decadence" and maintaining its "vigor."

Even before the war broke out, Roosevelt expressed his desire to see Britain become the pre-eminent power on the African continent. Most revealing were Roosevelt's letters to Cecil Arthur Spring Rice, the British diplomat and best man at Roosevelt's second wedding. The New York governor told his friend that England should "let some men like Kitchener deal in his own way with the Boers, if it is absolutely necessary," ensuring that "the future of the African continent will lie in your hands and be under your direction." "And what a splendid work this will be!" Roosevelt gushed. "It is of itself to establish a race for all time."[34] Roosevelt often repeated the idea that British victory in Africa was in the interest of "civilization," echoing a favourite theme of George Grant. "I have great sympathy for the Boers," Roosevelt wrote to a German friend, "but I think they are battling on the wrong side of civilization and will have to go under."[35] Clearly Roosevelt did not express to his Teutonic correspondent the need for English-speaking domination of the world. To his brother-in-law William Sheffield Cowles, Roosevelt wrote, "I feel it would be better for the Boers themselves and for all civilization to have affairs managed as they have been managed by the English in Natal and the Cape."[36] Once again he wrote to Spring Rice that although the Boers possessed "many fine traits ... it would be to the advantage of mankind to have English spoken south of the Zambesi just as in New York."[37] To another British friend Roosevelt called himself "a believer in the fact that it is for the good of the world that the English-speaking race in all its branches should hold as much of the world's surface as possible."[38] Being of mixed heritage, Roosevelt did not believe in the need for Anglo-Saxon racial purity, but in the assimilation and anglo-conformism of non-English-speaking peoples, whether in New York or Cape Town. He equated the English language with the higher forms of civilization, including self-government, and "civic morality."

While official American opinion echoed Roosevelt's sentiments, the possibility of Canadian participation in the war received much less scrutiny. With the rapprochement in place and American annexationism on the wane, most Americans seemed to accept that the Dominion would send troops. During the Venezuela crisis, Americans had viewed Canada's imperial connection as a violation of the Monroe Doctrine. Goldwin Smith had postulated that under the doctrine the United States would never allow Canada to participate in any imperial war. To a British friend he had written, "I must tell you that I do not believe that the Americans will ever willingly allow you to make this continent the scene, base, or highway of war, or to use the two Canadian railways – which in fact are as much American as Canadian – for the transmission of troops or munitions of war to be employed against any power with which the Americans are at peace."[39] Albert Shaw agreed with Smith, and characterized Canada as not just a mere dominion, but as England's most important military ally. "Canada is now looked upon as a part of the strategic and military strength of England," Shaw wrote in the *Review of Reviews*, "and as such available, at any time, for England's support in imperial conquest or in European war." According to Shaw, Canada's position meant that the Dominion "is to be dragged into the arena of European conflict, from which it is the object of the Monroe Doctrine to deliver her along with the rest of the western world." European powers would thus be justified "in making Canadian soil the theater of warlike operations. This dragging of European and Asiatic conflicts in the very heart of the continent of North America," Shaw continued, "would cause our Government great inconvenience. Canada's participation in the South African war, – a matter which was no concern of hers, directly or indirectly, – is the most flagrant violation of the Monroe Doctrine that has ever been committed, because it makes a precedent under which Canada will be deemed by Europe a party to all of England's quarrels, and therefore a legitimate fighting ground." Shaw indicated that the rapprochement had not made the forty-ninth parallel secure. For him the war underscored Canada's unnatural and anachronistic position. Shaw believed that "the one thing in the whole outlook for the United States that is in any degree whatever menacing or annoying is the arbitrary line across the continent, which checks its natural expansion, and beyond which a European power is building fortifications." Shaw's rhetoric indicated that American continental expansionism was alive and well. "Nature intended the far Northwest for the free and natural expansion of America," Shaw continued, while now England was "creating a military ally in Canada to thwart the expansion of the United States."[40] Shaw's comments paralleled ones he had made both in print and privately to William T. Stead during the Venezuela crisis. While Roosevelt may have altered his view of England because of the Spanish-American War, Shaw continued to view Great Britain as the "lion in the path" of American power. Specifically, the British empire continued to encroach upon American soil; and more dangerously, Canadian participation in the South African war indicated Canada's willingness to become England's most important military ally.

Like Shaw, other Americans questioned Canada's sending of troops to South Africa and illustrated continuing expansionism and anglophobia. In June 1900 a number of prominent New Yorkers, including Paul Dana and W. Bourke Cockran, formed the National Continental Union League to promote the political union of Canada and the United States. Their declaration included a paragraph that combined the Monroe Doctrine with Anglo-Saxonism: "In our opinion, the time has come when it is desirable that Europe should cease to direct or control the political or domestic affairs of any portion of this Continent, and we believe that such cessation will tend to unite all English-speaking communities throughout the world in one common effort to develop, promote, extend, and defend constitutional government, and will be for the best interests of humanity."[41] The founding of the League during the South African war certainly reflected the anglophobia of its founders. More importantly, the League indicated the persistence of the cornerstones of nineteenth century American ideology: anglophobia, expansionism, and the Monroe Doctrine.

Such sentiment even found its way into Senate debate over the South African war. In a highly anglophobic speech favouring recognition of the Boer belligerents, Senator Wellington praised the Boers for having reached "the sublimest height of moral and physical courage to which it is possible for mankind to ascend." Wellington then turned his attention toward Canada. "What nation holds and controls a great body of land in the north, governs islands above the United States and below them?" the Senator asked. "The answer will be, England." Like Shaw, Wellington suggested that a war between England and a European power would mean war in North America. In case of a European invasion of Canada, "what will we be forced to do?" Wellington asked – "Protect England in her American possessions? Would it not be better to acquire Canada ourselves and hold it instead of defending it for England?" Wellington answered his own question with reference to recent American expansion overseas. "If we have the right to conquer the unwilling Filipinos, 8,000 miles away," he said, "why not, for the safety of our frontier, strike down British rule in Canada and force Canadians to become a part of the United States?"[42] Once again, Wellington's speech reflected persistent American anglophobia and continental expansionism. Fresh from their heady victory only the year before, many Americans seemed to feel the time was ripe for fulfilling America's manifest destiny. Canada still irritated the sensibilities of many Americans.

Despite questioning the justice of the war and Canada's role in it, most Americans seemed to accept Canadian participation as of little consequence. The *New York Times* made note of Canada's enthusiastic support for England with very little comment. When the Canadian government decided to send a contingent of 1,000 men, the paper noted only that this constituted a larger number than any other colony and more than England had suggested.[43] With the Canadian decision to send a second contingent, the paper noted that two of the mounted rifle detachments would be recruited from the Northwest Mounted Police and from western cowboys. "These will be genuine 'Rough Riders,'" the paper declared with admiration, making a comparison with Theodore Roosevelt's outfit of the Spanish-American War.[44] The New York *Tribune* also expressed some admiration for the Canadian contingents, expressing an element of New World solidarity. The Canadian "fighters," according to the paper, were "picked men from all over the Dominion that are expected to compete favorably with the regular army." Moreover, as the British planned to incorporate the contingent as a whole it would "thus maintain its individuality as a distinctively Canadian organization," a fact destined to be "very gratifying to the pride of Canadians." Despite the Canadians' lack of battle experience, the *Tribune* fully expected them to "give a good account of itself."[45] A few weeks later, with more Canadian troops planned after the disastrous "Black Week," the paper noted the Canadian desire to bear its fair share. "This is a matter in which Canada is not counting dollars," the *Tribune* stated, "being content to pour out her last coin, if necessary, for the vindication of the Imperial cause."[46] Unlike some Americans who viewed Canadian participation in an imperial war as a violation of the Monroe Doctrine, the *Times* and *Tribune* offered little comment. When the papers did take note of Canadian participation, it was with positive characterizations of the Dominion's troops and its filial support of England. The American journal *Outlook* echoed this sentiment, praising the Canadian response to the war as "quick and full" and "generous in spirit."[47]

Despite the ongoing dispute over the Alaska boundary, the South African war witnessed a large degree of Canadian-American amity. Much of this goodwill might be attributed to the Canadian Prime Minister. During the previous year no Canadian had been more outspoken than Sir Wilfrid in decrying America's unjust stance on the boundary issue. In the House of Commons he had even speculated on war being the only other alternative to arbitration or compromise [see below]. The outbreak of the war, however, found the Prime Minister in Chicago to attend the ground-laying ceremony for the new post office. With the American and Mexican presidents also in attendance, the ceremony became symbolic of continental goodwill. Laurier displayed his usual rhetorical skills and struck a balance between maintaining Canada's rights and proclaiming Anglo-American unity. Laurier struck the familiar chord of Canadian-American racial ties: "We are of the same stock: we spring from the same races on one side of the line as on the other. We speak the same language. We have the same literature, and for more than one thousand years we have had a common history." Once again, Laurier utilized Anglo-Saxon rhetoric to appeal to an English-speaking audience. When the Prime Minister turned to Alaska, he spoke with a frankness softened by humour. While Laurier stated that "we do not want one inch of your land," which brought cheers from the Chicago crowd, he facetiously asked, "if I state, however, that we want to hold our land, would that be an American sentiment? I want to know." This drew laughs from the audience. Laurier also trotted out the old phrase "blood is thicker than water," and noted British sympathy toward America during the war with Spain "for no other reason than that we were of the same blood." Finally, Laurier concluded by envisioning the day Great Britain and the United States would join together "in the defence of some holy cause, in the defence of holy justice, for the defence of the oppressed, for the enfranchisement of the downtrodden, and for the advancement of liberty, progress and civilization."[48] Not only did Laurier echo the righteous rhetoric of the Spanish-American War, but with another war imminent in South Africa, the prime minister cast the war with the Boers in a similar vein, as a "holy crusade" – words that he would soon repeat in the House of Commons.

Laurier's biographer Joseph Schull states that upon the prime minister's departure for Ottawa, he left behind him "an atmosphere chill with righteous disapproval."[49] Schull means that Laurier's fine words could not undermine American sympathy for the Boers. Yet the American press received Laurier's speech very well. In Chicago, the *Times-Herald* called the speech the "most significant utterances of the festival" next to those of the president. The paper further referred to Laurier's speech as a "brilliant peroration" and his words about Anglo-American unity the "climax of the most strikingly significant incident of the fall ceremonies." The Chicago *Post* believed Laurier had mentioned the Alaska difficulty only to emphasize the fact that "between two nations so united by ties of sympathy, blood, comprehension and interest no quarrels and bickerings are capable of producing any real ill-feeling and hostility."[50] Finally, the New York *Tribune* gushed over Laurier's "eloquent address," especially his thoughts concerning Anglo-Saxon unity. "If that is the voice of Canada," the paper stated, "there should be no further bickering between the Dominion and the Union." In the prime minister's "ennobled and ennobling sentiments the voice of Canada and the voice of the United States are one."[51]

Anglo-American unity would be sorely tried during the South African war, with many expressions of anglophobia and sympathy for the Boers. For the most part, however, Canadians seemed to ignore such anglophobic sentiment while emphasizing "American sympathy" for the British cause. Moreover, English Canadians placed American sympathy within the context of Anglo-American unity, just as they had British sympathy toward the United States during its war the year before. *Methodist Magazine* believed that "the magnanimous sympathy shown the Americans ... has brought its reward in the warm sympathy shown by the American people."[52] Shortly after "Black Week," in an article entitled "American sympathy," the same journal stated that "Beyond the ties of blood and brotherhood between Great Britain and America, the intellectual and moral sympathy between these imperial democracies ... will bind them in a moral alliance."[53] The editor of *Canadian Magazine* went so far as to note the lack of protest against the war in the republic. "There can be no question that a general and outspoken objection to the war on the part of the people of the United States," John Ewan wrote, "would have been a greater obstruction to the war party in England than the hostile opinion of the rest of the world." Although both nations possessed innate sympathy for the underdog, Spain and the Boer republics had "forfeited a great deal of this natural feeling" by their actions. "Thus the two leaders of civilization have been an example and justification to each other."[54]

In *Queen's Quarterly* George Grant also viewed American sympathy as a positive outcome of the war. At the outbreak of the war Grant praised Joseph Chamberlain, the British Colonial Secretary, for his efforts to foster Anglo-American amity. The most "American" member of the British cabinet, Chamberlain had displayed, according to Grant, the "greatest sincerity and steadiness in his American sympathies," reflecting the "mind of the British people in general."[55] A few months later Grant speculated that any interference in the war would result in not merely an Anglo-American alliance, but "an alliance of the English-speaking peoples that would never be broken." British sympathy during the Spanish-American war had broken the average American out of his isolation. During the present crisis, Grant concluded, "the claims of blood, of descent, of common interest, and common moral aims, ideals and hopes can now exert their legitimate influence."[56] A year later Grant continued to preach the benefits of Anglo-Saxon solidarity, which he viewed as one of the most significant events of the previous century: "The great Republic has come of age. It is taking its place as one of the greatest of the World Powers. It has found out that there is neither honour nor political profit in twisting the lion's tail. The best gift the last century has left with us is the promise of a moral union and possibly a common citizenship between it and the Mother Country."[57] Grant's writing revealed the broad context in which English Canadians viewed the events of the turn of the century. British sympathy during the Spanish-American War had been reciprocated during the Boer War. Grant not only cheered the Anglo-American entente, but envisioned a greater, common destiny for the entire race. The wars with the Spanish, the Filipinos, and the Boers were not unconnected, but constituted parts of a larger, highly significant picture that drew the English-speaking peoples of the world inexorably closer together.

CANADA'S VOICE: THE MODUS VIVENDI AND CLAYTON-BULWER TREATIES

Despite the change in American opinion toward Great Britain after the Spanish-American War, problems still existed. The Joint High Commission had adjourned in early 1899 with no resolution of the Alaska boundary. Moreover, with new territories in the Pacific, the United States eagerly desired to begin building an isthmian canal. The Anglo-American Clayton-Bulwer Treaty of 1850, however, stipulated that the United States and Great Britain must build any canal in cooperation. Both in Canada and in Great Britain, American impatience to build a canal was seen as a bargaining chip. If the United States would concede on the Alaska boundary, Great Britain would agree to modify the 1850 treaty and allow the United States to build a canal independently. In the end, Canada refused to accept any settlement agreed to by both the United States and Great Britain. After all, with the United States champing at the bit in its desire to build a canal, all Canada need do was wait. In its resistance of American demands, the Canadian government enjoyed the support of the British government, namely Joseph Chamberlain, the Colonial Secretary. Moreover, Lord Salisbury, as historian H.C. Allen notes, "was very much the aristocrat and had some of the inclination of the old Tory aristocracy to despise all things American."[58] Moreover, Salisbury served as both prime minister and foreign secretary, a combination that often tended to complicate Anglo-American affairs, as during the Venezuela crisis. Apparent Canadian intransigence, then, provided the British with a convenient excuse to resist complete capitulation to American terms.

The coming of the war in South Africa, however, drastically changed the situation. With early British setbacks coupled with a threat by the United States Senate unilaterally to abrogate the Clayton-Bulwer Treaty, Great Britain found itself backed into a corner. Desirous of

American support in its critical hour, the British government agreed to abrogate the treaty without any *quid pro quo* regarding Alaska. Canadian historians have repeatedly referred to Great Britain "sacrificing" Canadian interests in the matter.[59] In reality, both Great Britain and the United States sought to "compartmentalize" Canadian-American relations. With relations between the dominion and the republic forming an apparent obstacle to Anglo-American relations at a critical hour, both British and American diplomats sought to cleave Canadian-American relations off into their own category. With increasing contact between Canadian and American officials, and the convening of the 1898–99 Joint High Commission composed largely of Americans and Canadians, Canadian-American relations already represented a separate category of diplomacy. Into this situation created by the rapprochement stepped Wilfrid Laurier to claim for Canada a measure of its own voice in the conduct of Anglo-Canadian-American relations. Still, Canada's inability to conduct its own external affairs directly placed the Dominion in a hopelessly inferior position. The fault lay not with grasping Americans or a callous British Foreign Office, but with Canada's disadvantaged position.

In early January 1899, John Hay and British ambassador Julian Pauncefote agreed on a modification of the Clayton-Bulwer Treaty allowing independent American construction of a canal. The British consulted the Laurier government, which rejected any modification of the treaty without some sort of Alaskan settlement. Almost immediately after the failure of the Joint High Commission, British and American diplomats set to work establishing a provisional boundary (*modus vivendi*) until the matter could be settled once and for all. In April Hay sent to Pauncefote a proposal to fix the boundary provisionally. Pauncefote initially accepted the proposal on condition that Canada agreed. The Canadian cabinet, and more specifically Minister of Interior Clifford Sifton, rejected the proposal. The Canadians demanded any provisional agreement be linked to a commitment to have the whole boundary submitted to arbitration.[60] Meanwhile, the territorial governor of Alaska reported that the Royal Canadian Mounted Police were encroaching on "American territory."[61] The situation was proving to be more than just inconvenient to the American and British governments.

Though an anglophile, the Secretary of State held little love for Canada during the negotiations over the Alaska boundary. On April 28 Pauncefote informed Hay that the Canadian cabinet had rejected the provisional boundary. Exasperated, Hay sent an angry letter to the American ambassador to Great Britain, Joseph Choate. Hay depicted the entire Alaska affair, the recently failed Commission, and Anglo-Americans relations generally, as prisoners to domestic Canadian politics.

[T]he whole matter is in a most unsatisfactory state, which has a tendency to become worse every hour. I do not believe we are asking anything unreasonable, and I am sure if the matter depended on direct negotiations between the United States and England, it would be very speedily and satisfactorily settled, but we were driven to the conclusion before the Conference closed that the Canadians did not wish any settlement, that they preferred the present risky and unsettled state of things to any decision which would leave them open to attack from the Opposition, as having shown a lack of spirit and a lack of regard for Canadian interests, in their negotiations with the Americans.

Hay stated that calling a new Commission would be useless unless the governments could reach some sort of an agreement beforehand. Hay then turned away from the Alaska boundary and expressed his dim view of both Canadian politics and the British habit of referring everything to Canada.

You are by this time probably aware of the great difficulties that surround the arrangement of any controversy in which Canada is concerned. The Dominion politicians care little for English interests. Their minds are completely occupied with their own party and factional disputes, and Sir Wilfrid Laurier is far more afraid of Sir Charles Tupper than he is of Lord Salisbury and President McKinley combined; while the habit of referring everything from the Foreign Office to the Colonial, followed by a consultation of the Canadian authorities by the Minister of the Colonies, produces interminable friction and delay. I hope it may be possible for you in your conversations with Lord Salisbury to cause him to feel the desirability of finding, if possible, some arrangement of these troubles, which, though intrinsically insignificant, are likely at any moment to embitter the relations between our two countries, solely in the interest of warring factions in Canada.[62]

For Hay, a few square miles of arctic wasteland were not worth endangering the momentous rapprochement, although he knew American politics demanded they remain under American control. The Secretary of State essentially asked Choate to convince Salisbury to come to an understanding over Alaska without letting Canadian politics interfere. At the same time, Hay sought the influence of key Washington figures.

Choate set to work almost immediately and agreed to Lord Salisbury's suggestion that the United States lease to Canada land on the Alaskan coast and give right-of-way to a Canadian railroad. While not owning the land outright, Canada would then possess her much-desired Yukon route, and break the virtual American monopoly on Yukon trade. On May 12 Choate cabled an exuberant Hay about the British plan. "I cannot exaggerate the feelings of satisfaction with which I received your despatches," Hay replied to the American ambassador. "I thought I saw in them the promise of an honourable conclusion of all the petty wrangling of the past year over the settling of the Alaska frontier." Even more importantly, Hay consulted with President McKinley, two members of the Joint High Commission, Senator Fairbanks and John Foster, and "the most prominent members within each of the Committees on Foreign Relations of the two Houses."[63] All agreed to Choate's proposal, except for Senator Davis, the chair of the Senate's Foreign Relations Committee – a key exception, indicating possible Senate opposition to any subsequent treaty. Once again, though, Hay had not figured Canada into the equation. Salisbury again insisted upon consulting the Canadian government. The Canadians once again demanded arbitration, with the added precondition that if any arbitration gave the United States the port towns of Dyea and Skagway, Pyramid Harbor would automatically revert to Canada. Choate expressed his disappointment to Hay that Canada had once again proved an obstacle to an amicable settlement.

I was assured that Lord Salisbury and Mr. Chamberlain would bring all reasonable pressure to bear upon Canada to bring about that result; and now it is manifest that whatever they have done in that direction, has been met by this astounding and unreasonable demand from Canada, ... and that if Pyramid Harbor was found to be within the territory and jurisdiction of the United States, it should be turned over to Great Britain, without rhyme or reason ... It is, as it seems to me, perfectly obvious that Canada has seized upon the opportunity of Great Britain and ourselves proceeding to an amicable arrangement of this vexed question, so as to permit the Joint High Commission to proceed and complete its labor – to produce an impossible bargain, by which they could secure the much-coveted port, to which they have no right.

Still, Choate remained optimistic that some solution could be found. "It is not possible that our present controversy can have anything but an amicable issue," Choate concluded, "although the Canadian intervention sometimes makes that seem somewhat distant."[64]

The next day Choate penned a note to the British ambassador in Washington, Julian Pauncefote. "Our apple-cart has been again upset," Choate stated, "and by running against the usual obstacle."[65] Choate did not need to explain of what "the usual obstacle" consisted. Pauncefote's reply revealed that the British representative to the United States viewed Canadian motives in the same light as Choate and Hay did.

I need not say how disturbed and disappointed I am at the failure of our efforts in the matter of the Alaskan Boundary. It only shows how difficult it is to satisfy politicians whose tenure of office is at stake. It is disheartening, but I do not despair. The Canadians must know ... it is quite certain that Dyea and Skagway must be and remain American territory; but they dare not put it in the Treaty in so many words as it looks as a Concession granted without an equivalent, for which they would be attacked by their opponents in Parliament and in the Press.[66]

Pauncefote's reply went beyond mere diplomatic niceties. After all, with the great volume of Canadian-American affairs that passed through the British embassy in Washington, Pauncefote acted essentially as Canada's ambassador to the United States. Yet in a note to his American counterpart in London, he freely expressed his dissatisfaction with the Canadian government and took the American side of the debate.

If the ambassadors in Washington and London were irritated at Canadian obstructionism, the Secretary of State was gravely disappointed. Hay wrote to Choate: "I was preparing a telegram to you announcing our unqualified acceptance of the proposals made in your despatch when Mr. Tower appeared at the department with a note from Lord Salisbury saying that, after consultation with the Canadian Government and a discussion in the Cabinet, the terms mentioned by you had been found unacceptable. I need not say it was a bitter disappointment," Hay lamented. With a settlement apparently likely, the Canadians had once again put up a roadblock. The phrase "after consultation with the Canadian Government" must have dripped from Hay's pen like bile. "The simple fact is," Hay continued, "that the whole Canadian claim was invented about a year ago for the purpose of getting a foothold on the ocean, the result of which would be to cut off southeastern Alaska from the rest of the Territory." Hay went on to lament the effect of Canada's stonewalling on the proposed revision of the Clayton-Bulwer Treaty.

A regrettable consequence of this failure of our negotiations as to Canada is the fact that it carries with it a failure of our convention as to the Clayton-Bulwer treaty. Of course it is absurdly illogical to make the one depend on the other ... The convention we made was entirely satisfactory to both of us, and yet Lord Salisbury informed Mr. White before your arrival that as a matter of tactics he would not care to go before Parliament with a convention modifying the Clayton-Bulwer treaty unless at the same time he was able to announce the settlement of all matters in which Canada was concerned.

Tellingly, Hay did not blame Canada for insisting upon linking the issues of Alaska and the inter-oceanic canal. Instead he referred to the political "tactics" of Lord Salisbury. Although often quick to condemn

Canada, Hay clearly saw British politics behind the scenes. Affixing responsibility on Laurier and Canadian politics provided anglophile Hay with a convenient means of preserving broader Anglo-American amity.

In the end, though, Hay continued to reserve his greatest excoriation for Canada.

The attitude of Canada as to such matters makes the whole affair hopeless. After a careful observation of two years I am convinced that the Canadians prefer that nothing shall be settled between the two countries. Sir Wilfrid Laurier and the Liberals came into power as the advocates of friendly reciprocal relations with the United States, but being in power and subject to the energetic attacks of Sir Charles Tupper and the rest of the opposition, they find it easier to sustain themselves as the stalwart defenders of Canadian rights and interests against the yankee encroachments than it would be to have the job of justifying a reasonable treaty, some provisions of which would necessarily be unpopular in certain quarters.

Once again Hay accused Laurier of "playing to the crowd" by maintaining a hard line toward the United States. Certainly there was an element of truth in this, as Laurier saw Canadian-American relations as a means of uniting a country sorely divided by language, religion, region, and political faction. Hay blamed the failure of the Joint High Commission on Laurier's fears that any settlement of Canadian-American disputes would be characterized by the Conservatives as the selling of Canadian interests: "Sir Wilfrid and his associates were absolutely afraid that they would have to return to Canada with a fair and honorable treaty on their hands, and the prospect was not agreeable to them." Once again Hay's words contained a kernel of truth, as nationalist members of the cabinet petitioned the Prime Minister to return to Ottawa without an agreement. Hay concluded his letter to Choate by praising the ambassador's work, where "success was only rendered impossible by the attitude of Canada."[67]

Meanwhile, in Canada, Laurier did his best to avoid answering questions about a proposed *modus vivendi*. News of various proposals had been leaked to the press, and on several occasions in April and May the Opposition leader, Sir Charles Tupper, raised the question in the House of Commons. Despite the fact that Canada had been consulted on a number of occasions, Laurier claimed ignorance of any plan to fix a temporary boundary. In April he stated that there was "no modus vivendi now pending or being discussed between the two countries," a position he adhered to for the next few months.[68] After the failure of the Joint High Commission the Tories had attacked the Liberals for not taking a firmer stand with the Americans. Perhaps Laurier wanted to avoid a potentially embarrassing subject, or perhaps he wanted to keep the cabinet's hands free in the negotiations. Tupper attempted to keep the pressure on with aggressive rhetoric. The Conservative leader suggested possibly cutting off America's supply of Canadian pulp wood or barring American miners.[69] Even after reports appeared concerning Anglo-American agreement to Ambassador Choate's plan, Laurier continued to dissemble. In early July Laurier responded to press reports of the plan by calling them "sensational despatches." "I do not believe there is any more truth in this than there has been in preceding despatches of the same character," Laurier said, although he knew the reports to be true.[70]

Finally, by late July, the facts had come out, and Canadian nationalist rhetoric reached a high pitch. Liberals and Conservatives united in lambasting both the American and the British handling of the affair. Tupper recalled his criticism of the government after the adjournment of the Commission when he had said, "They have forgotten what is due the people of Canada." Now Tupper withdrew the remark, saying he had not understood Laurier's steadfast refusal to reconvene the Commission unless the Alaska matter were settled. He called America's position "monstrous," and also questioned the absolute unwillingness of Great Britain "to allow any circumstance whatever to even threaten a collision with the United States." Echoing Canadian sentiment in the wake of the Venezuela crisis, Tupper conceded that an Anglo-American "armed conflict" would constitute "the most terrible event that the civilized world could witness." After all, Tupper said, "they are of our own blood to a large extent." Yet England could never understand the United States as well as Canada, and that in this instance "the diplomacy of England has failed." The Conservative leader concluded by praising the work of the Laurier Government: "The policy my right honorable friend [Laurier] has pursued up to the present is one to which I have given my hearty endorsement. The Government have only done what it was their absolute duty to do in the interests of Canada, in maintaining inflexibility, and against the pressure of England, I am afraid, the attitude it has assumed against the contentions of the United States."[71] Tory criticism of the United States was nothing new, but perhaps never had a Conservative party leader so attacked the British government on the floor of the House of Commons.

With Tupper's high level of rhetoric, Laurier felt compelled to stand and affirm Canadian rights on behalf of the Liberals. He stated that there existed only three methods of settling the Alaska boundary dispute: compromise, arbitration, or war. Although Laurier elaborated, "I am sure that no one would think of war," the damage had been done. Reports appeared that the Canadian Prime Minister suggested war as the only alternative to arbitration. "Canada Blames America," a headline in the *New York Times* ran: "Talk of War or Arbitration."[72] American reaction to Laurier's words was mixed. On the one hand, Americans resented the remark as a means of pressuring the United States to submit the boundary to arbitration. "Sir W. Laurier's declaration for arbitration or war was very ill timed and unfortunate," Senator Davis wrote to Hay. "It is regarded here as a threat to compel arbitration, and has aroused considerable resentment."[73] Writing to the Secretary of State, Davis probably referred to resentment in the Senate. In general, however, Laurier's comment caused very little outrage in the United States, perhaps indicating the new feeling of Anglo-American goodwill. The *Times* noted that Laurier's comment did not alarm the government.[74] Theodore Roosevelt, who only a few years before had itched to "take Canada" during the Venezuela crisis, played down Laurier's remark. Writing of Laurier's use of the word "war" to his friend Cecil Spring Rice, Roosevelt noted the change in feeling in the United States: "Two years ago this would have provoked frantic retaliatory denunciation on our part and action in the State legislatures and Congress, which really might have endangered the peace. Now it is for the most part dismissed by our papers and by all of our public officers with the good-humored remark that there is to be no interruption of the friendship between England and America, and that to talk of any rupture in their relations is mere nonsense."[75] Joseph Choate said essentially the same thing to the press, blaming Laurier's remarks on Canadian politics and affirming that "no amount of politics or politicians in either country could occasion war in this connection."[76] When informed of Choate's view, the Canadian High Commissioner in London, Lord Strathcona, called Laurier's remark "merely a figure of speech and not a political dodge, as intimated by Mr. Choate."[77] No doubt Strathcona was correct, and Laurier's reference to war constituted little more than a rhetorical device. Yet coming in the middle of the *modus vivendi* negotiations, in which Canada continually rejected Anglo-American settlements, Laurier's remarks were destined to be received by Americans as further proof of the Dominion's obstinacy.

Immediately after the uproar over Laurier's remarks faded, American papers reported that an American official had received a rather rude reception in Ottawa. F. W. Fitzpatrick of the Treasury Department had met with Laurier and invited Lord Minto and the premier to Chicago for a cornerstone-laying ceremony for the city's new post office. Fitzpatrick, the Assistant United States Architect, described his reception as "slightly chilly." According to Fitzpatrick Laurier called the official's visit "untimely" and declined the invitation fearing that any Canadian officials "might in a great gathering of such a character as the Chicago ceremony be subjected to some unpleasantness or indignity by thoughtless persons." Laurier supposedly added that he would also advise the Governor-General to decline the invitation.[78] The *Times* laughed at the prime minister's reported remarks, referring in an editorial headline to "The Hyperaesthesia of Wilfrid Laurier." "It is impossible to repress a smile at his excessive sensitiveness," the editorial smirked, "and the air of deeply offended dignity which he assumes." Americans, the paper stated, simply didn't care that much about the boundary dispute. "Sir Wilfrid evidently supposes that there is a popular tumult here over the question; that mobs roam the streets bellowing for his gore; that Americans are secretly arming for the conquest of Canada, and that all our people, having laid aside their ordinary pursuits, are working themselves into a fever over the question of the Canadian port on the Lynn Canal." The *Times* asserted that in spite of Laurier's talk of war, "we really like him very well." The paper speculated, in much the same manner as John Hay, that Laurier's remarks were once again "part of the game of home politics."[79]

Meanwhile Hay and Choate sought to keep alive the plan of leasing a port to Canada. Choate worked on Lord Salisbury in London,[80] while Hay worked on the Senate in Washington. The sole obstacle in the United States seemed to be Senator Davis, chair of the Senate Foreign Relations Committee. With the support of other important Republicans such as Whitelaw Reid, Davis told Hay that no treaty giving Canada a "foothold on the coast" would pass the Senate. Moreover, Davis said, an embarrassing Republican defeat on the eve of the 1900 election might pave the way for a Bryan victory.[81] Clearly, domestic politics played an important role for all three nations involved in the dispute.

While the Americans worked steadily for a compromise, Sir Louis Davies, Canadian Minister of Fisheries and member of the Joint High Commission, visited London to make clear Canada's views to the Foreign Office. Choate noted to Hay that the British would not take the matter any further until after Davies's visit.[82] While in London, Davies rejected Lord Salisbury's plan for the United States to lease Canada a port on the Alaska coast. Moreover, he impressed upon the British the intensity of Canadian opinion on the matter and the high political stakes involved. Writing to Laurier in October 1899 Davies reported on his conversation at the British Foreign Office: "I then stated that I was satisfied public opinion in Canada, believing we had a right to the territory at the head of Lynn Canal, would never sanction the voluntary surrender by us of Dyea and Skagway to the United States ... unless we had a reciprocal and distinct concession to Canada of the only other remaining harbour in Lynn Canal [Pyramid Harbor];

and I went further and said that it was not a matter of the present Government's existence, but of the existence of any government."[83] In the wake of Davies's visit Henry White and F.H. Villiers of the British Foreign Office discussed the Alaska dispute. White asked Villiers what the Canadians wanted, and Villiers replied, "more than they will get," displaying some impatience with the Canadians by the Foreign Office.[84] Clearly a permanent settlement was some time off. Impatient with the standoff and anxious for some temporary settlement, the State Department pressed for a *modus vivendi*, after which other questions might be discussed. On October 20, the British and Americans agreed to a temporary boundary, apparently without consulting Canada. As the *modus vivendi* did not give Canada any access to the Lynn Canal, the settlement, although temporary, was seen as a victory for the United States, establishing a precedent for keeping Dyea and Skagway American towns.

A month before the *modus vivendi* was completed, Hay wrote Henry White expressing his doubts about any possible abrogation of the Clayton-Bulwer treaty. "I wish I could believe that Lord Salisbury would let the Clayton-Bulwer Convention go through," Hay wrote, "independent of Canadian matters."[85] That seemed very unlikely, with the Canadian government sending emissaries to the Foreign Office and rejecting solutions agreed to by both the American and British governments. The isthmian canal was Canada's ace-in-the-hole; the Dominion would not give it up, and England backed its position. Time appeared to be on the Canadian side until the outbreak of war in South Africa in early October.

"At this instant, 11 a.m., while I write," the well-informed Henry Adams wrote to a friend in February, 1900, "Hay is probably signing with Pauncefote an abrogation of the Clayton-Bulwer Treaty! Hay himself actually trembles for fear that he should wake up and find that he dreamt it. He has given nothing for what a dozen Presidents have broken their necks to get. No doubt he is lucky to have a Transvaal war round the adjacent corner; but he got his *modus vivendi* without, or before, the war, which was a still greater relief, for Canada really threatened to be our Transvaal."[86] The temporary settlement of the Alaska boundary coincided with the outbreak of war in South Africa, and the consequent disbanding of the Joint High Commission. The State Department now turned to having the Clayton-Bulwer Treaty abrogated. With continuing Canadian demands, Hay and Choate's task seemed hopeless. Indeed, Canada's war contribution weighed heavily in the Dominion's favour when seeking support from the Foreign Office. Hay worried that Canadian opposition to the treaty's abrogation would not only block the canal's construction, but reveal

England as blocking the course of civilization. "It will be a great benefaction to the entire civilized world," Hay wrote to Choate of the proposed canal. "It would be a deplorable result of all our labor and thought on the subject if, by persisting in postponing the consideration of this matter until all the Canadian questions are closed up, England should be made to appear in the attitude of attempting to veto a work of such world-wide importance."[87] In January Choate spoke with Lord Salisbury about abrogating the treaty with some alacrity. Salisbury would not be rushed, and continued to claim the need to consult with Canadian authorities. According to Choate, Salisbury had stated "very emphatically that he would have to bring it up before the cabinet so as to give Mr. Chamberlain a chance to be heard for Canada." Choate protested that "Canada had nothing to do with it," while Salisbury replied that "the war and Canada's participation therein had changed the situation." Choate advised the Secretary of State that, "I think you must expect some difficulty here."[88]

Meanwhile, the Canadian Minister of Justice, David Mills, published two articles in the British press explaining Canada's position on the Clayton-Bulwer treaty. Instead of calling for a quid pro quo on Alaska, Mills asserted that any canal would affect Canada's trade and security. In the *Empire Review* Mills wrote "Canada is a North American State. Her commerce is far greater in proportion to her population than that of the neighbouring republic. The construction of a Central American canal would be as much called for in her interest, as in that of the United States, and we shall never be content to submit to any other rule in respect to such a canal than that of perfect equality. The provisions of the Clayton-Bulwer treaty in this regard," Mills continued, "are vital to Canada, and the government of the United Kingdom must not, for any political consideration, sacrifice the interests of Canada, and the future of the British Empire upon this continent." Departing from the convention of the Clayton-Bulwer treaty, Mills concluded, "would be a greater menace to our security and future progress than any other matter of controversy that now presents itself for solution."[89] Mills's words echoed Canadian sentiment during the Venezuela crisis. If Great Britain conceded hegemony in the western hemisphere to the United States, Mills argued, Canada would be forever placed in a disadvantaged position. Mills did not try to interest his British audience in a few square miles of arctic tundra, or pepper his article with alien-sounding names like "Chilkoot," "Dyea," and "Skagway." Instead, he appealed to Britons as fellow members of the British Empire with identical interests. The Canadian government seemed to be undertaking a rigorous campaign to sway British public and official opinion.

With no abrogation forthcoming, the House of Representatives took unilateral action, introducing a bill that authorized construction of an

American canal. If passed, the bill would have constituted a violation of the Anglo-American treaty. Despite Hay's unhappiness about Congress's hasty action, it appeared to break the deadlock with the British. With December's disastrous reverses at the hands of the Boers, known as Black Week, still reverberating throughout England, the British government pressed Canada to agree to an abrogation for the sake of maintaining American sympathy. Chamberlain informed Lord Minto that the Canadian government must give their consent, and with little choice in the matter, Laurier agreed. Lord Salisbury told Ambassador Choate that "Canada was very considerate and surrendered her special scruples." Choate agreed with Salisbury's evaluation of Canada's actions, and wrote to Hay, "you must give Canada a large credit mark for this, considering the great heed paid to her wishes by the Imperial Government in these days of ardent loyalty."[90] On February 5 Hay and the British ambassador signed the Hay-Pauncefote Treaty allowing the United States to build and own an isthmian canal. "Hay beams with relief," Adams observed. "He has euchred the canny-dians. He has gone one better on the *modus vivendi*."[91] No doubt Adams saw Hay's reaction correctly. Within four months Hay had successfully removed two major obstacles in the way of Anglo-American understanding. Moreover, he, or rather Congress and the British government, had successfully removed Canada from the equation.

The initial Hay-Pauncefote Treaty did not allow for the United States to fortify the canal, which resulted in a howl of protest throughout the United States. Theodore Roosevelt publicly called for the Senate to refuse ratification, leading to a "grieved protest" from his friend Hay.[92] The Canadian public also expressed a grieved protest upon hearing news of the treaty's abrogation. A year earlier Professor Adam Shortt had claimed Canada and Great Britain had "nothing to lose but much to gain by permitting the canal to be built and controlled by the United States." He cited the "better feeling in the Anglo-Saxon household."[93] Yet Shortt's seemed like a minority opinion. Major-general T. Bland Strange, formerly of the Canadian militia, responded to Shortt stating that even between "the best of friends, partners or relatives, it is desirable that each should keep their respective keys of the mutual safe." About the new Anglo-American understanding Strange wrote, "When a new-found friend asks to be allowed to put a pistol to your head as a proof of reconciliation, the man or nation that allows it has no brains worth blowing out."[94]

In the House of Commons Henri Bourassa, who had broken from the Liberal party over the Canadian contribution of troops to the war, questioned Laurier about the new treaty and the Alaska boundary. Laurier said that he could not produce any Alaska documents as the matter continued to be negotiated. When Bourassa asked for just the

Clayton-Bulwer correspondence, Laurier tellingly replied, "I am afraid that the two cannot be separated."[95] Of course, the two matters had been separated, placing Canada in a very disadvantaged position. Bourassa realized this, and excoriated the British authorities for yet another sacrifice of Canadian rights. The British had, Bourassa said, conceded its canal rights to the United States without a quid pro quo for Canada. "I say the position is most unfair for Canada," Bourassa stated. "Have we come to that point that Great Britain can count upon our devotion to such an extent that, even where we had acknowledged rights, she will not make the slightest efforts to have those rights acknowledged?" Laurier essentially agreed; "I am not," he said, "an admirer of British policy on the continent of America." S.E. Gourley used rather extreme rhetoric when he argued that the imperial authorities should have gone to war over Alaska and the Clayton-Bulwer Treaty. "I will go into the trenches," Gourley proclaimed, "and take my wife and family with me and stay there two years if need be to fight for the rights of Canada." The MP from Colchester went on to call the men of the Foreign Office "blockheads," and concluded by affirming his willingness to fight the "Yankees." If necessary, Gourley concluded, "we will fight them within twenty-four hours, and after six months we will capture their capital and annex their country to Canada."[96] While few other Canadians desired war with the United States, most would have agreed with Canadian politicians that their rights had once again been sacrificed.

With 1900 a presidential election year in the United States, the Senate duly noted American opinion and Democrats delayed ratifying the Hay-Pauncefote Treaty, supported by key Republicans such as Lodge. The treaty controversy resulted in a surge of anglophobia and pro-Boer sentiment. The State Department was roundly criticized by the American press and Hay offered his resignation, which President McKinley declined. In December the Senate added sweeping amendments to the proposed Hay-Pauncefote Treaty, which the British government quickly rejected. The issue lay dormant until the summer, when Henry Cabot Lodge and Henry White visited England. Salisbury repeated to White the need to compromise on Alaska in order to win a modification of the Clayton-Bulwer Treaty. When White protested, Salisbury conceded the advantage of separating the two issues; in regards to the canal, Salisbury said, "we should have only one antagonist, whereas in respect of Alaska there would be two – yourselves and Canada."[97] The British government agreed to allow the United States to fortify the canal, and Hay lobbied leading senators who agreed to approve the new convention.

Negotiations on a new canal treaty and on arbitrating the Alaska boundary now proceeded on two separate, parallel fronts. The treaty's prospects were aided by the new prime minister, A.J. Balfour, and the new foreign minister, Lord Landsdowne, both of whom were committed to an Anglo-American understanding. The goal now was to keep the two issues unconnected so that Canada could no longer hold up negotiations. When Landsdowne privately asked Ambassador Choate why the United States insisted upon a tribunal of six to settle the boundary question, Choate begged off answering in full, saying "don't let us bring up anything about Canada or Alaska until this Canal business is out of the way. Let's get the treaty ratified first before we take up anything else."[98] Landsdowne agreed, and the new Hay-Pauncefote treaty was signed in November and ratified by the Senate the following February. The United States would now be allowed to build, control and fortify the canal, and had not conceded anything to Canada regarding Alaska.

The abrogation of the Clayton-Bulwer treaty without any compromise on Alaska was met in Canada with some disappointment. In the face of an imperial crisis in South Africa, and American and British pressure, Laurier's government had little choice but to give in on the matter. Laurier had previously staked a firm position on the issue, as evidenced by his intense rhetoric, by the London visits of Sir Louis Davies, and by the courting of British public opinion by David Mills. With much to lose from the treaty's abrogation, Laurier attempted to soft-pedal the issue when confronted by Tory questions. In the House of Commons F.D. Monk demanded that all documents relating to the new Hay-Pauncefote treaty be released, claiming that "the interests of Canada were insufficiently and improperly guarded by this government."[99] Monk even cited the articles by David Mills, the former minister of Justice in Laurier's own cabinet, in affirming Canada's interest in the abrogation of the Clayton-Bulwer treaty. Laurier replied by calling Monk's reasoning "fallacious." "Canada had no interest in the Clayton-Bulwer treaty," Laurier claimed: "Canada had no interest in the Nicaragua canal. Canada had no more interest in the negotiations of a treaty which affected the Nicaragua canal than she would have in a treaty in reference to the Suez canal." Not only did this contradict the public statements by a member of Laurier's own cabinet, but Laurier's reply also minimized any connection between the Clayton-Bulwer abrogation and Alaska. With the two issues simultaneously facing Great Britain and the United States, Laurier said, "it was thought opportune that the two questions should be negotiated together."[100] Again, the three-month visit of Davies to London seemed to indicate that the Canadian government thought it more than just "opportune" or convenient to negotiate the two issues together. From the time of the Joint High Commission's adjournment in early 1899 until the signing of the new Hay-Pauncefote treaty in November 1901, Canada's primary external affairs goal (apart from the South African war) was pressing for a compromise on Alaska in exchange for a revision of the Clayton-Bulwer treaty. The Tories realized this and sought to exploit it.

Continuing the Commons debate, Conservative leader Sir Charles Tupper blamed the Laurier government for not insisting to the imperial authorities that the rights of Canada should not be sacrificed.[101] A.C. Bell of Pictou disputed Laurier's claim that Canada had no interest in a Nicaragua canal. "We, in Canada, have as large a part of the North American continent as the United States," Bell observed, "and our interests in the Nicaragua canal ... is at least as great as theirs." Clearly if Laurier failed to understand this, Bell said, "we need not be surprised if the interests of Canada in this matter were not safeguarded."[102] W.F. Maclean of East York said that if the Canadian government had insisted that the Foreign Office "stand by her guns" regarding the Clayton-Bulwer treaty, "we should have had the settlement of the Alaskan boundary at the time the final treaty was made." This was certainly not true, as no amount of Canadian insistence could have pressured the British government into sacrificing larger imperial interests for the sake of Canadian pride. Yet Maclean's remark, echoed by other Conservative MPs and the Conservative leader, represented a persistent misconception in Canada concerning its external affairs: that with recent displays of Canadian fealty, namely the Jubilee, British preference, and the South African war, Canada held a co-equal position in imperial councils. In early 1902 Laurier and many others knew differently. Yet it would take a more humiliating public defeat at the hands of the Americans and their seemingly willing cohorts in the Foreign Office, to impress upon a wider Canadian public Canada's disadvantaged position.

CONCLUSION

The years 1899–1902 witnessed the crest and crisis of North American Anglo-Saxonism. English-speaking Canadians and Americans began 1899 by singing "white man's burden" in the Philippines, and ended the year singing the same tune in South Africa. Anglo-Saxonism helped shape the anglophilia of important policy makers like John Hay and Joseph Choate, while it undermined the anglophobia of Theodore Roosevelt. These years also witnessed an eruption of Anglo-American conflicts, whose successful resolutions confirmed the two countries' rapprochement. While many Americans held a dim view of the war against the Boers, official American opinion reflected the "benevolent sympathy" of the British during the Spanish-American war. Americans and Britons exchanged condolences over the death of Queen Victoria and the assassination of President McKinley. Tensions in the disputed Alaska region were relieved by determining a temporary border, while Great Britain gave up its rights to a Central American canal under the Hay-Pauncefote treaty. The latter indicated further British acknowledgment of American hegemony in the western hemisphere. Following the abrogation of the Clayton-Bulwer treaty Great Britain reduced its West Indies fleet and garrison.[103] The Caribbean had become an American lake.

The various events of these years simultaneously underscored both the strength and the weakness of North American Anglo-Saxonism. Canadians and Americans employed the same "rhetoric of righteousness" during the Boer War as they had during the Spanish-American War, illustrating that they viewed the two wars as part of the same mission: to keep English the dominant language from "Cape to Cairo," and to keep Anglo-Saxon institutions the dominant form of African "civilization." Certainly, many English Canadians supported the war because of other motivations, such as imperialism, loyalty to Great Britain, and perhaps even anti-Americanism. And certainly not all Americans supported the war, using it as just another springboard for attacks on England and designs on Canada. Yet the similarity of Anglo-Saxon rhetoric heard across the continent cannot be denied, nor can the fact that Canadians and Americans drew a conscious link between these imperial wars. At the same time, however, domestic politics and the realpolitik of Anglo-American relations could just as easily have drowned out such talk of kinship and common mission. Like the on-going reciprocity debate, the Alaska *modus vivendi* and the abrogation of the Clayton-Bulwer treaty ran headlong into the perceived national self-interest of all three countries. The predetermined conclusion of such disputes had much more to do with the shifting balance of power in the hemisphere than with Anglo-Saxon idealism.

Hay's and Choate's displeasure over Canadian obstructionism during the Alaska negotiations illustrated a subtle shift in Canada's place in Anglo-American relations. No longer was Canada viewed merely as an offshoot of Great Britain. British and American diplomats went to great lengths to compartmentalize Canadian actions and official Canadian views emanating from Ottawa. It was striking to witness Ambassadors Pauncefote and Choate commiserating over their failed plans, and blaming Canadian politicians for the narrowness of their interests. This finger-pointing resulted in part from Canada's growing independence, including its contribution to the South African war. It also resulted from the British and American diplomats' earnest desire to preserve the tenuous rapprochement. Placing the blame for failed negotiations squarely upon Canada's shoulders made more diplomatic sense than blaming each other and ruining years of carefully cultivated friendship. Canadians, such as Laurier and Clifford Sifton, were aware of this, and sought to have Canada's voice heard in Anglo-American councils. Canada's ability to throw up obstacles in the Alaska and canal negotiations may have given Laurier and Sifton a false impression of their power to shape Anglo-American relations and of Canada's destiny on the continent. On the eve of the Alaska boundary tribunal, Henry Cabot Lodge stated that "Canada is in that worst of all possible positions of possessing power unaccompanied by any responsibility."[104] Indeed, the very reverse seemed true; Canada possessed growing responsibility unaccompanied by power. The Alaska boundary tribunal would certainly underscore the limits of Canadian power.

5 The Defeat (and Triumph) of North American Anglo-Saxonism: The Alaska Boundary Tribunal

> I shall perhaps turn up to see your grimaces as you writhe
> in the strong grasp of Colombia and Canada ... I suppose
> you can always buy your way out, but it will in the end come
> cheaper to buy Colombia outright, and rent Canada.
>
> Henry Adams to John Hay, 15 September 1903

> The Yankees have simply got a lust for power, territory
> and expenditure, and they are going to be the biggest bully
> the world has ever seen.
>
> Clifford Sifton to John W. Dafoe, September 1903

INTRODUCTION

Perhaps not since California in the 1840s had a New World territory captivated the imagination of North Americans as Alaska did at the turn of the century. As in California, the discovery of gold in the Yukon in 1897 and the consequent gold rush gave the cold wastelands of Alaska an aura of romance and adventure. "Ho, for the Klondike!" an article in *McClure's* magazine exclaimed in March, 1898, and claimed to inform readers of "The Various Ways In" and "How the Gold is Found and Where It is Got." "It is no place," the author warned, "for weak men, lazy men, or cowards."[1] A few months later the *Bookman* noted the release of three new books on Alaska, including one by A.P. Swineford, the former governor of the Alaska territory.[2] Alaska made the young Jack London a household name, while London made Alaska a household obsession. In 1897 London had left California State University to join the gold rush, and he quickly made a name for himself as a writer of adventure stories set in the Alaska region. In the January 1900 issue of *North American Review* London published his story "An Odyssey of the North," describing the adventures of the Malamute Kid.[3] The same month he published an essay

in the *Review of Reviews* entitled "The Economics of the Klondike."
London noted that the gold rush was over and welcomed the coming
of the "new Klondike," where "the frontiersman will yield to the
laborer, the prospector to the mining engineer, the dog-driver to the
engine-driver."[4] That April, London published his first book, a collection
of short stories called *The Son of the Wolf*, which invited comparisons
to Kipling's work.[5] The writings of London and others provided the
popular backdrop to official negotiations on the boundary question.
Although the rush to the Yukon quickly subsided, the continuing interest in the region sparked by books and journals arguably gave the issue
more attention than it deserved.

The Canadian claim in Alaska resulted from a desire to acquire
Pyramid Harbor on the Lynn Canal (or Lynn Channel, as it was a
natural waterway) as a deep-sea port for the Yukon, and thus break
the monopoly of the American Northwest states on transportation and
supplies to the region. The Canadian bargaining posture rested upon
two positions. First, by questioning the drawing of the boundary,
Canada hoped to cast into doubt ownership of the American towns
Dyea and Skagway at the head of Lynn Canal. The Canadians believed
that conceding ownership of the towns to the United States would lead
to a compromise on Pyramid Harbor. Second, the Canadian contention
rested upon the British ability to assert power in the western hemisphere. Especially after the Spanish-American War, the annexation of
the Philippines, and the subsequent American desire to unilaterally
build and own a Central American canal, Canadians assumed that the
British could win Alaska concessions in return for abrogation of the
Clayton-Bulwer treaty. On both counts, such reasoning was seriously
flawed. While debating the Yukon railway bill in March, 1898, Laurier
himself had conceded ownership of the towns to the United States.
Laurier noted that "from time immemorial" the Russians, and then
the Americans, had claimed Dyea, and that no protest had ever been
lodged over this occupation. "[I]t becomes manifest to everybody,"
Laurier concluded, that "we cannot dispute their possession."[6] While
holding out the possibility of their annexation to the Yukon might
have made for good press and politics in Canada, for the Americans
it simply constituted an empty and dangerous threat.

The Canadian failure to understand the hemisphere's shift in the
balance of power represented a more profound miscalculation. The
uproar in Canadian public opinion following the Alaska decision illustrated the widespread belief that the United States and Great Britain
possessed equal interests in the hemisphere, and that British power
remained undiminished. In reality, since the Washington Treaty of
1871, Great Britain had been gradually withdrawing from the western

hemisphere in order to shore up British interests elsewhere. This shift of power in favour of the Americans was underscored by the profound events of the turn of the century: the Venezuela crisis; the Spanish-American war; the annexation of Hawaii, Guam, Puerto Rico, and the Philippines; the abrogation of the Clayton-Bulwer treaty; and the signing of the second Hay-Pauncefote treaty allowing the United States to fortify the canal. Moreover, by the time of the Alaska tribunal's meeting in the autumn of 1903, recent events had only accentuated this shift. England and Germany sought the State Department's permission before blockading Venezuela in late 1902, and accepted an American offer to arbitrate the dispute in early 1903.[7] By the time of the Alaska decision in October, the United States was already preparing to support a Panamanian revolt against Colombia in order to proceed with the canal. Theodore Roosevelt's succession to the presidency in September, 1901, did not help the Canadian cause. A devout adherent to the Monroe Doctrine and a proponent of a "vigorous" American foreign policy, Roosevelt had long held the opinion that Canada had no case in Alaska. Moreover, he was willing to back this belief with American troops. While Roosevelt's manipulation of the tribunal represented a lack of good faith, it only reflected America's incontrovertible power in the western hemisphere.

Laurier was not completely unaware of the shift in power in North America, nor of the decreased importance of Yukon trade after 1898. Moreover, Laurier might conceivably have ended the dispute in 1899, taking the American offer of a leased port and claiming victory. Why, then, would his government place so much emphasis on the Alaska boundary? Why would Laurier talk of war, send Davies on a mission to London, have Mills publish articles in the British press, and reject Anglo-American offers to settle the dispute? By the end of the nineteenth century, few national issues existed to bind together Canadian public opinion. Within the Liberal party itself, Laurier needed to balance regional interests to maintain party cohesion. The Alaska boundary dispute represented not only one of the few national issues of the day, but one on which most Canadians could agree. Moreover, in the Liberal government, the Alaska question was largely the purview of the strong Canadian nationalist and anti-American Clifford Sifton, the Minister of the Interior. Sifton had been instrumental in bringing the Joint High Commission to a deadlock in February 1899, and from 1899 to 1903 continued to advocate the most extreme position.[8] Reacting to such national sentiment, the Laurier government placed Alaska at the top of its agenda, pressuring Great Britain and gambling much on intense rhetoric. In the short term this strategy was successful. The Conservatives had long made anti-Americanism a highly successful political position, accusing the Liberals of unpatriotically courting the republic's favour. By way of the Alaska issue, Laurier co-opted this position from the Conservatives. In the long term, however, a Canadian defeat on Alaska was inevitable. Laurier realized this by the summer of 1902 and sought to save face by quickly settling the issue. Yet in having pressed Canada's claims on Alaska over several years, Laurier helped carve out a new place for Canada within Anglo-American relations. The Anglo-American rapprochement, and the accompanying Anglo-Saxon rhetoric, created an ideological framework within which Canada could find a relatively secure position.

Roosevelt and the Americans had essentially the same political concerns as their Canadian counterparts. Needing to prove himself before the 1904 presidential election, Roosevelt coupled bluster with a level of dishonesty in his dealings with the British and the Canadians. He reluctantly agreed to the convening of a tribunal with "impartial jurists," only to name men with clear political ties to his administration. Moreover, like the Canadians, Roosevelt attempted to pressure the British, who held the deciding vote on the tribunal. While Laurier effectively pressed Canada's claims via the Colonial Secretary, Joseph Chamberlain, Roosevelt threatened military action and disruption of the rapprochement. In general terms, then, both Canada and the United States acted in parallel, with their leaders pressured by domestic concerns and, in turn, seeking to pressure the British. In the end, however, Laurier could not bring to bear on the British the same sort of coercion that Roosevelt could. Because of the rapprochement, Canada had gained increasing autonomy in the conduct of its external affairs. Yet, to paraphrase Henry Cabot Lodge, the Dominion did not have power to match the responsibility.

Canadian historians have analyzed the Alaska boundary dispute within a very narrow framework, concentrating primarily on the Canadian claim, Roosevelt's blustering, the partiality of the American delegates, and the failure of Alverstone to act in a judicial manner.[9] The main contention seems to be that, although the Americans had a stronger case, the Canadian claim never had a fair chance amid American pressure and British acquiescence – in short, that the 1903 commission was never "judicial."[10] Historians have failed to place the tribunal within the larger context of Canadian-American domestic politics and American hegemony in the western hemisphere. By 1903 the United States was far and away the ascendant power in the hemisphere, a fact apparently lost on Canadians of the day, and the Americans were never at any point going to risk losing an inch of Alaska territory, let alone two entire towns. Even before the American delegates were named, the tribunal was never "judicial," despite the wording of the Hay-Herbert treaty.[11] Roosevelt had repeatedly shown that he would not accept any body that might rule against the United States – hence his early demand for an even number of jurists, with at least one British representative.

The tribunal, then, was always a diplomatic construct and not a board of arbitration, with possibly significant political ramifications for both the Canadians and Americans. Even the Canadian delegates could not be said to have been "impartial." Laurier had long made the official Canadian position clear, and most informed Canadians had long made up their minds on the issue. On October 8, 1903, Aylesworth gave an interview to the Canadian Associated Press in which he stated, "I have told Lord Alverstone that we Canadians on the Tribunal would never sign any document giving away a single inch of territory which we considered to be British."[12] With both the Canadians and Americans unbudging in their positions, Alverstone rightly viewed his role as an umpire between the two sides. His personal diplomacy with the Americans, though insensitive to the feelings of the Canadian delegates, resulted in breaking the inevitable deadlock. No matter how the tribunal was constituted, Canada would have lost the award, but Alverstone's siding with the Americans allowed Laurier to deflect criticism away from his government and onto the British. His claim for Canada to have treaty-making power, and thus independent diplomatic relations with the United States, resulted not solely from Canada's disappointment over Alaska. In more general terms, Laurier sought a special, more independent place for Canada in the relations between the United States and Great Britain, a claim previously made by such Liberal Anglo-Saxonists as John Charlton and Sir Richard Cartwright.

Like the Reciprocity debate, the Alaska boundary controversy had little to do with Anglo-Saxon notions of North American kinship or common mission. Alaska was about power and politics. For the most part, Canadians and Americans did not utilize the Anglo-Saxon rhetoric that surrounded the Venezuela crisis, the Spanish-American War, the annexation of the Philippines, and the South African War. The Alaska dispute ended the relatively short-lived period that witnessed the predominance of Anglo-Saxonism as a means of accommodating North American opinion to the new realities of the Anglo-American rapprochement. Alaska, then, marked the general obsolescence of such rhetoric, as Canadians began a new nationalist chapter of their history, defining Canada as increasingly independent of Britain and the United States. At the same time, however, Alaska marked the general completion of the rapprochement, removing the last great obstacle to the Anglo-American friendship that would define the new century. By 1903 Canadians and Americans had generally accepted this rapprochement, and Americans generally accepted Canada's independent existence on the continent. No further accommodation seemed necessary. Anglo-Canadian-American relations emerged from 1903 on a new level, one that gave Canada a central place in preserving the goodwill between the two Atlantic powers. The Alaska boundary dispute, then, marked both the defeat and ultimate triumph of North American Anglo-Saxonism.

THE ALASKA DISPUTE:
A BRIEF OVERVIEW

In 1867 the United States purchased the Alaska territory from Russia, inheriting the Anglo-Russian treaty of 1825 that marked the boundary between the British Yukon territory and the Alaska panhandle (or "lisière," French for the word "selvage," the edge of cloth).[13] As in many nineteenth-century treaties that doled out largely unsurveyed tracts of land, and the indigenous occupants, among nations, the wording of the boundary proved unavoidably vague.[14] According to the treaty, the boundary ran "to the North along the channel called Portland Channel," yet failed to take into account the several small islands that lay within the channel. Once the boundary reached the coast at the 56th degree of north latitude, the line, the treaty continued, "shall follow the summit of the mountains situated parallel to the coast." Seeking to define the width of the Russian lisière more precisely, the treaty stated: "That wherever the summit of the mountains which extend in a direction parallel to the Coast ... shall prove to be at the distance of more than ten marine leagues from the Ocean, the limit between the British Possessions and the line of the Coast which is to belong to Russia, as above mentioned, shall be formed by a line parallel to the windings of the Coast, and which shall never exceed the distance of ten marine leagues."[15] In other words, the British did not want the Russian "panhandle" exceeding ten leagues in width. The Russians resented such "ungracious" terms, especially as they related only to "the occupation of a few leagues of land more or less." The dramatic "windings" of the Alaskan coast, often broken by deep inlets like Lynn Canal, complicated any interpretation of exactly what constituted the "Coast." In 1826 the Russian Admiralty published a map of the panhandle, with its interpretation of where the line ran. The Russian boundary ran around the heads of the inlets, including Lynn Canal.

The British did not protest this official Russian interpretation of the boundary, neither after 1826 nor after the 1867 transfer of Alaska to the United States. In the meantime, two towns, Dyea and Skagway, arose at the head of Lynn Canal. Before 1897 these small outposts had limited significance, but with the discovery of gold in the British Yukon territory, the towns, and the Lynn Canal itself, took on potential commercial importance. Three elements of the boundary, then, came into dispute: the southern boundary along the Portland Channel, and the ownership of four islands lying in the channel; the interior boundary along the mountain range; and the northern boundary, which either ran around the head of the Lynn Canal, leaving Dyea and Skagway in American hands, or cut across the channel, giving the towns to Canada. The last of the three elements proved most significant and symbolic: would the United States be allowed to maintain its monopoly on Yukon trade, or would some compromise be reached allowing Canada a Pacific outlet for the Yukon?

ROOSEVELT AND LAURIER

The Canadian position in the Alaska dispute was not aided by the assassination of President McKinley in September 1901. McKinley's successor, Theodore Roosevelt, had long felt that Canada had no claim. While still Vice President, Roosevelt had staked out firm positions in his correspondence. To a British friend in March 1901, Roosevelt wrote, "I have studied that question pretty thoroughly and I do not think the Canadians have a leg to stand on. We might just as well claim part of Newfoundland."[16] The very same day Roosevelt wrote Alfred Thayer Mahan to discuss England's "unwisdom" in refusing to accept American proposals concerning Alaska.[17] In April Roosevelt indicated his happiness with the *modus vivendi*, and his willingness to let it stand indefinitely instead of attempting to negotiate a permanent settlement.[18] Once President, Roosevelt continued to prefer to let the matter drift rather than submit the boundary to arbitration or accept an unpopular treaty. In January 1902, Hay, who remained Secretary of State after McKinley's assassination, wrote to Ambassador Choate, "I am afraid we shall not have any definite program to put forward in regard to Canadian matters at this time. The president seems to think that sufficient to the day is the evil thereof."[19] Yet increased disturbances in the disputed territory led the administration to send more troops to Alaska as well as change Roosevelt's mind as to the need for a permanent settlement.

The breakthrough came in the summer of 1902. Roosevelt had made it clear to American and British officials on both sides of the Atlantic that he had no respect for the Canadian claim and would uphold American rights in Alaska. With Laurier in London for the 1902 Colonial Conference, the Canadian Prime Minister met with the American embassy's First Secretary, Henry White, and Ambassador Choate. To White, Laurier confided what he had long realized: that the towns of Dyea and Skagway would remain American. Laurier wished to settle the matter quickly without great embarrassment to his government. White described the meeting to Hay, noting that Laurier needed to "'save his face' so to speak, vis-a-vis his people; his idea being that if the arbitrators were to decide that our view of the boundary is correct, there would be an end to the whole business, ... and he could say that he had done his best for them. If on the other hand the arbitrators should decide that our view was not the correct interpretation of the treaty, Canada would be entitled to compensation elsewhere, either in land or in *money*, for the Skagway district."[20] Hay informed Roosevelt of the Laurier interview, and Roosevelt responded with his previous opinions of the Canadian position. "In my judgement it is not possible to compromise such a claim," Roosevelt wrote to Hay. "I think the Canadian contention is an outrage pure and simple." Moreover, Roosevelt rejected any ideas of arbitration or compensation. "The fact that they have set up such an outrageous and indefensible claim," Roosevelt continued, "and in consequence are likely to be in hot water with their constituents when they back down, does not seem to me to give us any excuse for paying them in money or territory." The professional diplomat Hay was a little disturbed by Roosevelt's bluster, realizing that diplomacy dictated allowing the opponent to leave the battlefield with some honour. Roosevelt, though, would have none of it: "To pay them anything where they are entitled to nothing would in a case like this come dangerously near blackmail." The President indicated that he would accept the idea of an Anglo-American commission, with three members from each side, to try to fix the line. Yet as early as July 1902, Roosevelt stated that such a commission would not indicate arbitration or even the possibility of surrendering American territory. "I should definitely instruct our three commissioners that they were not to yield any territory whatsoever," Roosevelt concluded.[21] Thus months before the conclusion of the Hay-Herbert Treaty, the President of the United States clearly indicated to the Secretary of State that any appointed commissioners would enter negotiations with a predetermined position. No matter what Hay and the British ambassador, Michael Herbert, agreed upon concerning "impartial jurists," Hay already knew his President's mind.

Ambassador Choate was reluctant to talk to Laurier, but was pressed "very strongly" by Lord Landsdowne to meet with the Prime Minister and Lord Minto, the Canadian Governor-General. Laurier was just as frank with the American ambassador as he had been with White, and conceded a number of points. Laurier told Choate that Canada would not oppose the American way of constituting a "court" to arbitrate the boundary, saying, "that it was so important to get the matter settled that other things being satisfactory they would not stand out on that." Laurier also conceded that Dyea and Skagway would remain American towns. "If the Court found Skagway and Dyea to be British," Choate recounted to Hay, "they should remain American. They didn't want them and wouldn't take them. They were American towns, full of American people, and would be troublesome to govern." As he had with White, Laurier left Choate with "the impression that the Canadians are more anxious than heretofore to settle, and will yield more in the arrangement of the terms of arbitration than they have been willing to contemplate before."[22] During those few days in July, then, Laurier reversed the previous position of his government. Apparently Laurier made this decision almost alone. Before leaving for London, Sifton and other cabinet members told Laurier to hold to the previous Canadian position concerning arbitration by a commission with an odd number of members including a neutral umpire.[23] After Laurier's return, they pressured him to demand better terms, but to no avail. Having gambled on the Alaska dispute for a number of years, Laurier evidently felt that a quick settlement was better than no settlement at all.

The Hay-Herbert Treaty was signed in January 1903. It provided for a tribunal of six "impartial jurists of repute" – three from each side. The *New York Times* hailed the agreement as "another witness and a new pledge of the friendship of the two great English-speaking nations."[24] Yet the *Times* also recognized that Canadian politics continued to provide an obstacle to any settlement. "The question becomes almost grave by reason of the complication growing out of the Canadian interest," a February editorial stated. "We might hope to come to an amicable agreement with Great Britain, but the question has become one of Dominion politics to such an extent that no government there would venture to make concessions which in all probability we might readily secure from the British Government."[25] Indeed, the Alaska question continued to feature prominently in the minds of Canadians. In November 1902, Norman Patterson wrote a scathing characterization of the United States throughout the Alaska boundary dispute. The American government, Patterson stated, had continually refused to accept "any of those mutually acceptable methods of terminating disputes that suggest themselves to civilized countries in times of profound peace." Patterson depicted the republic as the pirate of North America. "It is the unwavering policy of the United States to claim, and if possible secure, by hook or by crook, every additional inch of territory in North America which may be obtained either by chance, by the indulgent weakness of the rightful owners, or, where feasible, by a little gentle buccaneering." Patterson held little hope for British diplomacy gaining a victory, however. "Always in the past confronted by Englishmen who were poorly equipped in knowledge of American questions as compared with the native American," Patterson wrote, "the victories secured by Washington diplomats were comparatively easy." As previous writers had sought to define Canadians as American Britons or North American Anglo-Saxons, now Patterson wrote of "native Americans" occupying the continent. He warned the British not to "trifle" with Canadian imperial sentiment. Despite America's long-time ownership of Dyea and Skagway, Patterson concluded, "occupation is no reason why the undoubted rights of Canada to her own territory should be abandoned."[26] Articles such as Patterson's did not help the Canadian cause. They made the Canadian claim appear more sound than it really was, and built up unreasonable expectations in the Canadian public mind. They certainly did not give Laurier much manoeuvring room by which he might "save face."

With the means for establishing a tribunal in place, Roosevelt set about appointing men he could be sure would reflect his view of the situation. Roosevelt claimed that only after the Supreme Court Justices declined his invitation to sit on the commission did he seek other delegates. While in Washington pressing for reciprocity, John Charlton visited the British embassy and found Sir Michael Herbert "greatly troubled" over the Justices having declined to serve on the tribunal and over the selection of American politicians instead. Charlton also echoed the British view concerning the futility of Canada's protesting. "It is a ticklish matter, however," Charlton wrote to Laurier, "to go beyond a certain limit in protesting against the president's choice, if Supreme Court Justices have declined to act."[27] Later, Charlton gathered more information, especially after a conversation with John Foster, a former secretary of state and member of the Joint High Commission. To Laurier, Charlton attempted to put a positive spin on the appointment to the tribunal of American Senators Lodge and Turner:

The appointment of Lodge and Turner, is probably due to influences that do not come to the surface. The ratification of the Treaty was for a time considered hopeless. Lodge engineered it through, and did it in a very skilful [sic] manner, practically taking the opponents by surprise, and getting snap judgment. Turner co-operated with him. Whether the appointment of Lodge as one of the Commissioners was a contingency following the ratification of the Treaty is not susceptible of demonstration, but may fairly be considered probable. General Foster told me that Lodge distinctly and emphatically repudiated having formed an opinion upon the merits of the case that would be impervious to argument and evidence, and he set light account upon two or three political speeches made in Massachusetts for purely political purposes, which he held had no interference at all with proper action in a judicial capacity.[28]

Charlton's account seemed plausible. After all, Roosevelt needed a two-thirds majority in the Senate to ratify the treaty. Moreover, the President had long indicated that he was taking no chances with the tribunal, and his appointment of American politicians made for a firm and united American position. Lodge himself would later state that the administration had made known the names of the delegates Roosevelt wanted to appoint in order to satisfy the Senate that such men would protect American interests.[29] Although most Canadians would not have agreed with Charlton on the need to pass a flawed treaty, Charlton was probably correct. Facing Henry Cabot Lodge across the negotiating table may have seemed a high price for Canada to pay, but, in the long run, a final settlement of the dispute may have been worth it.

Another account of the treaty's ratification came from Edward Farrer, Toronto *Globe* journalist and another Laurier agent in Washington. Unlike Charlton, Farrer placed the Senate's view of the Hay-Herbert Treaty within the larger context of Anglo-American affairs and the recent uproar over Venezuela. In December 1902, just as Hay and Herbert were concluding their convention, Britain and Germany (later joined by Italy) blockaded Venezuela in order to extract debt payments from the corrupt regime of Cipriano Castro. The Anglo-German force seized Venezuelan gunboats and bombarded forts. While the British Office had received tacit approval for the actions from Secretary Hay, a storm of protest erupted from both the British and American public. From Washington Farrer wrote, "If the Alaska treaty should come to grief in the United States Senate, it will be because of the growing anti-English feeling – a feeling arising out of the Venezuela affair." To his letter Farrer attached a clipping by the New York *Herald*'s Washington correspondent, whom Farrer described as "exceedingly close to the President and … careful to express the President's views, and none other, on all matters of international moment." The article stated: "Among officials here much of the gain which England has made in American friendship during the last four years has been dissipated by her course of action in the present crisis. This belief prevails in the highest administration circles." The article went on to say that the administration believed that the British Ministry "is entering on a pro-German policy."[30]

The British Ministry, however, had not counted on such a backlash from both the British and American public, and it reversed course almost immediately. Not only did the British accept an American proposal to arbitrate the Venezuela debts at the Hague, but Foreign Minister Landsdowne placed pressure on Germany to accept the proposal as well. British actions, and kind words about the Monroe Doctrine, quickly defused the situation.[31] Writing two weeks later, Farrer noted the change in attitude. He also illustrated his valuable contacts in Washington, informing Laurier of Elihu Root's membership on the tribunal three days before Chamberlain cabled that fact to Ottawa. "It seems to be pretty well settled that Mr. Root, Secretary of War and an able lawyer, will be the head of the American three on the Alaska boundary," Farrer wrote. "The action of the Senate in passing the Treaty was due in the main to the sudden clearing of the atmosphere surrounding the Venezuela question, and to the eagerness displayed by Great Britain in forcing Germany's hand at the critical moment."[32] Farrer's account seemed as plausible as Charlton's.

What, then, caused Roosevelt to appoint the three politicians: United States Senate politics, British actions in the western hemisphere, or Roosevelt's firm stand on Alaska? Probably it was a combination of all three, and Laurier's Washington agents had given the Prime Minister valuable tools for assessing the Canadian position within a larger context. Laurier, then, perhaps better than any other Canadian, and even better than later historians, knew the stark reality facing the Canadian claim in Alaska.

In the end, Roosevelt appointed Lodge, Turner, and Secretary of War Elihu Root. Certainly these were not "impartial jurists" – Lodge had previously stated his strong opinions on the issue, which, not surprisingly, reflected Roosevelt's; Turner represented the interests of the Pacific states, which had been at least partially responsible for the impasse of the Joint High Commission in 1899; and Elihu Root, though a lawyer of national repute, was clearly a mouthpiece for Roosevelt himself. The British were disappointed with the President's actions, and feared that Canada would refuse to take part in the proceedings. British Ambassador Herbert wrote to Lord Minto that "it will be inadvisable and useless to protest."[33] Yet Laurier personally protested to Hay, and Lord Minto protested to the British Foreign Office. It was too late, however, as the British had already accepted the convention. In the end the Canadians decided to follow the spirit of the convention and appointed two prominent jurists, Sir Louis Jetté, Lieutenant Governor and formerly a Quebec judge, and Justice John Douglas Armour of the Supreme Court of Canada. After Armour's death that summer he was replaced by A.B. Aylesworth. The sole British representative was the Chief Justice of England, Lord Alverstone.

The composition of the tribunal under the Hay-Herbert Treaty, giving Great Britain the deciding vote, along with the appointment of Lodge, Turner, and Root, sparked understandable concern in Canada. The Ottawa *Journal* called Lodge "a fiery jingo," while the Toronto *Mail and Empire* observed that the three Americans were neither "jurists of repute" nor "impartial." It would have been impossible, the paper continued, for President Roosevelt to have selected commissioners "more disqualified by avowed prejudice, or by official commitment, for passing judgment on the question before them." In an interview in the Toronto *Star*, Sir Charles Tupper stated that the United States had violated the terms of the treaty, thus releasing Canada from any obligation to proceed with the tribunal.[34] In the House of Commons, the Alaska dispute occupied much of the debate on the Speech from the Throne in March. The new Conservative leader Robert Borden attacked the Liberal government for continually placing Canada in a disadvantaged position regarding Alaska. Borden criticized the government's agreeing to the abrogation of the Clayton-Bulwer treaty and the composition of the tribunal. The Tory leader also questioned why the Canadian government had not undertaken to make the Canadian case clear to the American public mind. On the defensive, Laurier called the Hay-Herbert Treaty "a great victory," as it placed before the tribunal all aspects of the question, something the United States had previously refused. John Charlton, in one of his last appearances in the House, injected some Anglo-Saxon rhetoric into the proceedings, stating, "it is a matter of primary importance to maintain good relations with that great branch of the Anglo-Saxon family to the south of us." Charlton's defence of the Hay-Herbert treaty was punctuated by a number of disbelieving Tory interjections. Finally, Henri Bourassa gave voice to a growing Canadian sentiment concerning British handling of Canadian matters. "[S]o far as our relations with the United States are concerned," Bourassa told the House, "it is perfectly useless for us to expect any strong support from the British government ... [T]he one great object of British policy for many years to come is to secure at any cost the friendship of the United States."[35] Such expressions served Laurier's interests very well, as they deflected criticism away from the Liberal government.

"Laurier kicks hard against Cabot," Henry Adams wrote to a correspondent about his friend Henry Cabot Lodge. "He kicks also at Root and Turner, but I feel that Cabot is the real pill. Whenever Canada raises a bristle, Theodore roars like a Texas steer," Adams continued, referring to the President, "and ramps round the ring, screaming for instant war, and ordering a million men instantly to arms."[36] Adams exaggerated only a little. Roosevelt was not taking any chances with the Alaska boundary. He had agreed to a tribunal only after the situation in Alaska became intolerably dangerous, and because failure to settle the issue might factor into the 1904 election. He had insisted upon a tribunal of six, with at least one British representative. He had appointed men whose minds he already knew. Still, he set about making it as plain as possible to both the American delegates and the British that he would not concede an inch of American territory. On March 17, days after making their appointments public, Roosevelt wrote a letter to the three American delegates. To Lodge, Turner, and Root he called the Canadian claims "untenable" and affirmed, "there will of course be no compromise."[37] In June he wrote Hay essentially instructing Ambassador Choate to inform the British of his strong feelings. "I hope Choate will gently convey to them," Roosevelt wrote, "that I shall probably, if they fail to come to an agreement, bring the matter to the attention of Congress and ask for an appropriation so that we may run the line ourselves." Roosevelt demurred, "I do not want to make this as a threat," but of course that was exactly what it was.[38]

Roosevelt and most of the key Americans sincerely believed that the Canadians had no claim, and that their public outburst against the American appointments was mere political manoeuvring. In March Lodge wrote to Henry White: "The Canadian outburst seems to have blown over. It was largely political, and also arose from the fact that they know in their hearts that they have no case. I wish that the English Commissioners could be appointed so as to settle the organization of the tribunal, and I sincerely hope they will put on two Englishmen and one Canadian. It will be a real misfortune if they give a majority to the Canadians."[39] Clearly Lodge was not "impartial," as he told White the Canadians "have no case." A month later Hay wrote to White along similar lines. Although he called Lodge's appointment "regrettable," he too claimed that every thinking American, Briton, and Canadian regarded the Canadian claim as untenable.

To say that our members of the tribunal have an opinion on the subject is simply to say they are American citizens. There is not a man in the United States out of an idiot asylum who has not an opinion on the subject. I believe in my heart of hearts that there is not an intelligent Englishman who does not know they have no case. Sir Wilfrid Laurier sent me a private messenger the other day to protest against the appointment of Lodge and Turner, and in the course of the conversation the emissary said to me: "Sir Wilfrid knows, and all of us know, that we have no case."[40]

It is unclear who this "emissary" was, when he visited Hay, or why he would admit to the American Secretary of State, in the same breath that he protested the appointment of the American delegates, that Laurier and most of Canada knew they "had no case." Assuming he was not a figment of Hay's imagination, Hay's account gives further indication of Laurier's understanding of Canada's poor position. Moreover, the writings of Hay, Lodge, Roosevelt, and other Americans underscored the Americans' absolute certainty of their case. This American certainty, in the face of apparent Anglo-Canadian wavering, confirmed the Americans in their course and made the outcome even more inevitable.

THE TRIBUNAL

Preliminary to the tribunal's meeting in September 1903, Roosevelt continued his campaign to pressure the British. While the Supreme Court Justices may have turned down the invitation to sit on the tribunal, at least one of the Justices served Roosevelt's aims in another manner. On July 25, 1903, Roosevelt wrote to Oliver Wendell Holmes a letter he intended the Justice to show Secretary of the Colonies, Joseph Chamberlain. The President warned that in the event of an award unfavourable to the United States he would "request Congress to make an appropriation which will enable me to run the boundary on my own hook." He repeated his view that the "claim of the Canadians for access to deep water along any part of the Canadian coast is just as indefensible as if they should now suddenly claim the island of Nantucket." Roosevelt concluded his letter by saying that in case of a disagreement, "I wish it distinctly understood, not only that there will be no arbitration of the matter, but that in my message to Congress I shall take a position which will prevent any possibility of arbitration hereafter," and the United States would settle the matter "without any further regard to the attitude of England and Canada."[41] In other words, Roosevelt impressed upon the delegates and the British the idea that the upcoming tribunal represented the last chance for the boundary's peaceable settlement. A deadlock would not lead to arbitration or another tribunal. Immediately after the Alaska decision in October, Roosevelt wrote back to Holmes saying that "your showing the letter to Chamberlain and others was not without its indirect effect on the decision."[42] To John Hay he wrote that if the tribunal did not produce an agreement, "nothing will be left the United States but to act in a way which will necessarily wound British pride."[43] To Elihu Root, one of the American commissioners, the President wrote that "if on the main issue the British hold out and refuse to agree with us I shall at once establish posts on the islands and sufficiently far up the main streams to reduce all the essential points of our claim to actual occupancy." If Lord Alverstone failed to side with the Americans, Roosevelt essentially said, the United States would forcibly occupy all of the disputed territory, including the Portland Channel islands.

Despite Roosevelt's undiplomatic bluster and sabre-rattling, he did allow the commissioners some room to manoeuvre. On a number of occasions he expressed the view that a compromise might be reached over the Portland Channel islands. In his July 25 letter to Justice Holmes, and thus the British Ministry, Roosevelt wrote, "There is room for argument about the islands in the mouth of the Portland Channel."[44] Despite the later uproar in Canada about the islands' great strategic value, a point echoed by some Canadian historians, Roosevelt clearly viewed them as unimportant. As a naval historian and former Assistant Secretary of the Navy, his view of the islands appeared doubly important. In June he wrote to Lodge repeating his threats about American action in the face of a deadlock. Yet he also believed there was "room for doubt" concerning "those little islands down at the mouth of the channel." "They are of negligible value," Roosevelt wrote the Senator, "and I don't think there is the least importance to be attached to their possession."[45] Here Roosevelt left some room for Canada and Great Britain to save face. Apparently the President would have accepted a decision that allowed the United States to retain Dyea and Skagway while giving the Portland islands to Canada.

As Clifford Sifton's biographer D.J. Hall has noted, the Canadians and British were shockingly unprepared for the tribunal. When the Americans presented their case on May 11, the Canadians needed to ask for the right to photograph and examine nearly forty percent of the American documentation.[46] With the importance given to the Alaska issue over the previous half-decade, this oversight is difficult to understand. As a result, the British asked for a delay of the Commission, in order that Lord Alverstone "might go shooting," as Henry White explained to Lodge.[47] Lodge protested to the President that a delay of the Commission, which was to sit in early September under the terms of the Hay-Herbert Treaty, would cause Root and the Senator to miss the start of the next Congressional session. Although Roosevelt might have appointed new men to serve on the Commission in their stead, Lodge felt it "important" that "Root and I should act on that Commission on your account and on account of everything." In other words, it seemed important for Lodge and Root to remain commissioners in order to represent the President's views. Lodge recommended threatening to postpone the Commission until the following summer.[48] Yet if the British wanted no delay, Roosevelt desired it even less. By the summer of 1904 Roosevelt would be running for re-election, after becoming president only after McKinley's assassination. His "vigorous" foreign policy of 1903 may be viewed as reflecting Roosevelt's desire to be elected president on his own merits in 1904. On June 23 Roosevelt wrote to both Lodge and John Hay that he would not tolerate a "serious" delay that would mean having "the thing pending during a presidential campaign."[49] Before Lodge's departure for London, Roosevelt wrote the senator that the present Commission represented the last chance for a final settlement agreeable to both parties. "When Congress assembles I must be able to report the success or failure of the negotiations so that action can be taken accordingly," Roosevelt wrote. "I feel that I have gone very far in my endeavor to come to a friendly understanding with England; and this is the last chance for an agreement under which the two parties can act together."[50]

Upon his arrival in London, Lodge set about impressing Roosevelt's views on Henry White and Joseph Choate at the American embassy, and meeting with top British politicians. A few days after his arrival he dined with Lord Alverstone, the head of the Anglo-Canadian delegates, and the two men took an instant liking to one another.[51] Lodge found the Chief Justice "entirely obliging and not only willing but anxious to forward matters as much as possible."[52] During meetings with Chamberlain and Prime Minister Balfour, both men promised to put pressure on the Dominion leaders. His meetings with the British left Lodge with the impression that the British favoured a quick and friendly settlement. Any potential problems or delay would come from the Canadians, Lodge believed, and from British inability to stand up to the Dominion. "There is no trouble at all with the English part of it," Lodge wrote to Roosevelt. "The whole difficulty comes from the Canadians, and they are as timid about the Canadians as can possibly be; they are so afraid of injuring their sensibilities that they hardly dare say anything." Lodge viewed the British case as "extremely weak" compared to the American case, yet he still doubted that the commission could reach a settlement, questioning British "courage to decide against the Canadians." The ability of the Canadians to block Anglo-American agreements had long infuriated Hay and Choate. Now Lodge, in London taking the pulse of the British first-hand, reached the same conclusion about Canadian obstructionism. "[T]he Canadians are so perfectly stupid about it that they seem to fail utterly to see that a disagreement deprives them of their only chance to get out of the matter creditably," Lodge wrote, "and leaves the land in our possession where it will remain."[53] The Alaska Tribunal represented the first time the Massachusetts senator dealt with Anglo-Canadian affairs on an intimate level. The infamous anglophobe blamed not the British, but the Canadians, clearly differentiating between the motives of the men in London and those of the ones in Ottawa.

Before the tribunal met in September, Lodge travelled to Europe, and reported to Roosevelt that "German papers say that England is extending fortifications and naval provisions at Esquimalt and is adding 92 big guns to those already there." Apparently Lodge took this information at face value, although it completely contradicted Britain's acquiescent attitude in the hemisphere of the previous quarter century. "I wonder why," Lodge mused, "for the one thing I feel reasonably certain of is that England will not go to war with us and that slavish as she is to Canada she will draw the line there."[54] Of course, Lodge was perfectly correct in this assessment, one which most residents of the North Atlantic Triangle had accepted long ago. The Alaska affair apparently impressed upon Lodge for the first time the problems and intricacies of the Washington-Ottawa-London relationship. To Roosevelt, Lodge again wrote of his pessimism about any possible settlement based on Canadian intransigence and British timidity. Lodge hoped that Alverstone would side with the American delegates, but, he said, "England is in such mortal terror of Canada that I feel more than doubtful in regard to it." Lodge noted the need for an agreement so that Canada and Britain could avoid Roosevelt's more dire prescription for Alaska. "I hope they will act in the sensible way," Lodge wrote, "but I very much fear the reverse. The fact is that Canada is in that worst of all possible positions of possessing power unaccompanied by any responsibility. It seems she could force England to do anything short of going to war with us, and at that point England will draw the line. As she will draw the line at that point the Canadian insistence on a disagreement is excessively stupid."[55] Reflecting Roosevelt's view, the senator essentially claimed that only war could dislodge the United States from any territory in the Alaska panhandle. While Lodge realized the British knew this, he did not yet understand that key Canadians, such as Laurier, also accepted this fact. While White, Hay, and Choate had had the advantage of meeting Laurier concerning Alaska, very possibly Lodge's view of Canadian intransigence was formed by his contact with Clifford Sifton, Canadian agent in London for the tribunal.

Lodge also knew of Canadian opinion from press clippings given to him by John Foster, the American agent for the tribunal. In one article the Toronto correspondent for the London *Times* wrote that "if the decision goes against Canada it will be put down, rightly or wrongly, to Great Britain's lack of desire to protect her North American colony."[56] For Lodge, the clippings displayed "the concerted effort made through the press to bring political pressure to bear on Lord Alverstone" to support the Canadian claim.[57] Lodge feared that such pressure would sway the British Ministry as well as Lord Alverstone. To the President Lodge wrote, "The Canadians have been filling the newspapers with articles of the most violent kind, threatening England with all sorts of things if the decision should go against Canada. They are all aimed, I suppose, at Lord Alverstone. Under ordinary circumstances I should think they had overplayed their hand badly, and this public menace would simply have the effect of driving Lord Alverstone and the English Cabinet the other way, but England is so afraid of Canada that I fear the effect."[58] Lodge's continuing pessimism over reaching agreement on Alaska must have deeply impressed his friend the President. Moreover, another crisis affecting American hegemony in the hemisphere intruded upon Roosevelt's thinking and his attitude toward Alaska. On August 12 the Colombian senate had voted unanimously against ratification of the Hay-Herrán Treaty, by which the United States would have acquired the Panama Canal zone for a payment of $10 million. Roosevelt faced twin defeats on the foreign policy front on the very eve of an election year. From Paris, Henry Adams wrote to John Hay his typically laconic view of the situation. "I shall perhaps turn up to see your grimaces as you writhe in the strong grasp of Colombia and Canada," Adams wrote. "As everything is, at bottom, a matter of money, I suppose you can always buy your way out, but it will in the end come cheaper to buy Colombia outright, and rent Canada."[59] In a sense, Adams read the situation accurately as both Canada and Colombia desired to extract financial compensation for their territorial rights. Yet Adams had no idea of the President's anger regarding Canadian and Colombian "blackmail," a word he applied to both the Alaska and Panama disputes. As events would show, Roosevelt had no intention of either buying Colombia or "renting" Canada.

In September and early October, Roosevelt, aided by Lodge, continued his letter-writing campaign to press upon the Americans in London the dire consequences for England if the tribunal failed to reach a settlement. The letters illustrated the grim effect Canadian public pressure had on the Americans. On October 3 the President wrote to Root that the British must be made to understand "that this is the last chance," and that no matter how unpleasant using force might be for the United States, "if they force me to do what I must in case they fail to take advantage of this chance, it will be a thousandfold more unpleasant for them."[60] To Henry White, Roosevelt wrote a similar letter. "The Canadians have had some very ugly articles published, which I was afraid might influence English opinion," Roosevelt observed, possibly referring to Lodge's September 13 letter. "This would be unfortunate. It would be a bad thing for us if there was a deadlock in the present Commission," Roosevelt repeated, "but it would be a very much worse thing for the Canadians and English."[61] In early October Lodge wrote to White, "The course of the American Government in case of disagreement is inevitable. No administration can avoid it." Referring to the Canadian campaign, Lodge concluded, "This situation I think should be understood and should counterbalance the very crass influence brought to bear by the Canadians through threats of Canadian displeasure in case of a decision against them."[62] Arguably, Canadians expressed their growing discontent in reaction to previous American manoeuvrings and British acquiescence. Yet in competing to bring pressure to bear on the British, the Canadians could simply not match the Americans.

Caught in this vice of Anglo-American-Canadian pressure was Lord Alverstone. In private conversations with Alverstone, the American delegates pressed the President's firm view of the matter on the Chief Justice and quite possibly showed him Roosevelt's letters. Even before the arguments were finished, Alverstone told Lodge and Root that he accepted the American claim of the boundary going around the Lynn Canal inlets, which Lodge noted was "the main contention." Having agreed with the Americans, however, Alverstone also desired to "let the Canadians down as easily as possible," and narrow the American strip of territory around Dyea and Skagway, while giving Canada the four Portland Channel islands. Lodge indicated that the United States was willing to concede the islands, but not the narrower strip of land. The private discussions between Alverstone and Lodge underscored the fact that the Alaska commission was no judicial tribunal. Indeed, the lawyers' arguments had almost nothing to do with the settlement. In late September, after speaking with Alverstone privately, Lodge indicated to Roosevelt that "we shall reach a decision very soon, probably even before the arguments are completed."[63] Lodge's biographer, John Garraty, argued that Lodge's role in the proceedings was "mainly a personal one," as he developed close relations with the British principals, namely Alverstone and Prime Minister Balfour.[64] On October 15, feeling the pressure from the British Government, Alverstone took Lodge into his room and told him that "matters were reaching a crisis." Lodge replied that, in view of past conversations with the Chief Justice, they could not reach an agreement on the line of the boundary around the Lynn Canal inlets. Alverstone replied that a decision must be reached and that he "would make great sacrifices."[65] By the next day Alverstone and the Americans had privately settled the Alaska boundary dispute. Aylesworth and Jetté had not been included in these private talks, a point which added to their dim view of the proceedings.

THE DECISION

On the evening of 15 October 1903, days before the decision of the tribunal was handed down, the delegates attended a dinner at Claridge's Hotel given by the Pilgrims' Society. Attending the banquet were some of the most prominent public men of the North Atlantic Triangle.

Ambassador Choate, Field Marshal Lord Roberts, and Foreign Minister Lord Landsdowne, among others, joined the members of the Anglo-Canadian-American tribunal. One American paper called the gathering "the most notable assemblage of Englishmen, Americans and Canadians ever brought together in London."[66] Not surprisingly, at least one speaker utilized Anglo-Saxon rhetoric to emphasize the common interests of the English-speaking world. While Lord Roberts toasted the health of King Edward and President Roosevelt, Lord Landsdowne toasted the health of the Anglo-Saxon race, which, he said, had done more than any other nationality to promote just and equal government. "I may prophesy that our contribution toward the happiness and the good government of the world will not be less in the future than it has been in the past," Landsdowne continued. "The two great branches of the Anglo-Saxon race will be found working shoulder to shoulder, giving an example to the world of the mode of settling differences." Apparently Landsdowne's reference to only two branches of the race did not sit well with Aylesworth, who, answering the toast in the name of Canada, asked if the Foreign Minister had not lost sight of the fact that millions of Anglo-Saxons lived in Canada. Aylesworth intimated that Landsdowne had overlooked this fact in his speech, the Canadian judge essentially asserting that Canadians formed their own branch of the race.[67] This was not the last time that a Canadian would question the attention given to Canada by the British Foreign Office.

Aylesworth's pique may have resulted more from the status of the boundary question than from Landsdowne's speech. Roosevelt's bluster had had the desired effect on the British generally and on Lord Alverstone specifically. On October 17 Sifton cabled Laurier that Alverstone had sided with the Americans, giving the United States the head of Lynn Canal as well as two of the four islands in Portland Channel. The United States had compromised on the Portland Channel islands and on the placing of the interior line along the mountains, including leaving a 120-mile strip blank for want of precise surveys. Since both the Americans and Canadians had claimed all four islands, the decision smacked of a diplomatic compromise rather than a judicial decision. In his cable Sifton called the decision "wholly indefensible." As the two American islands commanded the entrance of the Portland Channel, Sifton believed they destroyed the "strategic value" of the two Canadian islands.[68] In his book on Sifton, Dafoe claimed it was a "reasonable theory that both the American and Canadian Commissioners foresaw a time when the two countries would be at war, and sought for advantages for their countries looking forward to this conflict."[69] Yet Sifton and Dafoe overstated the issue. Both the Canadians and the Americans had long been concerned with the commercial, not the strategic, value of the Alaska panhandle. When Lodge wrote the President that Alverstone considered giving all four islands to Canada, Roosevelt showed more concern about an American cannery on one of the islands than he did about any possible strategic value.[70] Moreover, Alverstone, Roosevelt, and many North Americans understood that the successful settling of the boundary dispute made any future Anglo-American conflict very remote.

Despite the later uproar over the Canadian delegates' refusal to sign the decision, initial Canadian reaction proved quite subdued. Of the decision the *Free Press* stated, "The net result is that things are precisely as they were." The paper noted that the two Portland Channel islands had been transferred to Canada, and stated that the islands, despite Sifton's belief, "are not without their military value." The Manitoba paper claimed that the decision had simply confirmed the status quo. "The decision will not cause much surprise in Canada," the paper concluded.[71] The Montreal *Gazette* conceded that however unfair the proceedings were, "there was more ground for the U.S. contentions and generally less expectation of any marked gain being made by this country."[72] The *Mail and Empire* called the decision "governed by reason." Other newspapers underscored the importance of clearing away a source of Anglo-American hostility. The Hamilton *Spectator* believed that any sacrifice of Canadian interests was justified "if the award results in enlisting the sympathy of ... the United States with Great Britain in certain schemes for the preservation of peace throughout the world." The London *Free Press* also stated "that the object gained in way of peace and concord by such a settlement would outweigh the advantage of possession."[73] The *Canadian Magazine* claimed that the most important matter of the tribunal was not the boundary, "but the preservation of the entente between Great Britain and the United States, and that a decision made in that direction also made for righteousness."[74] The Toronto *Globe* called the decision a "compromise" which would be accepted by Canadians with "frankness and dignity." Insisting upon the Canadian claims, the paper continued, would have resulted in no decision at all, a "regrettable and even dangerous" outcome. Finally, the paper claimed that the decision would "leave room for increasing friendliness such as should exist between two nations made up of kindred though alien peoples."[75] The Canadian press initially received news of the decision with calm forbearance, and actually welcomed a settlement that could pave the way for better relations between "kindred" peoples.

Still ignorant of the actual proceedings of the tribunal, the Canadian public largely accepted the results. The real uproar occurred after the Canadian delegates, Aylesworth and Jetté, refused to sign the award.

While most Canadian historians have depicted the two men as acting heroically in the face of American bluster and British treachery, they have generally failed to note Laurier's role in the matter. When Sifton cabled the Commission's "indefensible" decision to Laurier, he asked the Prime Minister, "What is your view?" On October 18, the day the decision was announced to the public, the Prime Minister cabled back, "Our Commissioners ought to protest in most vigorous terms."[76] Though "impartial jurists," Aylesworth and Jetté had been nominated by Laurier and must have taken the Prime Minister's cable as permission to stand against the Alaska decision. The Canadian delegates refused to sign the award, characterizing Alverstone's siding with the Americans as a diplomatic, and not a judicial, decision. They cited the fact that only days before the final decision, the British Chief Justice had declared himself in favour of giving Canada all four of the Portland Channel islands. The drawing of a zigzagging line through the channel, thus giving two islands to each nation, proved to the Canadian delegates and public that Alverstone had sacrificed Canadian rights for Anglo-American amity. The blame directed at Alverstone and the British Foreign Office served Laurier's interests well, deflecting blame away from the Liberal government and onto the British.

In his rather partisan account of the tribunal, Dafoe states, "Very little attempt was made by the opposition party to turn the public indignation against the government."[77] Yet a brief look at the Commons debates from October 23 illustrates that the Conservative opposition, led by Robert Borden, did indeed attack the government's handling of the entire affair all the way back to the 1898 Joint High Commission. Moreover, Borden was joined by prominent former Liberal Israel Tarte. The attack in the Commons, backed by an upswell of public outrage, placed Laurier on the defensive. While October 23 went down in history as the day Laurier called for Canada to have treaty-making power, he in fact asserted this right as just one of many counter-arguments to opponents' criticisms. Dafoe also states that Canadian ire was directed mainly at Great Britain, and not at the United States. Again, the Commons debate included many attacks against the United States by the Conservatives, while Laurier and others, including former Liberal Henri Bourassa, tried to direct the blame toward the British.

Indeed, Bourassa began the debate that day by faulting the British abrogation of the Clayton-Bulwer Treaty without an accompanying compromise on Alaska. Bourassa noted that "at a time when the sons of Canada were shedding their blood for the empire on the soil of Africa, Mr. Chamberlain was coldly sacrificing the interests of Canada."[78] England, Bourassa continued, had forced Canada to accept the Alaska tribunal. Bourassa concluded by claiming the need for independent Canadian representation in Washington. "[W]e should take the position as it is, coldly and firmly," Bourassa said, "that if we want to deal with the American government, we should deal directly through an agent at Washington appointed by the Canadian government."[79] Bourassa, thus, brought up the possibility of Canadian diplomatic independence hours before Laurier.

Before Borden rose to speak, a number of Tories punctuated the debate with anti-American outbursts. Gourley, who had proposed war after the abrogation of the Clayton-Bulwer Treaty, decried the "low Yankees," while R.G. Macpherson of Burrard described Americans as "our hereditary enemies."[80] Borden then rose to question what the Liberal leader had "accomplished for Canada in connection with the Alaskan boundary." Borden questioned Laurier's agreeing to the abrogation of the Clayton-Bulwer Treaty, supporting the Hay-Herbert Treaty, and failing to protest the bias of the American delegates. Far from blaming Great Britain, Borden blamed Laurier for not placing the various matters before Parliament. Borden expressed his regret that "without any consultation whatever with parliament my right hon. friend has seen fit to adopt a course, for which the government are absolutely responsible, and which has resulted so unfortunately for the best interests of Canada."[81] Borden did not even bother condemning the United States, reserving all his vitriol for Laurier.

Laurier defended his actions, claiming the need to settle the dispute once and for all, and stating that the British had ratified the Hay-Herbert Treaty before the Canadian protest could be considered. Laurier claimed the need to ask the British Parliament for more extensive power to protect Canadian rights, as well as stating that the United States had not gained everything it wanted in Alaska. This brought a cry of disbelief from Israel Tarte. "We are losing and ceding thirty-five miles, not of water, but of Canadian territory," Tarte protested. "Our case is lost, the sentence is given." Tarte sided with Borden in criticizing the government for not protecting Canadian rights under the Hay-Herbert treaty. Laurier, Tarte declared, "should have taken a firmer stand," and told the British, "We cannot possibly take part in proceedings of that character."[82] This ability to "stand firm" with the British, many Canadians believed, essentially constituted Canadian treaty-making ability. Tarte could not believe that "the British ambassador at Washington would have dared to sign a treaty dealing with the interests of Canada without even waiting for the answer of the Canadian government." Seymour Gourley agreed. Since Canada agreed to the Hay-Herbert Treaty, he said, Laurier "was just as much responsible for it as Sir Michael Herbert or Mr. Joseph Chamberlain, or any

other member of the British cabinet."[83] Despite the Liberals' attempt
to deflect criticism from themselves onto the British, the Tories made
the Alaska decision a political issue and attacked the Liberals, not the
British, for sacrificing Canadian rights.

Laurier was at least partially successful in deflecting criticism by
claiming Canada's right to make its own treaties. The October 23
Commons debate on the Alaska decision was best remembered for
Laurier's statement that Canada "should ask the British parliament for
more extensive power, so that if ever we have to deal with matters of
a similar nature again we shall deal with them in our own way, in our
own fashion, according to the best light that we have."[84] As a result
Laurier has been depicted as a great nationalist hero, marking an
important step in Canada's march toward nationhood. Surely, though,
Laurier did not mean for Canada to have the power to relate directly
to all nations of the world, but only to the United States. Laurier's claim,
then, must be seen in the light of Anglo-Canadian-American relations
in 1903, and not via some vague notion of inevitable national development. The assertion of Canadian treaty-making power was of itself
less important than the circumstances that allowed Laurier to make
such a claim. With the Alaska decision, the rapprochement was firmly
in place and Canada's position secure. Most Canadians did not react
to Roosevelt's threats and bluster by running into the arms of the
Mother Country, but, quite the reverse, by asserting a new level of
autonomy from Great Britain in order to treat independently with the
United States. If Laurier should be given credit for anything, it should
be for seizing the opportunity created by the rapprochement and pressing Canadian claims to direct the course of Canadian-American relations during the Joint High Commission, and for the negotiations over
the *modus vivendi*, and the Clayton-Bulwer treaty. By 1903 Anglo-
Saxonism had helped to create an ideological framework within which
Canada might play a unique national role in trans-Atlantic relations.

Laurier's comments caught the imagination of the country, still
rocked by the Alaska decision. Once again, Canadian opinion seemed
to split itself along political lines. The Liberal Toronto *Globe* supported Laurier, stating that Canada had been "treated throughout like
mere children," and calling the British ambassador at Washington "a
mere stool-pigeon for the United States."[85] The Conservative Montreal
Gazette blamed Laurier, "who allows his mouth to run away with his
brains," for the sacrifice of Canadian rights, and concluded that "Canada
should change her ministers before she goes shouting for fuller diplomatic powers."[86] The Toronto *Mail and Empire* represented much of
the Conservative press by condemning Laurier's comments as a "Sep-
aratist cry." Papers such as the Windsor (Ontario) *Record*, the St. John

Globe, and the *Eastern Chronicle* of New Glasgow, Nova Scotia, on the other hand, all agreed that Canada must begin moving toward independence.[87]

Moreover, the Liberal government did not let the matter drop from the public eye. On November 19, the Minister of Marine and Fisheries J.R.F. Prefontaine asked his audience at Laval University, an audience which included the Prime Minister, whether the time had come to negotiate with foreign nations "without the presence of an embarrassing third party, a useless presence"? In a December 9 interview with the London (Ontario) *Daily News*, Laurier repeated his desire to see Canada have the treaty-making power, calling the existing system "persistently, fatally, hostile to Canadian interests."[88] Once the initial uproar over the decision had diminished, Laurier let the matter drift. "Nothing was more foreign to Sir Wilfrid's ruling bias than to urge any policy on general and theoretical grounds," O.D. Skelton wrote.[89] Laurier's claim for treaty-making power resulted both from the dictates of domestic politics and from the reality of relations among the North Atlantic Triangle nations.

Initial partisan opinion following the House of Commons debate in October gradually gave way to a more reasoned consideration in Canada of the treaty-making power. Most of the opinion was quite favourable – Canada's obtaining the treaty-making power, many believed, was the natural course of the Dominion's political development, and did not indicate the dismemberment of the empire. The editors of *Canadian Magazine* viewed the treaty-making power as a natural "growth in self-government," which did not necessarily mean "a lessening of the affection for Great Britain." "The man who would propose an agitation for independence at the present moment," the magazine cautioned, "would find himself in a more hopeless minority than at any time during the past century."[90] In February 1904, Goldwin Smith wrote an article for the magazine entitled "Can Canada Make Her Own Treaties?" Smith believed that treaty-making power indicated independence. "To demand the treaty-making power is to demand the power of making peace and war," Smith wrote, "to which only a nation can aspire." Smith then discussed the possible results of such independence, including political union with the United States and a worldwide Anglo-Saxon union.[91] The next month Thomas Hodgins, a judge of the Admiralty Court, argued that the injustice of the Alaska decision underscored Canada's right to make its own treaties, "subject to the veto of the Sovereign."[92] Hodgins's formula seemed one that many Canadians would accept, as it allowed Canada to act independently while still within the imperial framework. In *Queen's Quarterly*,

John Cooper supported Canada's claim for treaty-making power, believing that "the unity of the Empire will be placed in a much safer position by the concession of this right." Still, adopting Hodgins's view, Cooper allowed that Canada would submit any treaty for British approval, "and only when so approved could it be regarded as involving the mother country in any obligations to assist Canada in maintaining its rights under the treaty."[93]

Surprisingly, the United States emerged largely unscathed in the eyes of many Canadians. While both Liberals and Conservatives condemned American dishonesty and the republic's grasping nature, the United States did not occupy a central position in the post-decision debate. When considering greater Canadian autonomy, at least a couple of writers turned toward the continent and the Anglo-Saxon race as the crucibles of Canada's destiny. "We are American in most of our habits, customs and manners," the *Canadian Magazine* boldly stated. "Socially, mentally and financially we are Americans; politically we are British." The journal continued, "Canada is part of the American continent and is swayed by the same natural influences as the United States, is confronted by the same great problems in the struggle against nature." This sounded very much like Goldwin Smith's geographical determinism as well as Turner's "Frontier Thesis." In *Queen's Quarterly* John Cooper looked beyond the growing Imperial Federation scheme of Joseph Chamberlain to a larger Anglo-Saxon federation:

Perhaps the new Imperialist now waiting quietly just beyond the horizon may have in hand a plea for an Anglo-Saxon Empire which shall have for its consolidating force that great, persistent Slav country which is now slowly gathering into its capacious maw large pieces of Asiatic territory. If self-government in the colonies is compatible with the binding together of the British Empire as a unit in commerce and in defence, there would seem to be no unsurmountable difficulty in the way of an Anglo-Saxon empire should the safety and the best interests of the Anglo-Saxon race demand the creation of a newer and greater Imperial power.[94]

Cooper's view deftly wove together the various early-twentieth-century conceptions of Canada's future: self-government, continued allegiance to the Crown, Imperial Federation, and the unity of the Anglo-Saxon race. With such views Cooper echoed the sentiments of his predecessor George Grant. Yet with the Alaska decision, Canadian Anglo-Saxonism largely passed away, becoming only a faint echo of what it had been in the previous century.

CONCLUSION

For their part, the Americans were, of course, pleased with the Alaska decision. The American press criticized the "huffy Canadian commissioners"[95] for their refusal to sign the award and for their criticism of Lord Alverstone. The Chicago *Tribune* believed the Canadian uproar signified Canadian separation from the empire, and its inevitable unification with the United States. Other journals welcomed the settling of a long-standing Anglo-American dispute. The Atlanta *Constitution* called the decision "a great triumph for the Anglo-Saxon idea of arbitration,"[96] while the Boston *Post* believed the main point of the matter was that the two English-speaking nations had settled the dispute between themselves.[97] In the *Review of Reviews*, Albert Shaw observed that any other remaining Anglo-American disputes were "too inconsiderable to be known by the average citizen of either country." He welcomed the fact that not since the American Revolution had the United States "been upon terms of such complete amity with the mother country."[98] Immediately upon hearing of the decision Joseph Choate wrote to John Hay, saying, "I regard the result of the decision as highly satisfactory both in the actual outcome of the decision and as establishing a precedent for the two nations settling their differences without calling in the neighbors."[99] Roosevelt agreed, saying in his annual Message to Congress in December that the settlement "removed from the field of discussion and possible danger a question liable to become more acutely accentuated with each passing year." Moreover, the Alaska decision "furnished a signal proof of the fairness and goodwill with which two friendly nations can approach and determine issues involving national sovereignty."[100] Although Canadians might not have realized it at the time, Roosevelt viewed the significance of the treaty correctly. Not only did it remove one of the last great obstacles to Anglo-American relations and North American harmony, but it paved the way for the future amity of the North Atlantic Triangle.

Canadian historians have largely refused to see the Alaska decision as being of any benefit to Canada, except for the resulting nationalism and claims for greater autonomy. This indicates the persistent failure of these historians to place the tribunal within a larger context of Canadian politics, Anglo-American relations, and the balance of power in the western hemisphere. The result has been a very narrow Canadian interpretation of Alaska diplomacy and of the tribunal itself: that Great Britain sacrificed Canadian interests in the Hay-Pauncefote and Hay-Herbert Treaties, and that the Lord Chief Justice made a mockery of the so-called "judicial" tribunal by siding with the Americans and drawing a zigzagging line down Portland Channel. Wilfrid Laurier has received great praise for standing up for Canada's rights from 1898 to 1903. Few have studied Canada's changing role during the Anglo-American rapprochement. Fewer still have placed Alaska within the larger context of American hegemony in the hemisphere. Never is the Anglo-German blockade of Venezuela mentioned in connection with the Hay-Herbert treaty, although Edward Farrer wrote to Laurier of its significance. Moreover, Roosevelt's apoplexy over the Panama negotiations with Colombia are never noted as touching upon the Alaska decision, although Roosevelt stepped up his pressure on the British after the Colombian Senate's rejection of the Hay-Herrán Treaty in August, 1903. The overall Canadian interpretation appears to be that the Alaska tribunal related only to a few square miles of the Alaska panhandle and a couple of small islands.

The fact is that the Alaska tribunal was never "judicial" at all. In the words of H.C. Allen, Canadian historians have been "purists" in their condemnation of American, and especially Roosevelt's, actions, and of Alverstone's "political" decision:

Purists may denounce this defiling of the legal process, but for the historian it is often hard to see the difference between legal and political decisions in international matters, and impossible to draw a precise line between international law and international policy. For the Lord Chief Justice to have taken the Canadian point of view might well have spelled disaster for Canada, as well as Britain; that he took the American, caused pain and vexation for a time, but reinforced in the end the fundamental Anglo-American concord upon which Canada's life depends.[101]

The Alaska decision essentially completed the Anglo-American rapprochement in the western hemisphere. While some Americans used the Alaska decision, and Canadian protests, as an excuse to revive talk of political union, most accepted the existence of Canada as an autonomous North American nation. Indeed, the Alaska dispute helped Americans distinguish between Canadian motives and actions, and those of Great Britain. With such acceptance, there was no longer any need to utilize Anglo-Saxon rhetoric to accommodate the old American anglophobia and manifest destiny to the rapprochement. In the long run, this proved of greatest value to Canada. "Canada had no alternative," Allen concludes, "but to accept the ironical axiom of her political existence, that though she might pay the highest price for Anglo-American friendship, she was also its greatest beneficiary."[102]

Conclusion: The Obsolescence of North American Anglo-Saxonism, 1903–14

The talk of Anglo-Saxonism begins to lose its relevancy.
Albert Shaw, *Review of Reviews*, 1903

The same years that witnessed the end of the British war in South Africa and the settlement of the Alaska boundary dispute also saw the publication of two books calling for Anglo-Saxon union. In 1902 William T. Stead, the editor of the English journal *Review of Reviews*, published his *The Americanization of the World, or the Trend of the Twentieth Century*. Stead called for "merging the British Empire in the English-speaking United States of the World," and substituting "the broader patriotism of the race" for "the insular patriotism of our nation." Such a union would usher in a new era of power and prosperity for the entire race, and allow Anglo-Saxons to "carry out the providential mission which has been entrusted to the English-speaking Race."[1] The following year John Dos Passos published *The Anglo-Saxon Century and the Unification of the English-Speaking People*, which echoed Stead's call for the union, or reunion, of the race. Dos Passos repeated old ideas about the common race, language, literature, and laws of the English-speaking world. He also called for Canada to voluntarily divide itself into states for admission into the American Union.[2] *Canadian Magazine* gave the book, and the idea of Anglo-Saxon union, a positive review, calling it "one of the sanest works on the relation of the United States to Great Britain and to Canada which has ever been written in the United States or out of it." "The idea is in the air," the journal noted about this sort of Anglo-Saxon Unionism.[3]

Dos Passos and Stead's call for Anglo-Saxon union reflected a fashionable idea of the day. The events of the Anglo-American rapprochement, Anglo-American sympathy during their respective wars, and the apparent menace of Slavic Russia, all tended to underscore Anglo-Saxon affinity and the benefits of closer association. Significantly, *Canadian Magazine*'s glowing review of the Dos Passos volume ("the most important contribution on the subject since Goldwin Smith's 'Canada and the Canadian Question'") appeared the month before the Alaska boundary decision was made. After the decision, few Canadians would have taken such a sanguine view of throwing in their lot with the Americans. Aside from the Alaska decision, many other aspects of North American life, Anglo-Canadian-American relations, and the shifting ideas of the English-speaking world contributed to a sharp decline in Anglo-Saxonism as a dominant turn-of-the-century ideology.

The core ideas of nineteenth-century Anglo-Saxonism came increasingly under attack at the turn of the century. Social Darwinism, which emphasized the effect of heredity, gave way to Progressivism, which emphasized the effect of environment.[4] Movements like the Anti-Saloon League called for government intervention to help reform individuals, while muckraking journalists like Lincoln Steffens called for reform of government itself.[5] In the fields of history and literature, Americans turned away from their supposed Teutonic origins in favour of a more "American" heritage. Frederick Jackson Turner's 1893 "Frontier Thesis" asked Americans to look for the nation's roots and character in the hinterland – which he simultaneously announced no longer existed.[6] Turner's stress on America's pioneer roots, rugged individuality, and personal freedoms was attractive to a nation in the midst of achieving world power status and glamourizing the "vigorous" exploits of Theodore Roosevelt, the Rough Rider President.

North American Anglo-Saxon rhetoric had largely resulted from the Anglo-American rapprochement, as Canadians and Americans sought to adapt their old rivalries to the new international reality. With the settlement of the Alaska boundary dispute in 1903, the rapprochement was essentially in place. The events of 1903 to 1914 only confirmed the two countries' identity of interests. Suspicious of Russian designs in Manchuria, the United States had approved the Anglo-Japanese Alliance of 1902, while Lord Landsdowne assured the State Department that Great Britain was "prepared to follow the United States step by step up to any point that may be necessary for the protection of our common interests in China."[7] When war between Japan and Russia broke out in February 1904 the United States and Great Britain proceeded in concert, warning the European powers that any action on behalf of Russia would lead to their siding with Japan. The decisive victory of Japan removed the spectre of the Far Eastern Russian threat, and the Slavic counter-threat to Anglo-Saxonism.

Anglo-Saxonism had also coloured Canadian and American perceptions of America's assertion of hegemony in the western hemisphere. Worried about encroachments upon the empire elsewhere, and happy to allow the United States to defend the status quo in the Americas, Great Britain had continually recognized American hegemony, often at the expense of Canada. By 1903 the British, and most Canadians, accepted the Monroe Doctrine as generally benign to British interests. From 1903 onward the United States took a very active role in the Caribbean and in Latin America. Almost immediately after the Alaska boundary settlement, the United States helped orchestrate Panama's revolution against Colombia, allowing the United States to negotiate an advantageous Canal Zone treaty with a newly independent Panama. Construction of the canal proceeded immediately, and was completed in 1914. Looking to protect America's "Isthmian viscera,"[8] the United States would no longer tolerate any hint of European intervention in Latin America, such as the 1903 Anglo-German blockade of Venezuela. Following a civil war, the Dominican Republic found itself bankrupt in 1904 and unable to pay its European creditors. In his annual message to Congress in December of that year, President Roosevelt outlined his "Corollary" to the Monroe Doctrine: "Chronic wrongdoing ... may in America, as elsewhere, ultimately require intervention by some civilized nation, and in the Western Hemisphere the adherence of the United States to the Monroe Doctrine may force the United States, however reluctantly, in flagrant cases of such wrongdoing or impotence, to the exercise of an international police power."[9] The United States went on to seize the customs houses of the Dominican Republic, as it later did in Nicaragua in 1911. The ill-will created in Latin America, especially after United States Marines landed in 1912, spurred Secretary of State P.C. Knox to undertake a goodwill tour of the Caribbean. "I beg to assure you ... that my Government does not covet an inch of territory south of the Rio Grande," Knox declared. Yet as Latin America increasingly came within the American economic, political, and strategic sphere, actual territorial occupation seemed unnecessary.

With Alaska out of the way, Canadian-American relations entered a new era of relative concord. The "Cleaning of the Slate," as it has been called, was greatly aided by the new Canadian Governor-General, Lord Grey (an Anglo-Saxonist believer in "race federation"); the new American Secretary of State, Elihu Root, who took over for John Hay in 1905; and the new British Ambassador to Washington, James Bryce. From 1906 to 1912, with close consultation among the three governments, more than a dozen long-standing disputes were resolved, including the bonding system, alien labour, the North Atlantic fisheries, Bering Sea sealing, and the complete demarcation of the border, the latter of some significance coming only a few years after the Alaska boundary dispute. In 1909 Bryce and Root signed the Boundary Waters Treaty, which set down principles for the shared use of all bodies of water along the Canadian-American border. More significantly, the 1909 treaty established the International Joint Commission as a permanent body to deal with Canadian-American disputes. Six years after the Alaska boundary settlement had displayed the apparent shortcomings of British diplomacy in Canadian-American affairs, the International Joint Commission removed the great mass of workaday cross-border disputes from the purview of the British embassy and put them under direct Canadian control. Moreover, the Alaska dispute had also shown Canada the great disadvantage of having public disputes with the United States, disputes which inevitably became politically charged. The International Joint Commission provided the further advantage of largely removing such disputes from the public eye. After the First World War, Canadian delegates to the League of Nations would point to the International Joint Commission as a model for other nations to follow in adjudicating international disputes. The Canadians may have been right, for the Commission still sits today and, according to C.P. Stacey, "appears in our time to be playing a valuable part in Canadian-American border relations."[10]

The events of 1911, however, illustrated that old Canadian-American rivalries could still come to bear in domestic politics. After negotiations in late 1910 and early 1911, Canadian and American representatives agreed to trading reciprocity, to be enacted by concurrent legislation in Ottawa and Washington. The American bill became law in July 1911 but the old reciprocity idea faced stiff opposition in Canada. Still smarting from the Alaska boundary embarrassment and generally suspicious of American motives, many Canadians viewed reciprocity as "the thin end of the wedge," only a preliminary measure to full annexation. Economic arguments were largely overshadowed by nationalist expressions, giving voice both to notions of Canadian autonomy and continued loyalty to the Crown and empire.[11] In English Canada reciprocity became a central issue of the 1911 election, an election marked by varying and interconnecting strains of English-Canadian nationalism, French-Canadian nationalism, and English-Canadian imperialism. The prominent Liberal Clifford Sifton defected from the party. Laurier had gambled that any lost support among Ontario manufacturers could be made up in Quebec and the prairie provinces. The Conservatives under Robert Borden, however, enlisted the support of French-Canadian Nationalists such as Henri Bourassa (reacting, in part, against Laurier's 1910 Naval Service Bill), and Sifton-led anti-Americanism gave Manitoba to the Conservatives.[12] The Liberals lost the election.

After years of resisting reciprocity advocates like John Charlton, Laurier had reversed himself and threw in his lot with the continentalists.

The defeat of reciprocity in 1911, and the alliance of Ontario imperialists with Quebec Nationalists, reflected the developing nature of a Canadian nationhood that had little time for the divisive ideology of Anglo-Saxonism. Through his journal *Le Devoir*, Bourassa led the way in reinventing Canada as a dualistic nation, recognizing both the British and French as the twin founding peoples. The 1905 Autonomy Bills, which established Alberta and Saskatchewan, had allowed for separate, denominational schools to educate the westward-migrating French-Canadian population. English Canada objected to allowing French Canadians to maintain such separateness, and to replacing a public school system with denominational schools. Laurier was forced to rewrite the bills, giving in to the notion that Canada should not be further split along racial or religious lines.

Bourassa also advocated a Canada independent of the British imperial connection, while most Canadians continued to define Canada through that very same connection (although the Imperial Federation scheme of Joseph Chamberlain never drew wide support in Canada). After a lengthy debate in Canada, the Liberal government introduced the Naval Service Bill, which made provisions for a Canadian naval college, for training officers, and for a separate Canadian navy which would, in the event of war, be placed at the disposal of imperial authorities if the Canadian Parliament chose. Borden's Conservatives opposed the bill as being of little use to the imperial authorities, and advocated instead the immediate contribution to the imperial navy of two dreadnoughts. Henri Bourassa objected to the bill as an imperialist measure that threatened to draw Canada into Britain's imperial wars. Although the bill passed, the Conservative-Nationalist alliance would help defeat Laurier in the next election. More importantly, the alliance reflected the growing inclination to reject Goldwin Smith's critique of Confederation as bringing together two "irreconcilable" peoples. Many English Canadians shared Bourassa's view of Canada as a dualistic nation as they accommodated French Canadians to their conception of Canadian nationhood. "It was not so much intellectual consistency that held this image together," Carl Berger has written, "but rather the nationalistic determination to think of Canada as 'one people.'"[13] In the end, Anglo-Saxonism could not provide Canadians with a viable alternative to a national sentiment that included both English and French Canada.

In Canada and the United States, the Anglo-Saxon conception of the continent also became increasingly eroded by the waves of non-English-speaking immigrants. From 1901 to 1911, nearly 1,750,000 immigrants entered Canada, a number equal to almost forty percent of the 1901 population.[14] In order to attract immigrants to fill the vast open spaces of the Canadian northwest, the government had long observed an open-border policy. While the immigrants came from all ethnic backgrounds, Clifford Sifton's Department of the Interior placed a premium on Anglo-Saxons. The head tax on the Chinese was eventually raised to $500 per head by 1903, while Sifton was prevented from placing a similar tax on the Japanese only by the Anglo-Japanese alliance. Furthermore, Sifton's department gave bonuses to European agents who diverted agricultural emigrants to Canada. Responding to the influx of immigrants in the first decade of the twentieth century, the Canadian government ended its open-border policy, placing ever-tighter controls on immigration through the 1906 and 1910 Immigration Acts. It also negotiated "voluntary quotas" on Japanese emigrants with the Japanese government. The United States' experience paralleled that of Canada. In 1907 alone, 1,285,000 immigrants found their way to the United States, and by 1910, 13,345,000 Americans, or one out of seven of the total population, were foreign-born.[15] Like Canadians, Americans had a particular fear of Asian immigrants. In 1906 the San Francisco Board of Education established a separate school for Asian pupils, arguing that all ninety-three of them were crowding out white students. Theodore Roosevelt then negotiated a series of "Gentlemen's Agreements" with the Japanese government by which it would not issue passports for Japanese labourers headed for the American mainland.[16] The anti-immigrant sentiment was a driving impulse of progressivism. Immigrants supposedly threatened old-stock "native" Americans across a wide spectrum of issues: economically, by working for less money and breaking strikes; politically, by selling their votes to the urban machines; and racially, by reproducing in such numbers as to overwhelm Anglo-Saxons.[17]

At the same time, however, many Canadians and Americans worried more about adequately assimilating the immigrants. "If large communities of foreigners are to be enfranchised without being assimilated," one writer stated in Queen's Quarterly, "the result will be the creation of innumerable sectional interests which will prevent any national question being decided on its merits."[18] In the United States, the 1912 platform of Theodore Roosevelt's Progressive "Bull Moose" party called for the "Americanization" of the immigrants. In 1901 Theodore Herzl, the founder of modern Zionism, wrote the play "The Melting Pot," which gave Americans a new conception of their unique character. Being American was based less on race than on the ideas and cultural norms of the dominant "Yankee tradition." Indeed, Americans set themselves apart from Europeans by their mixed heritage, which ensured the continued vigour of the American race. While some still worried about racial purity and equated the corruption of Anglo-Saxon blood with the corruption of society, the sheer number of immigrants forced Americans, especially politicians, to adapt their view of what it meant to be American. Anglo-Saxonism was out; Anglo-conformism was in.

Perhaps nothing indicated the obsolescence of North American Anglo-Saxonism more than the death or old age of so many of its prominent advocates. In Canada, the years following the Alaska boundary dispute saw the deaths of Goldwin Smith, John Charlton, George Grant, and Sir Richard Cartwright. John Hay died in 1905, and after that point, writers such as Josiah Strong and Alfred Thayer Mahan held much less sway in the nations' intellectual debates. Theodore Roosevelt and Albert Shaw gave much less prominence to Anglo-Saxon rhetoric. In 1903, observing the influx of eastern and southern Europeans, Shaw wrote that "the talk of Anglo-Saxonism begins to lose its relevancy."[19] In the English-speaking North Atlantic Triangle, the death or decline of prominent British Anglo-Saxonists also had some effect. Chamberlain resigned from the cabinet in 1903 and died from a stroke in 1906, while Arthur Balfour, who became Prime Minister in 1902, was turned out of office in 1905.[20] Such men, and their ideas of racial affinity and determinism, belonged to the nineteenth century.

The Anglo-American rapprochement of 1895–1903 forced English-speaking North Americans to reconcile old animosities with the new international realities. In 1895, Canadians and Americans viewed each other across a border marked on the one side by Canadian Loyalism and imperialism, and on the other by American anglophobia and Manifest Destiny. Some events of the rapprochement, such as the Venezuela crisis, the Spanish-American War, the annexation of the Philippines, and the South African War, were viewed in the context of common Anglo-American interests in an age marked by the threat of new and growing powers. The threat of Russia in the Far East, Germany in South Africa, or a combination of European powers anywhere, created an identity of interest between the United States and Great Britain. This era of Anglo-American understanding depended upon North American concord. Canadians and Americans searched for an area of common ground and found it in Anglo-Saxonism. The ideas of Anglo-Saxon kinship, affinity, and a common mission to bring civilization, Protestant Christianity, and political liberty to the world allowed Canadians and Americans to view each other with a level of tolerance and camaraderie not seen before on the continent.

Anglo-Saxonism was an extremely flexible notion that could incorporate ideas of gender, religion, science, literature, and history. Roosevelt and his contemporaries used the terms "Anglo-Saxon" and "English-speaking" virtually synonymously. Such flexibility was one of Anglo-Saxonism's strengths as well as one of its weaknesses. Many elements of Anglo-Saxon affinity were very superficial, and broke down in the face of serious national issues. Most Americans and Canadians only scoffed when John Charlton used Anglo-Saxon rhetoric to argue for reciprocity. Anglo-Saxonism was no longer anywhere to be found in official dispatches or in the correspondence of men like Secretary of State John Hay. Anglo-Saxonism, then, was a rhetorical device that provided an easily understood and widely recognized context by which one could discuss friendly Canadian-American relations, thus the frequent use of Anglo-Saxon rhetoric by Sir Wilfrid Laurier, who could hardly be mistaken for an Anglo-Saxonist. Still, despite its limitations, North American Anglo-Saxonism was not simply a device of the speechmakers, but constituted an important strand of thought that existed side-by-side with nationalism and imperialism. As racial conceptions constituted an important element of Canadian nationalism and imperialism, a politician like Richard Cartwright, or an intellectual leader like George Grant, could easily include the United States within their vision of Canada's national and imperial future. Canadian nationalism, imperialism, and Anglo-Saxonism were not mutually exclusive, but formed concentric circles of self-definition for a young Canadian nation: Anglo-Saxonism could easily encompass the United States, the empire, and an autonomous Canadian nation.

While Canadians might not have realized it at the time, Anglo-Saxonism and the Anglo-American rapprochement placed Canadian-American relations on a more equal footing and ensured Canadian security. Only with the events of the rapprochement did Americans come to see Canada as a self-governing nation with a right to an independent existence, and not just a fragment of a European empire. Moreover, although Americans had initially applied the Monroe Doctrine to Canada, Anglo-Saxonism helped differentiate the English-speaking Dominion from what were seen as the corrupt and backward Latin American republics. This, in turn, aided in differentiating Canadian and British national interests in the conduct of North American diplomacy, and the compartmentalization of Canada within Anglo-American affairs. In the short term this did not serve Canada's interests as it helped bring about a settlement of the Alaska boundary unfavourable to Canada. In the long term, however, such compartmentalization provided Canada with greater control of its external affairs, leading to the Dominion sending its first credentialed minister to a foreign capital in 1927. By that time, many Canadians had adopted the idea of Canada as a living link, or linch-pin, between the two great Atlantic powers. Yet decades earlier, advocates of Anglo-American friendship had utilized Anglo-Saxon rhetoric to give Canada a special place in fostering that friendship. Just as inter-war Canadians became Atlanticists for the sake of Canadian security, turn-of-the-century Canadians became Anglo-Saxonists in order to protect Canada's place on the continent and the empire's place in the Far East and Africa. Once again, a Canadian Anglo-Saxonism that encompassed the United States actually served British imperial interests.

While perhaps not entirely relevant to recent "borderlands" histories of Canada and the United States, Anglo-Saxonism certainly appears relevant to the broader field of "transnational" history.[21] After all, such racial ideology resounded throughout the English-speaking world, crossing borders as easily as Goldwin Smith or John Charlton. Perhaps because of this, historians of Anglo-Saxonism portray its advocates as progenitors of the modern British Commonwealth. "In his vision of a free association of the English-speaking peoples of the world, linked by common bonds of language, literature, and law," Elizabeth Wallace writes of Goldwin Smith, "he was a prophet of the modern Common-wealth of Nations."[22] Since it has been pointed out that the British Commonwealth was neither British, nor shared common wealth, Anglo-Saxonism seems inapplicable.

Much more important was the effect of Anglo-Saxonism on the Anglo-American entente, and the unity of action of the North Atlantic Triangle. While Anglo-Saxonism did not cause the rapprochement, in setting out Anglo-American affinity in terms of moral and political responsibilities, Anglo-Saxonism's legacy can be seen in the events of the twentieth century, marked as it was by Anglo-American concert of action.[23] With the effectiveness of U.S.-British interaction proven by World War I and the later failure of the League of Nations, the idea of an English-speaking Union returned to vogue.[24] In 1926 the Anglo-American English-speaking Union could claim 10,000 members in each country, with Lord Balfour and former president William Taft presidents of the British and American branches.[25] In 1939 American journalist Clarence Streit published his highly popular *Union Now* which called for a union of the United States, Great Britain, and the self-governing Dominions.[26] Though never bound politically, the Anglo-American alliance shaped the history of the twentieth century. From World War II and the founding of the United Nations to a united policy in Iraq and Serbia at the end of the century, the United States and Great Britain sought to establish a world based on Anglo-American notions of political and individual liberty. While not racially based, the rhetoric of Anglo-American policy often seems to have antecedents in turn-of-the-century Anglo-Saxonism.

During the Second World War, Canadian Prime Minister William Lyon Mackenzie King stressed his role as a personal linch-pin between Winston Churchill and Franklin Delano Roosevelt. Whether visiting England or hosting the two leaders in Quebec, Mackenzie King relished Churchill's praise for "helping to bring English-speaking peoples together."[27] "We all look to you as the link to America," Churchill told the Canadian Prime Minister. "That fraternal association must be kept up."[28] Churchill, for his part, liked to remind Roosevelt and American audiences that his mother was American. Mackenzie King's mother had also been born in the United States while her father, and Mackenzie King's namesake, had been living there in exile. Even at a meeting of Commonwealth prime ministers in 1944, Churchill praised Canada's effort to maintain "the fraternal association of the United States and British Commonwealth and Empire."[29] Nearly half a century after the Anglo-American rapprochement, the idea of English-speaking kinship remained a powerful rhetorical device. For many, Anglo-Canadian-American cooperation during the war represented the natural culmination of familial feelings shared by people who viewed themselves as sharing a common mission, and linked by a common religion, language, and civilization.

Notes

INTRODUCTION

1 In Dyer, 69–88.
2 James Cappon (who succeeded Queen's University Principal George
   M. Grant as editor in 1901), "Current Events," *Queen's Quarterly* 9, 4,
   (April 1902), 321.
3 Henry Adams to John Hay, 28 July 1896, in *Henry Adams*, 376;
   and to Brooks Adams, 12 June 1899, ibid., 465.
4 Goldwin Smith Papers, Smith to [?] Mowbray, undated.
5 Roosevelt to Francis Parkman, 22 May 1892, in Morison, *Volume I*, 282.
6 Schurman, 6.
7 Barbara Tuchman, *A Distant Mirror*; Carlos Fuentes, *The Buried
   Mirror*; Ronald Takaki, *A Different Mirror*.
8 Reginald Horsman, *Race and Manifest Destiny: The Origins of American Racial Anglo-Saxonism*.
9 Edward Augustus Freeman, *History of the Norman Conquest of
   England* (1867–79); Charles Kingsley, *The Roman and the Teuton*
   (1864). Nell Irvin Painter also notes the popularity of the medieval
   genre of fiction, which included Charles Major, *When Knighthood
   Was in Flower* (1898) and F. Marion Crawford, *Via Crucis: A Romance
   of the Second Crusade* (1898). Painter, 150.
10 Strong, *Our Country*, 165.
11 Strong, *The New Era*, 56.
12 Carl Berger discusses the widespread popularity of natural history in
   nineteenth-century Canada, and argues it represented an effort to come

to terms with Darwinism. Berger notes that by the end of the century Darwinism had triumphed and natural history began its decline. Berger, *Science, God and Nature in Victorian Canada.*

13 Quoted in Richard Hofstadter, *Social Darwinism*, 21.

14 Hobsbawm, 102. Also Greenfeld, 12–13, and Ignatieff, 9.

15 Fredrickson, *Comparative Imagination*, 83.

16 Hofstatder, 101.

17 Jones, 144.

18 Adams, 165.

19 A.E. Campbell, *Great Britain and the United States*; H. C. Allen, *Great Britain and the United State*; Charles S. Campbell, *Anglo-American Understanding*; John A.S. Grenville and George Berkeley Young, *Politics, Strategy, and American Diplomacy*; Lionel Gelber, *The Rise of Anglo-American Friendship.*

20 Roger Sarty, "Canada and the Great Rapprochement;" Peter Neary, "Grey, Bryce, and the Settlement;" Alvin C. Gluek, Jr., "Pilgrimages to Ottawa;" Kenneth Bourne, *Britain and the Balance*; C.P. Stacey, *Canada in the Age of Conflict.*

21 Stacey, 151.

22 Stuart Anderson, 66–67, 201n.

CHAPTER ONE

1 Morison, 501.

2 Charlton, "Canada and the Venezuela Settlement."

3 Dexter Perkins, *A History of the Monroe Doctrine*, 356–67.

4 Lodge, "Our Blundering Foreign Policy."

5 Widenor, 107.

6 Lodge, "England, Venezuela, and the Monroe Doctrine."

7 The previous secretary of state, Walter Gresham, had died suddenly in May. Gresham had been diplomatic, whereas Olney was characterized by "his natural acerbity of temper" (Dexter Perkins, 174). Although Olney's temperament may have made his communications with the British more hostile in tone, Cleveland approved of Olney's message. Moreover, Republican attacks made it difficult for the President to take anything but a firm stand.

8 "That Olney was definitely influenced by the language of Lodge is something that cannot be proved," Dexter Perkins writes. "But the note which he prepared for Lord Salisbury was written in a similar spirit." (Dexter Perkins, 174–75).

9 See Dexter Perkins.

10 Lodge, "Our Blundering Foreign Policy," 16–17.

11 Grover Cleveland Letters, Cleveland to Olney, 7 July 1895.

12 Nevins, *Letters of Grover Cleveland*, Cleveland to Bayard, 29 December 1895, 417–18.

13 "Message of the President," December 27, 1895, *Papers Relating to Foreign Relations of the United States*, 542–45.

14 See Woolsley, "The President's Monroe Doctrine"; Moore, "The Monroe Doctrine"; Cassatt, "The Monroe Doctrine: Defence, Not Defiance"; Burgess, "The Recent Pseudo-Monroeism."

15 Editorial, "The Presidency and Mr. Olney," *Atlantic Monthly*, 680.

16 Lodge, *Selections* Volume I, Roosevelt to Lodge, 20 December 1895, 200.

17 Adams to Olney, 17 December 1895, *Henry Adams*, Volume 4, 346.

18 Atlanta *Constitution*, 18 December 1895.

19 New Orleans *Times-Democrat*, reprinted in Atlanta *Constitution*, 20 December 1895.

20 New York *Tribune*, 30 December 1895.

21 *New York Times*, 22 December 1895.

22 Atlanta *Constitution*, 22 December 1895.

23 *New York Times*, 21 December 1895.

24 The most comprehensive work on Shaw is Graybar, *Albert Shaw of the Review of Reviews*. While noting Shaw's Anglo-Saxonism, Graybar colours Shaw as an American nationalist walking "hand in hand" with Roosevelt.

25 Beveridge's friendship with Shaw and the Shaw-Beveridge correspondence receive much attention in Bowers, *Beveridge and the Progressive Era*.

26 Albert Shaw Papers, Shaw to Stead, 27 November 1895.

27 Shaw, "Is England an 'American Power'?" 645.

28 Stead, "Preface"

29 Albert Shaw Papers, Shaw to Stead, 20 January 1896.

30 Halifax *Herald*, 21 December 1895.

31 See Carl Berger, *The Sense of Power*. Berger notes that by the end of the nineteenth century Grant had "attained the stature of a Christian statesman and moral guardian by speaking out on public questions." (25) Berger is careful to differentiate the imperialism of Grant from that of his fellow Canada First member, Colonel George Denison. (171)

32 Grant Papers, vol. 25, clipping from the Toronto *Mail* 14 February 1887, in Berger, *The Sense of Power*, 171.

33 *Free Press*, 23 December 1895.

34 "Current Events," *Queen's Quarterly* 3, 3 (January 1896), 238.

35 George Grant, "Our Origins," *Methodist Magazine* 43, 2, 143.

36 Ottawa *Evening Journal*, 31 December 1895, and Montreal *Gazette*, 25 December 1895.

37 Quoted in Montreal *Gazette*, 26 December 1895.

38 Manitoba *Free Press*, 23 December 1895.

39 Manitoba *Free Press*, 8 January 1896.

40 George Grant, "Our Origins," *Methodist Magazine* 43, 1, (January 1896), 142.
41 "Current Events," *Queen's Quarterly* 3, 3 (January 1896), 237–8.
42 "Current Thought," *Canadian Magazine* 6, 2, (December 1895).
43 Toronto *Globe*, 18 January 1896.
44 Ibid., 21 December 1895.
45 Ibid., 23 December 1895.
46 Ibid., 24 December 1895.
47 Montreal *Daily Star*, 23 December 1895.
48 Ibid., 28 December 1895.
49 F.P.B., "Fratricide," *Canadian Magazine* 6, 4, (February 1896), 380.
50 Toronto *Mail and Empire*, 28 December 1895.
51 Ibid., 1192–3.
52 Ibid., 1194.
53 Ibid., 1199.
54 James, Bayard to Olney, 13 January 1896, 228.
55 Ibid., Olney to Bayard, 14 January 1896, 229.
56 Henry White Papers, Lodge to White, 12 March 1896.
57 Nevins, *Letters of Grover Cleveland,* Bayard to Cleveland, 29 January 1896, 426.
58 Wolcott's speech, quoted in Toronto *Mail and Empire*, 23 January 1896.
59 Morison, Roosevelt to Anna Roosevelt Cowles, 26 January 1896, Volume I, 510–11.
60 Ibid., Roosevelt to Henry White, 30 March 1896, Volume I, 523.
61 Carnegie, "The Venezuelan Question." Carnegie's article was followed by the British author James Bryce's article, "British Feelings on the Venezuelan Question." Bryce wrote of British horror at the thought of war with the United States, "for we and the Americans come of the same stock, speak the same language, read the same books, think upon similar lines, are connected by a thousand ties of family and friendship." (150)
62 Sherwood.
63 Phelps.
64 Powell.
65 Shaw, "The Progress of the World."
66 Albert Shaw Papers, Shaw to W.T. Reid, 23 March 1896.
67 Toronto *Mail and Empire*, 24 January 1896.
68 *Saturday Night*, 11 January 1896.
69 "Current Thoughts," *Canadian Magazine* 6, 5, (March 1896), 482.
70 Bailey, Thomas A., *A Diplomatic History,* 446.
71 Toronto *Globe*, 12 November 1896.
72 "Current Events," *Queen's Quarterly* 4, 3, (January 1897), 238.
73 Manitoba *Free Press*, 12 November 1896.

74 Toronto *Mail and Empire*, 14 November 1896.
75 "Current Thoughts," *Canadian Magazine 8*, 2, (December 1896), 187.
76 Manitoba *Free Press*, 12 and 13 January 1897.
77 *Monetary Times*, 15 January 1897.
78 Ottawa *Evening Journal*, 14 January 1897.
79 Toronto *Mail and Empire*, 14 January 1897.
80 "Current Thoughts," *Canadian Magazine 8*, 4, (February 1897).
81 Blackstock, "Canada and the Venezuelan Settlement."
82 "Current Thoughts," *Canadian Magazine 9*, 4, (August 1897), 350–51.
83 Tansill, 600 and 661.
84 Thomas Bayard Papers, John Bassett Moore to Bayard, 30 March 1893, in Tansill, 655–56.
85 *Nation 64*, 1668, 17 (June 1897).
86 Tansill, *Foreign Policy*, 656.
87 Ibid., 691.
88 Walter Gresham Papers, Bayard to Gresham, 28 December 1893, in Tansill, 660–61.
89 Bayard to Cleveland, 4 December 1895, in Tansill, 716.
90 White had been First Secretary at the American embassy in London under Bayard's predecessor. Tansill notes that White had enemies in the new Cleveland administration that took office in May 1893. On Cleveland's orders Bayard asked for White's resignation upon his arrival in England. White's biographer Allan Nevins blames Bayard for White's dismissal, as did White's friends at the time, including Theodore Roosevelt and William McKinley. Tansill believes this episode influenced the Republican criticism levelled at Bayard as well as Olney's hostile attitude. (Tansill, 658n.)
91 Smith, *Reminiscences*, 41.
92 Tansill, *Foreign Policy*, 745n.

CHAPTER TWO

1 Advocates of Canadian-American free trade used the technically different terms "Commercial Union" and "Unrestricted Reciprocity" synonymously. As Goldwin Smith wrote to the New York *Independent* in a letter that appeared January 24, 1888, "'Commercial Union,' 'Unrestricted Reciprocity,' 'Continental Free Trade,' are three different names for the same or nearly the same thing." *Handbook of Commercial Union*, 245. Technically, while Unrestricted Reciprocity indicated free trade only, Commercial Union included common North American areas of commerce such as the Atlantic fisheries. Advocates of Commercial Union adopted the name, as Smith notes, "in direct contradistinction to political union, and for the special purpose of guarding against any

such idea." Goldwin Smith, "Letters on Commercial Union," 233.
The name apparently backfired, with opponents of free trade associating
Commercial Union with American annexation.

2 Smith, "Introduction," ibid., xxxi.
3 Smith, "Letters," ibid., 199 and 219.
4 Ibid., 199 and 237.
5 "Speech by the Hon. Sir Richard Cartwright, K.C.M.G.," ibid., 35.
6 Ibid., 39.
7 Ibid., 44.
8 Ibid., 48.
9 Ibid., 53.
10 Ledyard, "Commercial Union and the Mining Interests of Canada,"
   ibid., 85.
11 Janes. "How Unrestricted Reciprocity with the United States Would
   Affect the Prosperity of Toronto," ibid., 98.
12 Lockhart Gordon, "The Effect of Commercial Union on Our Relations
   with Great Britain," ibid., 100.
13 Longley, "Current Objections to Commercial Union Considered," ibid.,
   115 and 121.
14 John Charlton, "Reply in the House of Commons to the Disloyalty
   Cry," ibid., 139–40.
15 Graham, "Sir Richard Cartwright," 1.
16 Haultain, Smith to George William Curtis, 17 December 1884, 108.
17 Smith, The Schism in the Anglo-Saxon Race.
18 Smth, Canada and the Canadian Question.
19 Robert Craig Brown, "The Commercial Unionists," 119.
20 Graham persuasively argues against Charles Tansill who says Laurier
   "was opposed to the idea of commercial union," and Laurier biographer O.D. Skelton who notes that Laurier "stood aloof" from the
   movement. Graham, 16.
21 Ibid., 13–14.
22 English, 25–26; Forster, A Conjunction of Interests.
23 J.W. Dafoe was one of the first to describe Laurier as "Machiavellian."
   Dafoe, Laurier, 15.
24 Ibid., 5–11. For more on the regional nature of Canadian national party
   politics, see also Dawson, The Government of Canada, 508–10; Brady,
   Democracy in the Dominions, 104; and Siegfried, The Race Question
   in Canada, 113.
25 Graham, 18; Stevens, "Laurier and the Liberal Party in Ontario," cited in
   Miller, "Mowat, Laurier, and the Federal Liberal Party;" Dafoe, Laurier, 97.
26 Graham, 17.
27 Gillis and Roach call Charlton an "aggressive businessman" who advocated free trade out of self-interest, in Lost Initiatives, 84; Skelton calls
   Charlton "indiscreet" during the Joint High Commission and accuses

him of promoting "local interests," in *Life and Letters of Sir Wilfrid Laurier*, 209n; Brown notes that when Charlton "did appear to speak for the Canadian Liberals he often did so without their knowledge or advice," in *Canada's National Policy*, 184; Schull calls Charlton a "dubious asset" at the Joint High Commission of 1898–99 as he was "totally preoccupied with lumber and pressing for his own interests," in *Laurier, The First Canadian*, 371.

28 *Our Country* had sold 176,000 copies by 1916, Muller, 488.

29 Hofstadter, *Social Darwinism in American Thought*, 178–79; Commager, *The American Mind*, 47. Muller disputes this notion, believing Strong did not advocate American expansion, but rather "evangelizing the world through the persuasive power of example and practice of civilization carried by its people to all parts of the world as they traveled or migrated – but not by the extension of political power or force" (489–90). Muller emphasizes the missionary aspect of Strong's writings and points out that he wrote *Our Country* at the request of the American Home Missionary Society. Meyer ("The Fear of Cultural Decline: Josiah Strong's Thought about Reform and Expansion") points out that Strong was an early leader of the Social Gospel movement, and came to emphasize internal American reform over expansion in his later writings. Meyer, however, fails to cite Strong's *The New Era*.

30 Hofstadter, *Social Darwinism*, 178.

31 Strong, *Our Country*, 165.

32 Ibid., 178.

33 Strong, *The New Era*, 74–75.

34 See the "Introduction" to Charlton's *Speeches and Addresses*. Also see Ferns and Brown, "John Charlton."

35 Charlton Papers, Diary, 16 December 1896.

36 Ibid., 12 August 1901.

37 Ibid., 5 December 1895.

38 Ferns and Brown, 189.

39 Ibid., 188–9.

40 Charlton Papers, Diary, 1893 summary.

41 Ferns and Brown, 188. The authors note that Prime Minister John A. Macdonald "facetiously observed that the legislation would cause thousands of young men to leave the country."

42 Schull, 226. Schull recounts the Charlton-Laurier confrontation over the bill. Charlton told Laurier that Canada should be a country of one race. Laurier rounded on Charlton: "I am of French origin but I am a British subject. Well, what race would that be? Is it the British lion that is to swallow the French lamb or the French lamb that is to swallow the British lion? There can be more than one race, but there shall be but one nation."

43 Charlton Papers, Diary, 1897 summary.

44 Charlton told the House: "Now these are British provinces. The design was that these should be Anglo-Saxon commonwealths." Quoted in Ferns and Brown, 189.

45 Speech to North Norfolk Liberals at Simcoe, Ontario, 19 October 1900. Reprinted in Toronto *Globe*, 20 October 1900.

46 Charlton, "American Trade Relations," 506.

47 Charlton, "The Anglo-American Joint High Commission," 165–66.

48 Charlton Papers, Diary, 30 April 1897.

49 Ibid., 16 January 1893.

50 Ibid., 12 January, 1893.

51 Charlton, "The Anglo-American Joint High Commission," 166.

52 Charlton, "Canadian Trade Relations with the United States," 371.

53 Goldwin Smith Papers, Charlton to Smith, 17 September 1897.

54 Charlton, *Diary*, 16 March 1892.

55 Ibid., 17 April 1896, and Ferns and Brown, 189.

56 Stacey, 30.

57 New York *Tribune*, 3 July 1896.

58 Ibid., 19 January 1897.

59 Laurier Papers, Laurier to Charlton, 18 January 1897.

60 Ibid., Charlton to Laurier, 30 April 1897.

61 Charlton Papers, Diary, 9 July 1897.

62 Ibid., 11 July 1897.

63 Laurier Papers, Charlton to Laurier, 1 September 1897: "Report to the Rt. Ho. Sir Wilfred [sic] Laurier By John Charlton, M.P."

64 *Nation* 64, 1655, 18 March 1898.

65 Ibid., 64, 1669, 24 June 1897. "It is no longer the 'manifest destiny' of the United States to absorb Canada."

66 Ibid., 65, 1675, 5 August 1897.

67 Ibid., 65, 1677, 19 August 1897.

68 Laurier and Davies had not been invited by the Americans, and their impromptu visit caused some anxiety at the British embassy. Callahan, 453.

69 "Sir Wilfrid Laurier at Washington," 349.

70 Toronto *Globe*, 26 May 1898.

71 New York *Tribune*, 23 May 1898.

72 Halifax *Herald*, 23 May 1898.

73 *New York Times*, 1 June 1898.

74 Ibid., 13 July 1898.

75 Montreal *Daily Witness* cartoon, reprinted in *American Monthly Review of Reviews* 19, 6, (June 1898), 654.

76 Toronto *Globe*, 30 July 1898.

77 Farrer, "Appendix A, Reciprocity with Canada, Statement by Hon. Edward Farrer, of Toronto," 76.

78 Farrer, "The Anglo-American Commission."

79 Laurier Papers, Charlton to Laurier, 30 June 1898.

80 Schull, 370.

81 Laurier Papers, Charlton to Laurier, 7 July 1898.

82 Ibid., Laurier to Charlton, 11 July 1898.

83 Ibid., Charlton to Laurier, 19 July 1898.

84 Ibid., Laurier to Charlton, 23 July 1898.

85 Charlton, "Canada and the Dingley Bill"; "The Anglo-American Joint High Commission."

86 Laurier Papers, Laurier to Charlton, 23 July 1898.

87 Foster, *Diplomatic Memoirs*, Volume 2, 187.

88 Atlanta *Constitution*, 25 August 1898.

89 *New York Times*, 29 and 30 August 1898.

90 Toronto *Globe*, 3 August 1898.

91 Ibid., 19 August 1898.

92 Ibid., 24 August 1898.

93 Montreal *Daily Star*, 22 August 1898.

94 *American Monthly Review of Reviews* 18, 4, (October 1898), 389–91.

95 Shaw Papers, Shaw to Agnes C. Laut, 30 September 1898. "You may make it just as frankly from the Canadian point of view as you like, because I could readily enough get an article of, say, two or three thousand words by some one from this side of the line ... I am not, however, planning at present for any article except yours."

96 McConnell, 198–201.

97 Henry Adams, Adams to Elizabeth Cameron, 21 November 1898, 622.

98 National Archives of Canada, F.C.T. O'Hara Papers, "Diary Extracts," 24 January 1899.

99 Charlton Papers, Diary, 1898 summary.

100 Henry Adams, Adams to Cameron, 21 November 1898, 622.

101 O'Hara Papers, "Diary Extracts," 10 and 30 January 1899.

102 Ibid., 3 January to 1 March 1899.

103 Henry Adams, Adams to Charles Milnes Gaskell, 1 March 1899.

104 Montreal *Gazette*, 25 February 1899.

105 Toronto *Globe*, 21 February 1899.

106 Ibid., 22 February 1899.

107 Toronto *Mail and Empire*, 22 February 1899.

108 Richard Clippingdale rightly notes that at this time, Willison and the *Globe*'s Canadianism "was part of a broader Anglo-Saxonism" that included the United States. See Clippingdale; see also Berger, *The Sense of Power*, 173. After Willison left the *Globe* in 1902 he published *Anglo-Saxon Amity* (Toronto, 1906), and a pamphlet, *United States and Canada*, (American Branch Association for International Conciliation, October, 1908).

109 Willison, "Relations between Britain and America."

110 *New York Times*, 21 February 1899.
111 Chicago *Tribune*, 21 February 1899.
112 *New York Times*, 22 February 1899.
113 Laut, "Canada's Claims before the Anglo-American Joint High Commission," 445–50.
114 *Review of Reviews* 20, 1, (July 1899), 10–11.
115 Goldwin Smith Papers, Charlton to Smith, 11 May 1903.
116 O'Hara Papers, "Diary Extracts."
117 Charlton speculated that Davies had tried to have him removed from the commission, remarking "I have reason to suppose he was not friendly to me, and his influence over Laurier seems to be great." Charlton also revelled in the fact that he was better prepared than Cartwright: "It was amusing to see Sir Richard bringing out his statistics for 1897 for a time only to find I had the information on every point nearly a year later." Charlton Papers, Diary, 1898 summary.
118 The Ontario Export Log Law, passed in late 1897 to become active in April 1898 essentially prohibited the export of Ontario sawlogs, the very foundation of Charlton's business. With the adjournment of the commission in early 1899, Charlton embarked upon a vigorous campaign to have the law disallowed. Charlton wrote scathing indictments of the law both in the *North American Review*, writing again as "A Canadian Liberal," and in *Canadian Magazine*. He appealed directly to the Ontario government, to Laurier, and finally to the British embassy in Washington – to no avail. Charlton's actions resulted only in frustration and his further disfavour among the Liberal leadership. See Robert Peter Gillis, "The Ottawa Lumber Barons," 14–31; and Nelles, "Empire Ontario: The Problems of Resource Development."
119 Toronto *Globe*, 20 October 1900.
120 Charlton Papers, Diary, 1898 summary.
121 Charlton, "Reciprocity with Canada," 582–93.
122 *Canadian Annual Review, 1902*, 132.
123 Charlton, "The Growth of Reciprocity Sentiment," 483.
124 *Canadian Annual Review, 1902*, 172.
125 Laurier Papers, Charlton to Laurier, 21 February 1903.
126 Charlton Papers, Diary, 20 February 1903.
127 Ibid., Laurier to Charlton, 17 November 1903.
128 House of Commons *Debates*, 7 February 1893, 369.
129 See Neary; Gluek, "Pilgrimages to Ottawa"; and Sarty, 12–47.
130 Baker, "A Case Study of Anti-Americanism."
131 *Canadian Annual Review, 1903*, 382.

CHAPTER THREE

1 LaFeber, *The New Empire*, 99.

2 May, 57–58; Hofstadter, *Social Darwinism*, 172.

3 Kennedy, 306–7; Leuchtenburg, , 483–504; Walden, 222–32.

4 Hudson, 111.

5 Stuart Anderson, 112. Anderson overstates the matter when he claims that "no factor was more important than Anglo-Saxonism in promoting good feelings between the British and American peoples." Ibid., 112. See also A.E. Campbell, *Great Britain and the United States 1895–1903*, 140–55; and Seed, "British Reactions," 254–72, and "British Views," 49–64.

6 Callahan, *American Foreign Policy in Canadian Relations*; Glazebrook, *A History of Canadian External Relations*.

7 Stacey, *Canada and the Age of Conflict*, 74, 86, 90; and Penlington, *Canada and Imperialism*, 97–108.

8 Penlington, *Canada and Imperialism*, 107–08; Robert Craig Brown, 326.

9 Mount, 59–70.

10 Penlington, *Canada and Imperialism*, 102; Whitely, 68–75.

11 Fry, 10–11.

12 Millis, 98.

13 Manitoba *Free Press*, 14 February 1898.

14 Toronto *Mail and Empire*, 12 February 1898.

15 Montreal *Gazette*, 26 March 1898.

16 Toronto *Globe*, 1 March 1898.

17 Clifford Sifton Papers, Richard Cartwright to Sifton, 30 August 1897; with enclosed letter, from [?] Dryden, Department of Agriculture, 27 August 1897.

18 Hall, 181.

19 Toronto *Mail and Empire*, 8 and 9 March 1898; Ottawa *Evening Journal*, 7 March 1898.

20 Toronto *Mail and Empire*, 8 March 1898; Ottawa *Evening Journal*, 12 March 1898.

21 House of Commons *Debates*, Volume 46, 7 March 1898, 1276.

22 Ibid., 1328.

23 Toronto *Globe*, 7 and 8 March 1898.

24 Ibid., 8 March 1898.

25 Manitoba *Free Press*, 28 March 1898.

26 Halifax *Herald*, 4 March 1898.

27 Ibid., 4 April 1898.

28 Ibid., 7 April 1898.

29 Ibid., 9 April 1898.

30 Manitoba *Free Press*, 12 March 1898. See also Toronto *Mail and Empire* 10 March 1898.

31 "An Anglo-American Alliance," *The Speaker*, reprinted in *Living Age* 217, 2805, 9 April 1898, 126–28.

32 Alfred Austin, "America and England," ibid., 66.

33 Manitoba *Free Press*, 22 March 1898.

34 Montreal *Gazette*, 22 March 1898.

35 Halifax *Herald*, 21 March 1898.

36 Toronto *Mail and Empire*, 3 April 1898.

37 Toronto *Globe*, 18 March 1898.

38 Goldwin Smith Papers, Smith to [?], undated (probably April 1898).

39 Ibid., Smith to Mowbray, 18 March 1898.

40 Ibid., Smith to [?] Munro, 10 March 1898.

41 Ibid., Smith to John Foster, 11 November 1898.

42 Montreal *Gazette*, 14 April 1898.

43 Toronto *Globe*, 20 April 1898.

44 Ottawa *Evening Journal*, 27 April 1898.

45 Halifax *Herald*, 6 May 1898.

46 Allen, 575.

47 *Papers Relating the Foreign Relations of the United States*, 1898, 237.

48 "England's Attitude and the War," *The Spectator* cited in *Living Age*
    217, 2811, (21 May 1898), 555–56.

49 "The Collision of the Old World and the New," *The Contemporary
    Review*, cited in *Living Age* 217, 2815, (18 June 1898), 779.

50 Toronto *Globe*, 20 April 1898.

51 Manitboa *Free Press*, 18 April 1898.

52 Montreal *Star*, 23 April 1898.

53 Toronto *Globe*, 20 April 1898.

54 Ibid., 17 May 1898.

55 Montreal *Star*, 21 April 1898.

56 Toronto *Globe*, 15 April 1898.

57 Manitoba *Free Press*, 21 April 1898.

58 Toronto *Globe*, 4 May 1898.

59 Halifax *Herald*, 20 April 1898.

60 "Must It be War?," *Canadian Churchman*, 28 April 1898.

61 "Why Spain is Cruel," *Presbyterian Record*, October 1898, 274.

62 "Current Events," *Queen's Quarterly* 5, 4, April 1898.

63 Toronto *Globe*, 7 May 1898.

64 Abbott, 513–21.

65 Allen notes that as a "self-made Birmingham businessman and Dis-
    senter, he had in some ways more in common with Americans than with
    such colleagues as the aristocratic Salisbury and the aloof Balfour."
    Allen, 565–66.

66 Davis, 140–99 (pages 176–99 are appendices listing Anglo-American
    marriages of peers, baronets, and landed gentry). Davis notes that
    the American women who married Britons were a force "in bringing
    the sea-change in Anglo-American relations at the turn of the
    century" (175).

67 Full text of speech in Toronto *Globe*, 24 May 1898.

68 New York *Journal* and British papers quoted in B.O. Flower, "The Proposed Federation of the Anglo-Saxon Nations," *Arena* 20, 105.

69 Robert Craig Brown, *Canada's National Policy*, 326.

70 Ibid.

71 "Mr. Chamberlain's Speech," *The Economist*, in *Living Age* 217, 2814, (11 June 1898), 750–2; Manitoba *Free Press*, 16 May 1898.

72 Manitoba *Free Press*, 18 and 21 May 1898.

73 Toronto *Globe*, 17 May 1898.

74 Ibid., 17 May 1898.

75 Ibid., 31 May 1898.

76 *Canadian Churchman*, 26 May 1898.

77 Montreal *Gazette*, 16 May 1898.

78 Halifax *Herald*, 20 May 1898.

79 Toronto *Mail and Empire*, 17 May 1898.

80 *Monetary Times*, 20 May 1898.

81 Mills, "Which Shall Dominate?," 729–39.

82 Colquhoun, 932–38.

83 Ridpath, 145–67.

84 Waldstein, 223–38.

85 Greenwood, 563–70.

86 Bryce, "The Essential Unity of Britain and America."

87 Goldwin Smith Papers, Smith to [?], undated [probably April 1898].

88 See also Henry Norman in the Halifax *Herald*, 4 July 1898; and G.S. Clarke, "England and America," *Nineteenth Century* reprinted in *Living Age* 218, 2827, (10 September 1898), 691–97.

89 Frank E. Anderson, "America and the European Concert," 433–44.

90 Dicey, 327–40.

91 Flower, 237.

92 Toronto *Mail and Empire*, 22 August 1898.

93 Toronto *Globe*, 20 September 1898.

94 McLeod, "Universal Empire for Anglo Saxon Stock."

95 "Current Events," *Methodist Magazine* 48, 3, (September 1898), 279–80.

96 "Religious Intelligence," ibid., 284.

97 Allen, 580.

98 "The Fate of the Philippines," *Spectator* reprinted in *Living Age* 217, 2815, (18 June 1898), 837–39.

99 "Current Events," *Queen's Quarterly* 6, 1, (July 1898), 83.

100 Allen, 577–78.

101 *Monetary Times*, 12 August 1898.

102 *Canadian Churchman*, 25 August 1898.

103 Toronto *Globe*, 11 August 1898.

104 Montreal *Star*, 17 August 1898.

105 Harrington, 211.
106 Ibid., 221.
107 Schurz, "Our Future Foreign Policy," in Bancroft, ed., pps. 481 and 485, quoted in Merriman, 376.
108 Carnegie, "Distant Possessions," 239, quoted in ibid., 377.
109 New York Public Library, Manuscript Division, W. Bourke Cockran Papers, Smith to Cockran, 10 November 1899.
110 Bancroft, *Speeches*, Volume V, Smith to Schurz, 6 November 1898, 529.
111 Ibid., Schurz to Smith, 530.
112 Clowes, 31–38.
113 Fisher, 552–59.
114 "Spanish Rule in the Philippines," from *Missionary Review*, cited in *Presbyterian Record*, (November 1898), 300–1.
115 Seed, "British Views," 52.
116 Ibid., 52.
117 Toronto *Globe*, 7 February 1899.
118 Ibid., 22 June 1899.
119 Manitoba *Free Press*, 7 February 1899.
120 Ibid., 9 February 1899.
121 Montreal *Daily Star*, 3 February 1899.
122 Rudyard Kipling, "The White Man's Burden," *McClure's Magazine* 12, 4, (February 1899), 1.
123 Anderson, 57–58.
124 Lodge, *Selections*, I, Roosevelt to Lodge, 12 January 1899, 384.
125 Ibid., Lodge to Roosevelt, 14 January 1899, 385.
126 Anderson, 58.
127 Montreal *Gazette*, 9 February 1899.
128 "Editorial Comment," *Canadian Magazine* 12, 5, (March 1899), 467.
129 "Current Events," *Queen's Quarterly* 6, 4, (April 1899), 321–22.
130 "The World's Progress," *Methodist Magazine* 44, 4, (April 1899), 377.
131 "The Philippines," *Canadian Churchman*, 9 March 1899.
132 "Editorial Comment," *Canadian Magazine* 12, 5, (March 1899), 467.
133 Burwash, "1799–1899 – The Contrast and Outlook," *Methodist Magazine* 50, 5, (November 1899), 406.
134 Hughes, "The Mobilization of Methodism," *Methodist Magazine* 50, 3, (September 1899), 236–41.

CHAPTER FOUR

1 Morison, I, Roosevelt to James Harrison Wilson, 12 July 1899, 1032.
2 Hochschild, 21–33.
3 Stanley, 249–58.
4 Penlington, *Canada and Imperialism*, 240–1.

5 Miller, *Painting the Map Red*, 3–8. See also Magney.

6 Biggar, 27.

7 Ibid., 29.

8 Stuart Anderson, 132; Olasky, 420–4.

9 Olasky, 420.

10 Miller, "English-Canadian," 422.

11 Haultain, 67.

12 Cockran Papers, Smith to Cockran, 10 November 1899.

13 Ibid., Smith to Cockran, 21 March 1899.

14 Goldwin Smith Papers, Cockran to Smith, 22 May 1900.

15 Cockran Papers, Smith to Cockran, 23 June 1899.

16 *Party Platforms*, "Democratic Platform of 1900," 113, 115.

17 Pitcher, 460.

18 Ewan, "Current Events Abroad," *Canadian Magazine* 17, 1, (May 1901), 79.

19 "The World's Progress," *Methodist Magazine* 50, 6, (December 1899), 573.

20 Neatby, 32.

21 "The World's Progress," *Methodist Magazine* 50, 5, (November 1899), 467–8.

22 Ibid. 6, December 1899, 573.

23 Pitcher, 456–60.

24 "World Wide Work," *Presbyterian Record*, (September 1900), 269.

25 Grant, "Current Events," *Queen's Quarterly* 7, 1, (July 1899), 78–79.

26 Grant, "Current Events," *Queen's Quarterly* 7, 2, (October 1899), 158–164.

27 *Papers Relating to the Foreign Relations of the United States* 1899, 350–1.

28 Allen, 591.

29 Beale, 97.

30 Knee, 200.

31 Morison, Volume 1, Roosevelt to John St. Loe Strachey, 27 January 1900, 1144.

32 Ibid., Roosevelt to Frederick Courteney Selous, 7 February 1900, 1175–76.

33 Ibid., Roosevelt to William Archer, 31 August 1899, 1064.

34 Ibid., Roosevelt to Cecil Arthur Spring Rice, 11 August 1899, 1052.

35 Ibid., Roosevelt to Hermann Speck von Steinberg, 27 November 1899, 1098.

36 Ibid., Roosevelt to Cowles, 2 March 1900, 1208.

37 Ibid., Roosevelt to Spring Rice, 2 December 1899, 1103.

38 Ibid., Roosevelt to Selous, 7 February 1900, 1176–77.

39 Goldwin Smith Papers, Smith to Mowbray, 19 December 1895.

40 "The Progress of the World," *American Monthly Review of Reviews* 25, 3, (March 1902), 264.

41 *New York Times*, 19 June 1900.

42 Government Printing Office, *Congressional Record*, Senate, 28 May 1900, 6131–32.

43 *New York Times*, 14 October 1899.

44 Ibid., 30 December 1899.

45 New York *Tribune*, 29 October 1899.

46 Ibid., 14 January 1899.

47 *Outlook* 64, 21 (April 1900), 891.

48 Toronto *Globe*, text of Laurier's speech, 10 October 1899.

49 Schull, 381.

50 Quoted in Toronto *Globe*, 12 October 1899.

51 New York *Tribune*, 11 October 1899.

52 "The World's Progress," *Methodist Magazine* 50, 6, (December 1899), 570.

53 "American Sympathy," *Methodist Magazine* 51, 1, (January 1900), 90.

54 Ewan, "Current Events Abroad," *Canadian Magazine* 17, 1, (May 1901), 80.

55 "Current Events," *Queen's Quarterly* 7, 2, (October 1899), 166–67.

56 Ibid., 3, (January 1900), 253.

57 "Current Events," *Queen's Quarterly* 8, 3, (January 1901), 239.

58 Allen, 523.

59 Penlington, *Alaska*, 126.

60 *Papers Relating to the Foreign Relations of the United States* 1899, 321–23.

61 Joseph Choate Papers, John Hay to Choate, 28 April 1899.

62 Ibid., Hay to Choate, 28 April 1899.

63 Ibid., Hay to Choate, 22 May, 1899.

64 Ibid., Choate to Hay, 19 May 1899.

65 Ibid., Choate to Pauncefote, 20 May 1899.

66 Ibid., Pauncefote to Choate, 22 May 1899.

67 Ibid., Hay to Choate, 22 May 1899.

68 House of Commons *Debates* 48, 4 April 1899, 1074. See also May 4, 2536; and vol. 49, May 26, 3668.

69 Ibid. 49, 27 May 1899, 3783.

70 Ibid. 50, 10 July 1899, 6937.

71 Ibid. 50, 22 July 1899, 8154–62.

72 *New York Times*, 23 July 1899.

73 Joseph Choate Papers, Davis to Hay, 31 July 1899.

74 *New York Times*, 25 July 1899.

75 Morison, Volume 1, Roosevelt to Spring Rice, 11 August 1899.

76 *New York Times*, 9 August 1899.

77 Ibid.
78 *New York Times*, 5 August 1899
79 Ibid., 6 August 1899.
80 Choate to Salisbury, 9 August 1899, in Tansill, *Canadian–American Relations*, 201.
81 Joseph Choate Papers, Hay to Choate, 18 August 1899.
82 Ibid., Choate to Hay, 20 September 1899.
83 Robert Craig Brown, *Canada's National Policy*, 401.
84 Tansill, *Canadian–American Relations*, 215.
85 Henry White Papers, Hay to White, 9 September 1899.
86 *Henry Adams and His Friends*, Volume 5, Adams to Elizabeth Cameron, 5 February 1900, 84.
87 Joseph Choate Papers, Hay to Choate, 15 January 1900.
88 John Hay Papers, Choate to Hay, 27 January 1900.
89 Quoted by Henri Bourassa in House of Commons *Debates*, 7 March 1902, 819.
90 Ibid., Choate to Hay, 7 February 1900.
91 Henry Adams, Adams to Elizabeth Cameron, 5 February 1900, 84.
92 Morison, Volume 1, Roosevelt to Albert Shaw, 15 February 1900.
93 Adam Shortt, 386.
94 Strange, 481.
95 House of Commons *Debates*, 19 February 1900, 143.
96 Ibid., 148–51.
97 Henry White Papers, White to Hay, 24 July 1901.
98 Joseph Choate Papers, Choate to Hay, 2 October 1901.
99 Canada House of Commons *Debates*, 5 March 1902, 754.
100 Ibid., 757.
101 Ibid., 764–6.
102 Ibid., 770–1.
103 Thomas A. Bailey, 488.
104 Lodge, *Selections*, 2, Lodge to Roosevelt, 30 August 1903, 48.

CHAPTER FIVE

1 Garland, 443, 454.
2 A.P. Swineford, *Alaska: Its History, Climate and Natural Resources*, (New York and Chicago: Rand, McNally and Co., 1898); Bushrod Washington James, *Alaska: Its Neglected Past, Its Brilliant Future*, (Philadelphia: Sunshine Publishing Co., 1898); Harry De Windt, *Through the Gold Fields of Alaska to Bering Straits*, (New York and London: Harper and Brothers, 1898); all cited in "The Bookman's Table," *Bookman* 7, 4, (June 1898), 357.
3 London, "An Odyssey of the North," 85–100.

4 London, "The Economics of the Klondike," 71.

5 *Bookman* 11, 3, (May 1900), 200.

6 Canada House of Commons *Debates*, 7 March 1898.

7 Dexter Perkins, *Monroe Doctrine*, 218–20.

8 Hall, *Clifford Sifton*. Studying the dispute through Sifton's eyes offers
one of the most thorough views of the Canadian side of the dispute.
Hall offers a relatively critical view of the Canadian claim as well as
Sifton's anti-Americanism and failure to prepare adequately for the
tribunal. Dafoe, in *Clifford Sifton in Relation to his Times,* essentially
acts as Sifton's hagiographer, as well as an apologist for Laurier and
the Liberal party.

9 The historiographical emphasis on American motives and actions may
result from the simple preponderance of material available from the
American side, including the letters of Theodore Roosevelt, John Hay,
Joseph Choate, Henry White, and Henry Cabot Lodge. The result has
been that in any consideration of the dispute, the Americans, and not
the Canadians, become the primary figures. Gibson, in "The Alaskan
Boundary Dispute," 25–40, gives only passing attention to Prime Minister Laurier, while focusing on Lord Alverstone's motives. Creighton, in
Dominion of the North, concedes the importance of the tribunal's decision in creating Anglo-American friendship, but still gives the standard
account of Canada paying "a heavy price" in the face of American "big
stick" diplomacy and British "imperialist power politics." Skelton, in
David Farr, ed., *The Life and Letters of Sir Wilfrid Laurier, Volume II,
1896–1919*, describes the Canadian reaction as "the just anger of the
man who considered himself the victim of a confidence game" (65).
Tansill calls Alverstone's conduct "far from commendable," and mocks
his reference to "Senator Oliver Lodge" in his later memoirs: "If he
could not distinguish between the great British physicist and the American
politician with the same surname, it might seem evident that the case of
Canada had a distinctly poor chance of being understood." Tansill also
calls Laurier "the herald of [the] new imperial order," in *Canadian-
American Relations, 1875–1911*, 261, 263, and 265. Stacey notes that
Alverstone had been Attorney-General in three Conservative administrations and states that he "reverted to type, and under pressure from his
government acted the part of a politician rather than a judge." Stacey
goes to some length to place the decision within the context of Anglo-
American relations, concluding that Canadian interests in the Alaska
affair "consisted in a basis being found for a sure and lasting peace
between Great Britain and the United States," in *Canada and the Age of
Conflict*, 98 and 100. See also Thomas Bailey, "Theodore Roosevelt and
the Alaska Boundary Settlement," 123–30. Bailey believes that Roosevelt
could have acted less rashly and received essentially the same decision,

without creating Canadian ill-will. Nearly all historians agree that memories of the Alaska decision aided in the defeat of Reciprocity in 1911.

10 The one notable exception to this is Penlington's *The Alaska Boundary Dispute: A Critical Reappraisal.* Penlington views the Canadian claim as weak, and criticizes the Canadian failure to take into account the diplomatic context of the tribunal.

11 See Carroll, "Robert Lansing and the Alaskan Boundary Settlement," 271–90. Lansing, who was John Foster's son-in-law, one of the American counsels for the Alaska tribunal, and a future Secretary of State, gave an address to the American Geographical Society in New York, entitled "The Questions Settled by the Award of the Alaskan Boundary Tribunal." The address was published in the *Bulletin of the American Geographical Society* 36, (1904), 65–80, and reproduced in John A. Munro, ed., *The Alaska Boundary Dispute.* Lansing concluded that the tribunal "was not in reality an arbitration, but a joint high commission with judicial duties and powers." This paralleled Roosevelt's view, as he always pointedly referred to the tribunal as a "commission."

12 *Canadian Annual Review, 1903,* 360.

13 Penlington, *The Alaska Boundary Dispute,* 12.

14 The 1895 Venezuela crisis resulted from similar circumstances, while the notorious 1885 Berlin Conference divided most of "unoccupied" Africa among the European powers.

15 Penlington, 11–12.

16 Morison, Volume 2, Roosevelt to Arthur Hamilton Lee, 18 March 1901, 20.

17 Ibid., Roosevelt to Mahan, 18 March 1901.

18 Ibid., Roosevelt to Lee, 24 April 1901.

19 Tansill, 222–3.

20 Tansill, 224.

21 Morison, Volume 2, Roosevelt to Hay, 10 July 1903.

22 John Hay Papers, Choate to Hay, 5 July 1903.

23 Hall, 113.

24 *New York Times,* 27 January 1903.

25 Ibid., 6 February 1903.

26 Patterson, 59–62.

27 Wilfrid Laurier Papers, Charlton to Laurier, 21 February 1903.

28 Ibid., 24 February 1903.

29 Washburn, "Memoir of H. C. Lodge," 334.

30 Wilfrid Laurier Papers, Farrer to Boudreau, 2 February 1903. Although Farrer addressed many letters to Rodolphe Boudreau, Laurier's personal secretary, the letters appear to be directed at Laurier. Quite possibly Farrer addressed them to Boudreau for greater confidentiality, especially when writing from the American capital.

31 For an account of the 1902–03 Venezuela incident see Allen, 603–7. He underscores how American displeasure stopped the British action "dead in its tracks" and induced British praise for the Monroe Doctrine.

32 Wilfrid Laurier Papers, Farrer to Boudreau, 15 February 1903.

33 Tansill, 233.

34 Quoted in *Canadian Annual Review, 1903*, 356–7.

35 House of Commons *Debates*, 13 March 1903, 31–88.

36 *Henry Adams*, Volume 5, 1 March 1903, Adams to Elizabeth Cameron, 464.

37 Morison, Volume 2, Roosevelt to Elihu Root, Henry Cabot Lodge, and George Turner, 17 March 1903, 448–9.

38 Ibid., Roosevelt to Hay, 29 June 1903, 507.

39 Henry White Papers, Lodge to White, 13 March 1903.

40 Ibid., Hay to White, 10 April 1903.

41 Morison, Volume 2, Roosevelt to Oliver Wendell Holmes, 25 July 1903, 529–30.

42 Ibid., Roosevelt to Holmes, 20 October 1903, 634.

43 Ibid., Roosevelt to Hay, 29 July 1903, 533.

44 Ibid., Roosevelt to Holmes, 25 July 1903, 530.

45 Lodge, *Selections*, II, Roosevelt to Lodge, 29 June 1903, 37.

46 Hall, 116.

47 Lodge, *Selections*, II, Lodge to Roosevelt, 23 June 1903, 32.

48 Ibid., 32.

49 Ibid., Roosevelt to Lodge, 29 June 1903, 37; and Roosevelt to Hay, 29 June 1903, 507.

50 Lodge, *Selections*, II, Roosevelt to Lodge, 16 July 1903, 39.

51 Garraty, 247.

52 Lodge, *Selections*, II, Lodge to Roosevelt, 30 July 1903, 41.

53 Ibid., 42.

54 Ibid., 20 August 1903, 46.

55 Ibid., 30 August 1903, 48–9.

56 Garraty, 251.

57 Lodge Papers, Lodge to C. L. Gardner, 19 September 1903, in Garraty, 250.

58 Lodge, *Selections*, II, Lodge to Roosevelt, 13 September 1903, 56.

59 *Henry Adams*, Adams to Hay, 15 September 1903, 512.

60 Morison, Volume 2, Roosevelt to Root, 3 October 1903, 613.

61 Henry White Papers, Roosevelt to White, 26 September 1903.

62 Ibid., Lodge to White, 2 October 1903.

63 Lodge, *Selections*, II, 24 September 1903, 58.

64 Garraty, 253.

65 Lodge Papers, Lodge to Gardner, 19 October 1903, in Garraty, 254.

66 Atlanta *Constitution*, 16 October, 1903.

67 Ibid.
68 Dafoe, *Clifford Sifton and His Times*, 233.
69 Ibid., 242.
70 Lodge, *Selections*, II, Roosevelt to Lodge, 5 October 1903, 66.
71 Manitoba *Free Press*, 19 October 1903.
72 Montreal *Gazette*, 21 October 1903.
73 Quoted in Montreal *Star*, 21 October 1903.
74 "Current Events Abroad," *Canadian Magazine* 22, 3, January 1904, 295–6.
75 Toronto *Globe*, 19 October 1903.
76 Dafoe, 233.
77 Ibid., 235.
78 Canada House of Commons *Debates*, 23 October 1903, 14785.
79 Ibid., 14789.
80 Ibid., 14788–90.
81 Ibid., 14794, 14810.
82 Ibid., 14821–2.
83 Ibid., 14824; 14828.
84 Ibid., 14817.
85 Toronto *Globe*, 23 October 1903.
86 Montreal *Gazette*, 27 October 1903.
87 In *Canadian Annual Review, 1903*, 32.
88 Ibid., 328–9.
89 Skelton, 68.
90 "Canadian, but British," *Canadian Magazine* 22, 3, (January 1904), 300.
91 Goldwin Smith, "Can Canada Make Her Own Treaties?," 331–5.
92 Hodgins, 482.
93 "Current Events," *Queen's Quarterly* 11, 4, April 1904, 326–7.
94 Cooper, "Self-Government and Imperialism," 246.
95 Chicago *Tribune*, 21 October 1903.
96 Atlanta *Constitution*, 20 October 1903.
97 *Canadian Annual Review, 1903*, 377.
98 *Review of Reviews* 29, 1, (January 1904), 10.
99 John Hay Papers, Choate to Hay, 20 October 1903.
100 *Canadian Annual Review, 1903*, 378.
101 Allen, 613.
102 Allen, 614.

CONCLUSION

1 From "Preface," Stead, *The Americanization of the World*.
2 Dos Passos, *The Anglo-Saxon Century*.
3 "Book Reviews," *Canadian Magazine* 21, 5, (September 1903), 478.

4 Stuart Anderson, 175.

5 Hofstadter, *The Age of Reform*, 174–214.

6 Turner, *The Frontier in American History*.

7 Allen, 615.

8 Bailey, 504.

9 Ibid., 505.

10 Stacey, 113.

11 Baker, 426–49.

12 Stacey, 148. See also *The Canadian Annual Review, 1911*, for an account of the election.

13 Berger, *The Sense of Power*, 138.

14 Bothwell, Drummond, and English, 40.

15 Hofstadter, *Age of Reform*, 177.

16 Bailey, 521–3.

17 Ibid., 180.

18 Conn, "Immigration," *Queen's Quarterly 8*, 2, (October 1900).

19 Shaw, "The Progress of the World," *Review of Reviews 27*, 5, (May 1903).

20 Stuart Anderson, 176.

21 See Lecker, *Borderlands*; Adelman and Aron, "From Borderlands to Borders"; Thelen, "The Nation and Beyond"; Buckner, "How Canadian Historians Stopped Worrying and Learned to Love the Americans!"; Tyrrell, "Making Nations/Making States." In particular, Anglo-Saxonism allows the exploration of, in David Thelen's conception of transnational history, "how a people in a nation balance their national identities against other ones and what those other identities might be." Thelen, 969.

22 Wallace, 183.

23 See Phillips, *The Cousins' Wars*.

24 Beer, *The English-Speaking Peoples*, 1917; Walston, *The English-Speaking Brotherhood*, 1919.

25 The English-Speaking Union, 3–7.

26 Hoopes and Brinkley, 20; Divine, *Second Chance*.

27 Pickersgill, 237.

28 Ibid., 675.

29 Ibid., 680.

Bibliography

Abbott, The Reverend Lyman. "The Basis of an Anglo-American Understanding." *North American Review* 166, 498, May 1898, 513–21.

Adams, Henry. *Henry Adams and His Friends: A Collection of His Unpublished Letters*, Boston: Houghton Mifflin Company, 1947.

Adelman, Jeremy and Stephen Aron. "From Borderlands to Borders: Empires, Nation-States, and the Peoples in Between North American History." *American Historical Review* June 1999, 814–41.

Allen, H.C. *Great Britain and the United States: A History of Anglo-American Relations, 1783–1952*. New York: St. Martin's Press Inc., 1955.

Anderson, Frank E. "America and the European Concert." *Arena* 20, 107, October 1898, 433–44.

Anderson, Stuart. *Race and Rapprochement: Anglo-Saxonism and Anglo-American Relations, 1895–1904*. London and Toronto: Associated University Presses, 1981.

Armstrong, Christopher. "The Mowat Heritage in Federal-Provincial Relations." In Donald Swainson, ed. *Oliver Mowat's Ontario*. Toronto: Macmillan of Canada, 1972, 93–118.

Ashcroft, Bill, Gareth Griffiths, and Helen Tiffin. *The Empire Writes Back: Theory and Practice in Post-Colonial Literatures*. London: Routledge, 1989.

Baehr, Harry W., Jr. *The New York Tribune Since the Civil War*. New York: Dodd, Mead and Co., 1936.

Bailey, Thomas A. *A Diplomatic History of the American People*, tenth edition. Englewood Cliffs, NJ: Prentice-Hall, Inc., 1980.

Bailey, Thomas. "Theodore Roosevelt and the Alaska Boundary Settlement." *Canadian Historical Review* 18, 2, June 1937, 123–130.

Baker, W.M. "A Case Study of Anti-Americanism in English-Speaking Canada: The Election Campaign of 1911." *Canadian Historical Review 51*, 4, December 1979, 426–49.

Bancroft, Frederic, ed. *Speeches, Correspondence, and Political Papers of Carl Schurz*. New York, 1913.

Beale, Howard K. *Theodore Roosevelt and the Rise of America to World Power*, third edition. New York, 1967.

Beer, George Louis. *The English-Speaking Peoples: Their Future Relations and Joint International Obligations*. New York: Macmillan and Co., 1917.

Berg, Meredith W., and David M. Berg. "The Rhetoric of War Preparation: The New York Press in 1898." *Journalism Quarterly 45*, 4, 1968, 653–60.

Berge, William H. "The Impulse for Expansion: John W. Burgess, Alfred Thayer Mahan, Theodore Roosevelt, Josiah Strong and the Development of a Rationale," Ph.D. thesis, Vanderbilt University, 1969.

Berger, Carl C. "Race and Liberty: The Historical Ideas of Sir John George Bourinot." *The Canadian Historical Association Annual Report, 1965*. Toronto: 1965, 87–104.

– *The Sense of Power: Studies in the Ideas of Canadian Imperialism, 1867–1914*. Toronto: University of Toronto Press, 1970.

– *Science, God and Nature in Victorian Canada*. Toronto: University of Toronto Press, 1983.

– *The Writing of Canadian History: Aspects of English-Canadian Historical Writing since 1900*. Toronto: University of Toronto Press, 1986.

Biggar, E.B. *The Boer War: Its Causes, and Its Interest to Canadians*. Toronto, 1900.

Blackstock, George Tate. "Canada and the Venezuelan Settlement." *Canadian Magazine 8*, 2 December 1896, 170–175.

Bothwell, Robert, Ian Drummond, and John English. *Canada, 1900–1945*. Toronto: University of Toronto Press, 1987.

Bourinot, John George. "Canada's Relations with the United States, and Her Influences in Imperial Councils." *Forum* 25, May, 1898, 329–40.

Bourne, Kenneth. *Britain and the Balance of Power in North America, 1815–1908*. Berkeley: University of California Press, 1967.

Bowers, Claude G. *Beveridge and the Progressive Era*. New York: The Literary Guild, 1932.

Brady, Alexander. *Democracy in the Dominions*. Toronto: University of Toronto Press, 1958.

Brebner, John Bartlett. *North Atlantic Triangle: The Interplay of Canada, the United States and Great Britain*. New Haven: Yale University Press, 1945.

Brown, Gerald H., ed. *Addresses Delivered Before the Canadian Club of Ottawa, 1903–1909*. Ottawa: The Mortimer Press, 1910.

Brown, Robert Craig. "The Commercial Unionists in Canada and the United States." *Canadian Historical Association Annual Report, 1963*, 116–24.

- *Canada's National Policy, 1883–1900: A Study in Canadian-American Relations.* Princeton, NJ: Princeton University Press, 1964.

Bryce, James. "British Feelings on the Venezuelan Question." *North American Review 162,* 471, February 1895, 145–153.

- "The Essential Unity of Britain and America." *Atlantic Monthly 82,* 489, July 1898, 22–29.

Buckner, Phillip. "How Canadian Historians Stopped Worrying and Learned to Love the Americans!" *Acadiensis 25,* 2, Spring 1996, 117–40.

Burgess, John W. "The Recent Pseudo-Monroeism." *Political Science Quarterly 11,* 1, March 1896, 44–67.

Burns, Edward McNail. *The American Idea of Mission: Concepts of National Purpose and Destiny.* New Brunswick, New Jersey: Rutgers University Press, 1957.

Burton, D.H. "Theodore Roosevelt and the 'Special Relationship' with Britain." *History Today 23,* 8, 1973, 527–35.

Burwash, Reverend N. "1799–1899 – The Contrast and Outlook." *Methodist Magazine 50,* 5, November 1899, 406.

Callahan, James Morton. *American Foreign Policy in Canadian Relations.* New York: The Macmillan Company, 1937.

Campbell, A.E. *Great Britain and the United States, 1895–1903.* London: Longmans, Green and Co., 1960.

Campbell, Charles S. *Anglo-American Understanding, 1898–1903.* Baltimore: Johns Hopkins Press, 1957.

Campbell, Wilfred. *The Collected Poems of Wilfred Campbell.* Toronto: William Briggs, 1905.

Canada House of Commons. *Official Report of Debates.*

Canada Senate. *Debates of the Senate of the Dominion of Canada.*

Carnegie, Andrew. "The Venezuelan Question." *North American Review 162,* 471, February 1895, 129–144.

- "Distant Possessions: The Parting of the Ways." *North American Review 167,* 501, August 1898, 237–39.

Carr, Graham. "'All We North Americans': Literary Culture and the Continentalist Ideal, 1919–1939." *American Review of Canadian Studies 17,* 2, 1987, 145–57.

Carroll, F.M. "Robert Lansing and the Alaskan Boundary Settlement." *The International History Review 9,* 2, May 1987, 271–90.

Cartwright, Richard. *Reminiscences.* Toronto: Morang and Co., Ltd., 1912.

Cassatt, Alfred C. "The Monroe Doctrine: Defence, Not Defiance." *Forum 20,* December 1895, 456–64.

Charlton, John. "Canada and the Venezuela Settlement: A Reply to Mr. Blackstock." *Canadian Magazine 8,* 3, January 1897, 258–61.

- "Canada and the Dingley Bill." *North American Review 165,* 491, October 1897, 418–30.

- "American Trade Relations," *Canadian Magazine* 9, 6, October 1897, 502–06.
- "Canadian Trade Relations with the United States," in J.C. Hopkins, ed. *Canada: An Encyclopedia of the Country 1*, Toronto, 1898.
- (Writing as "A Canadian Liberal"). "The Anglo-American Joint High Commission." *North American Review* 167, 501, August 1898, 165–75.
- "Reciprocity with Canada." *Forum 32*, January 1902, 582–93.
- "The Growth of Reciprocity Sentiment." *Outlook 73*, 9, 28 February 1903, 483–88.
- *Speeches and Addresses: Political, Literary and Religious.* Toronto: Morang and Co., Ltd., 1905.
- *Diary.* John Charlton Papers. Thomas Fisher Rare Book Library, University of Toronto.

Choate, Joseph. Joseph Choate Papers. Manuscript Division, Library of Congress.

Clark, S.D. *The Developing Canadian Community.* Toronto, Macmillan and Company, 1962.

Clarke, G.S. "England and America." *Nineteenth Century.* In *Living Age 218*, 2827, 10 September 1898, 691–97.

Cleveland, Grover. Grover Cleveland Letters. Microform Department, New York Public Library.

Clippingdale, Richard. "J.S. Willison and Canadian Nationalism, 1886–1902." *Canadian Historical Association Historical Papers* 1969, 74–93.

Clowes, William Laird. "American Expansionism and the Inheritance of the Race." *Fortnightly Review* in *Living Age* 220, 2844, 7 January 1899, 31–8.

Clymer, Kenton J. *John Hay: The Gentleman as Diplomat.* Ann Arbor: University of Michigan Press, 1975.

Cockran, W. Bourke. W. Bourke Cockran Papers. Manuscript Division, New York Public Library.

Cole, Douglas. "Canada's 'Nationalistic' Imperialists." *Journal of Canadian Studies 5*, 2, 1970, 44–49.

- "Introduction." *Canadian Review of Studies in Nationalism 7*, 1, 1980, 1–3.

Colquhoun, Archibald R. "Eastward Expansion of the United States." *Harper's 97*, 582, November 1898, 932–38.

Commager, Henry Steele. *The American Mind: An Interpretation of American Thought and Character Since the 1880s.* New Haven: Yale University Press, 1952.

Cook, J.G. *Anglophobia: An Analysis of Anti-British Prejudice in the United States.* Boston: The Four Seas Company, 1919.

Cook, Ramsay. *The Politics of John W. Dafoe and the "Free Press."* Toronto: University of Toronto Press, 1963.

Cook, Ramsay, general editor. *Dictionary of Canadian Biography. Volume 13, 1901 to 1910.* Toronto: University of Toronto Press, 1994.

Cooper, John. "Self-Government and Imperialism." *Queen's Quarterly 11*, 3, January 1904, 246.

Cortissoz, Royal. *The Life of Whitelaw Reid*, two volumes. New York: Charles Scribner's Sons, 1921.

Cowles, Anna Roosevelt, ed. *Letters of Theodore Roosevelt to Anna Roosevelt Cowles 1870–1918.* New York, 1924.

Crapol, Edward P. *America for Americans: Economic Nationalism and Anglophobia in the Late Nineteenth Century.* Westport, CT: Greenwood Press, Inc., 1973.

– "Book Reviews." *Journal of American History* 69, 2, September 1982, 481–2.

– "Coming to Terms with Empire: The Historiography of Late-Nineteenth-Century American Relations." *Diplomatic History 16*, 4, 1992, 573–97.

Creighton, Donald. *Dominion of the North*, New Edition. Toronto: Macmillan of Canada, 1966.

Crook, D.P. *Benjamin Kidd: Portrait of a Social Darwinist.* Cambridge: Cambridge University Press, 1984.

Dafoe, John W. *Laurier, A Study in Canadian Politics.* Toronto: Thomas Allen, 1922.

– *Clifford Sifton in Relation to His Times.* Toronto: The Macmillan Co., 1931.

Dallek, Robert. "National Mood and American Foreign Policy: A Suggestive Essay." *American Quarterly 34*, 4, 1982, 339–61.

Davies, Barrie. "'We Hold a Vaster Empire Than Has Been': Canadian Literature and the Canadian Empire." *Studies in Canadian Literature*, 14, 1, 1989, 18–29.

Davis, Richard W. "'We Are All Americans Now!': Anglo-American Marriages in the Later Nineteenth Century." *Proceedings of the American Philosophical Society 135*, 2, 1991, 140–99.

Dawson, R. Macgregor. *The Government of Canada.* Toronto: University of Toronto Press, 1947.

DeConde, Alexander. *Ethnicity, Race, and American Foreign Policy: A History.* Boston: Northeastern University Press, 1992.

Dennis, Alfred L.P. *Adventures in American Diplomacy, 1896–1906.* New York: E.P. Dutton and Co., 1928.

Department of State. *Papers Relating to Foreign Relations of the United States, with the Annual Message of the President to Congress (1895–1905).* Washington: Government Printing Office, 1896–1906.

De Ricci, J.H. *The Fisheries Dispute and Annexation of Canada.* London: Sampson Low, Marston, Searle and Rivington, 1888.

Dicey, Edward. "The New American Imperialism." *Nineteenth Century.* In *Living Age 219*, 2835, 5 November 1898, 327–40.

Dingley, Edward N. *The Life and Times of Nelson Dingley, Jr.* Kalamazoo: Ihling Brothers and Everand, 1902.

Divine, Robert A. *Second Chance: The Triumph of Internationalism in America During World War II.* New York: Atheneum, 1967.

Dos Passos, John R. *The Anglo-Saxon Century and the Unification of the English-Speaking People.* New York: Knickerbocker Press, 1903.

Douglas, James. *Canadian Independence, Annexation and British Imperial Federation*. New York: G.P. Putnam's Sons, 1894.

Dulebohn, George Roscoe. *Principles of Foreign Policy Under the Cleveland Administrations*. Philadelphia, 1941.

Duncan, George William. "The Diplomatic Career of William Rufus Day, 1897–1898," Ph.D. thesis, Case Western Reserve University, 1976.

Dyer, Thomas G. *Theodore Roosevelt and the Idea of Race*. Baton Rouge: Louisiana State University Press, 1980.

Eggert, Gerald G. *Richard Olney: Evolution of a Statesman*. University Park: Penn State University Press, 1974.

Einstein, Lewis. "British Diplomacy in the Spanish-American War." *Proceedings of the Massachusetts Historical Society* 76, 1964, 30–54.

English, John. *The Decline of Politics: The Conservatives and the Party System, 1901–20*. Toronto: University of Toronto Press, 1977.

English-Speaking Union, The. *The English-Speaking Union: To Draw Together in Comradeship the English-Speaking Peoples of the World*. London, 1927.

Farrer, Edward. "Appendix A, Reciprocity with Canada, Statement by Hon. Edward Farrer, of Toronto." *Report of the Committee on Ways and Means Concerning Reciprocity and Commercial Treaties*, House of Representatives, 54th Congress, 1st Session, June 6, 1896, Washington: Government Printing Office, 1896.

– "The Anglo-American Commission." *Forum* 25, August 1898, 652–663.

– Edward Farrer Papers. National Archives of Canada.

Farwell, Byron. "Taking Sides in the Boer War." *American Heritage* 27, April 1976, 21–25, 92–97.

Ferguson, John H. *American Diplomacy and the Boer War*. Philadelphia, 1939.

Ferns, Thomas H., and Robert Craig Brown. "John Charlton," in Ramsay Cook, general editor, *Dictionary of Canadian Biography. Volume 13, 1901 to 1910*, Toronto: University of Toronto Press, 1994, 187–9.

Field, James A., Jr. "American Imperialism: The 'Worst Chapter' in Almost Any Book." *American Historical Review* 83, 3, June 1978, 644–68.

Fisher, Horace N. "The Development of our Foreign Policy." *Atlantic Monthly* 82, 492, October 1898, 552–9.

Flower, B.O. "The Proposed Federation of the Anglo-Saxon Nations." *Arena* 20, 105, 223–38.

Foner, Philip S. "Why the United States Went to War with Spain in 1898." *Science and Society* 32, 1, 1968, 39–65.

Forster, Ben. *A Conjunction of Interests: Business, Politics, and Tariffs, 1825–1879*. Toronto: University of Toronto Press, 1986.

Foster, John W. *Diplomatic Memoirs*. 2 vols. Boston: Houghton Mifflin, 1909.

Fredrickson, George. *The Black Image in the White Mind: The Debate on Afro-American Character and Destiny, 1817–1914*. New York: Harper and Row, 1971.

– *The Comparative Imagination: On the History of Racism, Nationalism and Social Movements.* Berkeley: University of California Press, 1997.

Fry, Michael G. *Illusions of Security: North Atlantic Diplomacy, 1918–22.* Toronto: University of Toronto Press, 1972.

Fuentes, Carlos. *The Buried Mirror: Reflections on Spain and the New World.* Boston, 1992.

Gaddis, John Lewis. "New Conceptual Approaches to the Study of American Foreign Relations: Interdisciplinary Perspectives." *Diplomatic History* 14, Summer 1990, 411–16.

Garland, Hamlin. "Ho, for the Klondike!" *McClure's* 10, 5, March 1898, 443–454.

Garraty, John A. *Henry Cabot Lodge: A Biography.* New York: Alfred A. Knopf, 1953.

Gelber, Lionel. *The Rise of Anglo-American Friendship: A Study in World Politics, 1898–1906.* London: Oxford University Press, 1938.

Gibson, F.W. "The Alaskan Boundary Dispute." *Canadian Historical Association Report,* 1945, 25–40.

Gillis, R. Peter. "John Bertram," in Ramsay Cook, general editor, *Dictionary of Canadian Biography. Volume 13, 1901 to 1910,* Toronto: University of Toronto Press, 1994, 65–67.

– "The Ottawa Lumber Barons." In Donald Swainson, ed., *Oliver Mowat's Ontario.* Toronto: Macmillan of Canada, 1972, 14–31.

Gillis, R. Peter, and Thomas R. Roach. *Lost Initiatives: Canada's Forest Industries, Forest Policy and Forest Conservation.* New York: Greenwood Press, 1986.

Glazebrook, G.P. deT. *A History of Canadian External Relations, Revised Edition, Volume 1: The Formative Years to 1914.* Toronto: McClelland and Stewart Ltd., 1966.

Gluek, Alvin C. *Minnesota and The Manifest Destiny of the Canadian Northwest: A Study in Canadian-American Relations.* Toronto: University of Toronto Press, 1965.

– "Pilgrimages to Ottawa: Canadian-American Diplomacy, 1903–13." *Canadian Historical Association Historical Papers, 1968,* Toronto, 1969, 65–83.

Gooch, John. "Great Britain and the Defence of Canada, 1896–1914." *The Journal of Imperial and Commonwealth History* 3, 3, May 1975, 369–85.

Gould, Lewis L. *The Presidency of William McKinley.* Lawrence: Regents Press of Kansas, 1980.

– and Craig H. Roell. *William McKinley: A Bibliography.* Westport, Conn.: Meckler, 1988.

Graham, W.R. "Sir Richard Cartwright, Wilfrid Laurier, and Liberal Party Trade Policy, 1887." *Canadian Historical Review* 33, 1, March 1952, 1–18.

Granatstein, J.L. *Yankee Go Home? Canadians and Anti-Americanism.* Toronto: Harper Collins, 1996.

Grant, George M. "Our Origins." *Methodist Magazine* 43, 2, January 1896, 142–45.

– "Our Origins." *Queen's Quarterly* 3, 1, January 1896, 54–58.

Graybar, Lloyd J. *Albert Shaw of the Review of Reviews.* Lexington, KY: The University Press of Kentucky, 1974.

Greenfeld, Liah. *Nationalism: Five Roads to Modernity.* Cambridge, MA: Harvard University Press, 1992.

Greenwood, Frederick. "The Anglo-American Future." *Nineteenth Century*, in *Living Age* 218, 2825, 27 August 1898, 563–70.

Grenville, John A.S., and George Berkeley Young. *Politics, Strategy, and American Diplomacy: Studies in Foreign Policy, 1873–1917.* New Haven, CT: Yale University Press, 1966.

Gwynn Stephen, ed. *The Letters and Friendships of Sir Cecil Spring Rice*, two volumes. Boston and New York, 1929.

Hall, D.J. *Clifford Sifton*, two volumes. Vancouver: University of British Columbia Press, 1981.

Handbook of Commercial Union: A Collection of Papers Read before the Commercial Union Club, Toronto, with Speeches, Letters and other Documents in Favour of Unrestricted Reciprocity with the United States, Toronto: Hunter, Rose and Company, 1888.

Hansen, Marcus Lee (completed and prepared for publication by John Bartlet Brebner). *The Mingling of the Canadian and American Peoples, Volume 1: Historical.* New Haven: Yale University Press, 1940.

Harrington, Fred H. "The Anti-Imperialist Movement in the United States, 1898–1900." *Mississippi Valley Historical Review* 22, September 1935, 211–30.

Hartz, Louis. *The Founding of New World Societies: Studies in the History of the United States, Latin America, South Africa, Canada, and Australia.* New York, 1964.

Haultain, Arnold. *Goldwin Smith: His Life and Opinions.* London: T. Werner Laurie, 1912.

Hay, John. *Addresses of John Hay.* New York: The Century Co., 1906.

– John Hay Papers. Manuscript Division, Library of Congress.

Hobsbawm, Eric. *Nations and Nationalism Since 1780: Programme, Myth, Reality.* Cambridge: Cambridge University Press, 1990.

Hochschild, Adam. *King Leopold's Ghost.* New York: Houghton Mifflin Company, 1998.

Hodgins, Thomas. "Canada and the Treaty-Making Power," *Canadian Magazine* 22, 5, March 1904, 482.

Hofstadter, Richard. *The Age of Reform.* New York: Vintage Books, 1955

– *Social Darwinism in American Thought.* Boston: Beacon Press, 1992 [reprint of 1944 University of Pennsylvania Press edition].

Holbo, Paul S. "Economics, Emotion, and Expansion: An Emerging Foreign Policy." In *The Gilded Age.* H. Wayne Morgan, ed. Revised edition. Syracuse: Syracuse University Press, 1970.

Hoopes, Townsend and Brinkley, Douglas. *FDR and the Creation of the United Nations.* New Haven: Yale University Press, 1977.

Horsman, Reginald. *Race and Manifest Destiny: The Origins of American Racial Anglo-Saxonism.* Cambridge: Harvard University Press, 1981.

Hudson, Winthrop S. "Protestant Clergy Debate the Nation's Vocation, 1898–1899." *Church History* 42, 1, 1973, 110–18.

Hughes, Reverend Hugh Price. "The Mobilization of Methodism." *Methodist Magazine* 50, 3, September 1899, 236–41.

Hunt, Michael H. *Ideology and U.S. Foreign Policy.* New Haven and London: Yale University Press, 1987.

Hyman, Ronald. "The Colonial Office Mind 1900–1914." *The Journal of Commonwealth and Imperial History* 8, 1, October 1979, 30–55.

Ignatieff, Michael. *Blood and Belonging: Journeys into the New Nationalism.* New York: Farrar, Straus, and Giroux, 1993.

James, Henry. *Richard Olney and His Public Service.* Boston: Houghton and Mifflin Co., 1923, reprint, New York: DeCapo Press, 1971.

Jenkins, Brian. "Anglo-American Relations before the First World War." *Canadian Journal of History,* 19, 3, 1984, 407–9.

Jessup, Philip C. *Elihu Root,* two volumes. New York: Dodd, Mead, 1938.

Johnson, Donald B., and Porter, Kirk H., compilers. *National Party Platforms, 1840–1972.* Urbana, IL: University of Illinois Press 1973.

Jones, Greta. *Social Darwinism and English Thought: The Interaction Between Biological and Social Theory.* New Jersey: Humanities Press, 1980.

Jordan, David Starr. *Imperial Democracy.* New York: D. Appleton and Co., 1899.

Kennedy, Philip W. "Race and American Expansionism in Cuba and Puerto Rico, 1895–1905." *Journal of Black Studies* 1, 3, 1971, 306–316.

Kidd, Benjamin. *Social Evolution.* Boston: Macmillan and Co., 1894.

King, Peter Henry. "The White Man's Burden: British Imperialism and its Lessons for America as Seen by American Publicists, From the Venezuela Crisis to the Boer War," Ph.D. thesis, University of California at Los Angeles, 1958.

Kipling, Rudyard. "The White Man's Burden." *McClure's Magazine* 12, 4, February 1899, 1.

Klinck, Carl Frederick. *Wilfred Campbell: A Study in Late Provincial Victorianism.* Toronto: The Ryerson Press, 1942.

Knee, Stuart E. "Anglo-American Understanding and the Boer War." *Australian Journal of Politics and History* 30, 2, 1984, 196–208.

Knuth, Helen E. "The Climax of American Anglo-Saxonism, 1898–1905," Ph.D. thesis, Northwestern University, 1958.

Krenn, Michael, ed. *Race and U.S. Foreign Policy.* New York: Garland Press, 1998.

LaFeber, Walter. *The New Empire: An Interpretation of American Expansionism, 1860–1898.* Ithaca and London: Cornell University Press, 1963.

– "The 'Lion in the Path': The U.S. Emergence as a World Power," *Political Science Quarterly 101,* 5, 1986, 705–18.

Lansing, Robert. "The Questions Settled by the Award of the Alaskan Boundary Tribunal." *Bulletin of the American Geographical Society 36,* 1904, 65–80.

Laurier, Wilfrid. Wilfrid Laurier Papers. National Archives of Canada.

Lecker, Robert. *Borderlands: Essays in Canadian-American Relations.* Toronto: ECW Press, 1991.

Leuchtenburg, William E. "Progressivism and Imperialism: The Progressive Movement and American Foreign Policy, 1898–1916." *The Mississippi Valley Historical Review 39,* December 1952, 483–504.

Lodge, Henry Cabot. "Our Blundering Foreign Policy." *Forum 19,* March 1895, 8–17.

– "England, Venezuela, and the Monroe Doctrine." *North American Review 160,* 463, June 1895, 651–58.

– ed. *Selections from the Correspondence of Theodore Roosevelt and Henry Cabot Lodge, 1884–1914,* two volumes. New York: Charles Scribner's Sons, 1925.

London, Jack. "An Odyssey of the North." *North American Review 85,* 507, January 1900, 85–100.

– "The Economics of the Klondike." *Review of Reviews 21,* 1, January 1900, 71.

Mackie, J.H.W., ed. *Addresses Delivered Before the Canadian Club of Toronto, 1906–07.* Toronto: Warwick Brothers and Rutier, Ltd., 1907.

Magney, William H. "The Methodist Church and the National Gospel, 1884–1914." *The Bulletin 20,* Toronto: The Committee on Archives of the United Church of Canada, 1968.

Mahan, Alfred T. *Lessons of the War with Spain and Other Articles.* London: Sampson, Low, Marston and Co., Ltd., 1900.

Marburg, Theodore. *Expansion.* New York: John Murphy Co., 1900. Reprint by Garland Publishing, Inc., New York and London, 1971.

Marotta, Gary. "The Academic Mind and the Rise of Imperialism: Historians and Economists as Publicists for Ideas of Colonial Expansion." *American Journal of Economics and Sociology 42,* 2, April 1983, 217–34.

Martin, Edward Sandford. *The Life of Joseph Hodges Choate.* New York: Charles Scribner's Sons, 1921.

May, Ernest R. *Imperial Democracy: The Emergence of America as a Great Power.* New York: Harcourt, Brace and World, Inc., 1961.

McConnell, Robert. "Commercial Relations Between Canada and the United States." *Canadian Magazine 12,* 3, January 1899, 198–201.

McLeod, R.R. "Universal Empire for Anglo Saxon Stock." Halifax *Herald*, 13 August 1898, 1.

Merriman, Allen H. "Racism in the Expansionist Controversy of 1898–1900." *Phylon 39*, 4, 1978, 369–80.

Meyer, Paul R. "The Fear of Cultural Decline: Josiah Strong's Thought about Reform and Expansion." *Church History 42*, 3, 1973, 396–405.

Miller, Carman. "Mowat, Laurier, and the Federal Liberal Party, 1887–1897," in Donald Swainson, ed. *Oliver Mowat's Ontario*, Toronto: Macmillan of Canada, 1972, 68–92.

– "English-Canadian Opposition to the South African War as seen through the Press." *Canadian Historical Review 55*, 4, December 1974, 422–38.

– *The Canadian Career of the Fourth Earl of Minto: The Education of a Viceroy*. Waterloo, Ontario: Wilfrid Laurier University Press, 1980.

– *Painting the Map Red: Canada and the South African War, 1899–1902*. Canadian War Museum, 1993.

Millis, Walter. *The Martial Spirit*. The Literary Guild of America, 1931.

Mills, David. "Which Shall Dominate – Saxon or Slav?" *North American Review 166*, 499, June 1898, 729–39.

Moore, John Bassett. "The Monroe Doctrine." *Political Science Quarterly 11*, 1, March 1896, 1–29.

Morison, Elting E., ed., *The Letters of Theodore Roosevelt: The Years of Preparation, Volume 1* and *Volume 2*, Cambridge, MA: Harvard University Press, 1951.

Moser, John. *Twisting the Lion's Tale*. New York: NYU Press, 1993.

Mount, Graeme S. "Friendly Liberator or Predatory Aggressor? Some Canadian Impressions of the United States during the Spanish-American War." *Canadian Journal of Latin American and Caribbean Studies 11*, 22, 1986, 59–70.

Mulanax, Richard. *The Boer War in American Politics and Diplomacy*. Maryland: University Press of America, 1994.

Muller, Dorothea R. "Josiah Strong and American Nationalism: A Reevaluation." *The Journal of American History 53*, 3, 1966, 488–501.

Munro, John A., ed. *The Alaska Boundary Dispute*. Toronto: Copp Clark Publishing Co., 1970.

Naanami, Israel T. "The 'Anglo-Saxon Idea' and British Public Opinion." *Canadian Historical Review 32*, 1, March 1951, 43–60.

Neale, Robert G. "British-American Relations during the Spanish-American War: Some Problems." *Historical Studies: Australia and New Zealand 6*, 21, November 1953, 72–89.

Neary, Peter. "Grey, Bryce, and the Settlement of Canadian-American Differences, 1905–1911." *Canadian Historical Review 49*, 4, December 1968, 357–380.

Neatby, Blair. "Laurier and Imperialism." *Canadian Historical Association Report 1955*, 24–32.

Nelles, H.V. "Empire Ontario: The Problems of Resource Development." In Donald Swainson, ed. *Oliver Mowat's Ontario*. Toronto: Macmillan of Canada, 1972, 189–210.

Nevins, Allan. *Henry White: Thirty Years of American Diplomacy*. New York: Harper and Brothers, 1930.

– ed. *Letters of Grover Cleveland, 1850–1908*. Boston: Houghton Mifflin, 1933.

Nye, Russell B. *This Almost Chosen People: Essays in the History of American Ideas*. Toronto: Macmillan and Co., 1966.

O'Hara, F.C.T. F.C.T. O'Hara Papers. National Archives of Canada.

Olasky, Marvin. "Social Darwinism on the Editorial Page: American Newspapers and the Boer War." *Journalism Quarterly* 65, 2, 1988, 420–4.

Olcott, Charles S. *The Life of William McKinley*, two volumes. Boston: Houghton Mifflin, 1916.

Page, Robert. "Canada and the Imperial Idea in the Boer War Years." *Journal of Canadian Studies* 5, 1, 1970 33–49.

Painter, Nell Irvin. *Standing at Armageddon: The United States, 1877–1919*. New York: W.W. Norton and Company, 1987.

Parker, George F. *Recollections of Grover Cleveland*. New York: Century, 1909.

Patterson, Norman. "The Alaskan Boundary," *Canadian Magazine* 20, 1, November 1902, 59–62.

Penlington, Norman. *Canada and Imperialism: 1896–1899*. Toronto: University of Toronto Press, 1965.

– *The Alaska Boundary Dispute: A Critical Reappraisal*. Toronto: McGraw-Hill Ryerson Ltd., 1972.

Perkins, Bradford. *The Great Rapprochement: England and the United States, 1895–1914*. New York, 1968.

Perkins, Dexter. *A History of the Monroe Doctrine*. Boston: Little, Brown and Company, 1963.

Phelps, E.J. "Arbitration and our Relations with England." *Atlantic Monthly* 78, 465, July 1896, 26–34.

Phillips, Kevin. *The Cousins' Wars: Religion, Politics, and the Triumph of Anglo-America*. New York: Basic Books, 1999.

Pitcher, The Reverend J. Tallman. "The Transvaal." *Methodist Magazine* 50, 5, November 1899, 460.

Porritt, Edward. "The New Administration in Canada." *Yale Review* 6, August 1897, 151–168.

Powell, E.P. "International Arbitration." *Arena* 17, 85, December 1896, 97–111.

Preston, Richard A. *Canada and "Imperial Defense": A Study of the Origins of the British Commonwealth's Defense Organization, 1867–1919*. Durham, NC: Duke University Press, 1967.

– *The Defence of the Undefended Border: Planning for War in North America, 1867–1939*. Durham, NC: Duke University Press, 1977.

Reid, Whitelaw. Whitelaw Reid Papers. Manuscript Division, Library of Congress.

Report of the Committee on Ways and Means Concerning Reciprocity and Commercial Treaties. House of Representatives, 54th Congress, 1st Session, June 6, 1896. Washington: Government Printing Office, 1896.

Ricard, Serge, and Helene Christol, eds. *Anglo-Saxonism in U.S. Foreign Policy: The Diplomacy of Imperialism, 1899–1919.* Aix-en-Provence, France: Université de Provence, 1991.

Ridpath, John Clark. "The United States and the Concert of Europe." *Arena* 20, 105, August 1898, 145–67.

Roberts, Charles G.D. *A History of Canada.* Boston: Lamson, Wolffe, and Co., 1897.

Russell, John W. "Wilfrid Laurier: A Character Sketch." *Arena 17,* 88, March 1897, 615–22.

– "Our Trade Relations with Canada." *North American Review 164,* 487, June 1897, 713.

Sarty, Roger. "Canada and the Great Rapprochement, 1902–1914." B.J.C. McKercher, and Lawrence Aronsen, eds. *The North Atlantic Triangle in a Changing World: Anglo-American-Canadian Relations, 1902–1956.* Toronto: University of Toronto Press, 1996.

Schull, Joseph. *Laurier: The First Canadian.* Toronto: Macmillan of Canada, 1965.

Schurman, J.G. "The Manifest Destiny of Canada." *Forum 7,* March 1889.

Seed, Geoffrey. "British Views of American Policy in the Philippines Reflected in Journals of Opinion, 1898–1907." *Journal of American Studies 2,* 1, 1975, 49–64.

– "British Reactions to American Imperialism Reflected in Journals of Opinion, 1898–1900." *Political Science Quarterly 73,* June 1958, 254–72.

Sewell, Mark. "'All the English-Speaking Race is in Mourning': The Assassination of President Garfield and Anglo-American Relations." *The Historical Journal 34,* 3, 1991, 665–86.

Shaw, Albert. "Is England an 'American Power'?" *Review of Reviews 12,* 12, December 1895.

– "The Progress of the World." *Review of Reviews 13,* 3, March 1896, 266–67.

– Albert Shaw Papers. Manuscript Division, New York Public Library.

Sherwood, Sidney. "An Alliance with England the Basis of a Rational Foreign Policy." *North American Review 162,* 473, April 1896, 89–99.

Shields, R.A. "Imperial Policy and Canadian-American Reciprocity, 1909–1911." *The Journal of Imperial and Commonwealth History 5,* 2, January 1977, 151–71.

Shortt, Adam. "The Nicaragua Canal and the Clayton-Bulwer Treaty." *Canadian Magazine 12,* 3, January 1899, 386.

Shortt, S.E.D. *The Search for an Ideal: Six Canadian Intellectuals and Their Convictions in an Age of Transition, 1890–1930.* Toronto and Buffalo, 1976.

Sifton, Clifford. Clifford Sifton Papers. National Archives of Canada.

Sinkler, George. *The Racial Attitudes of American Presidents: From Abraham Lincoln to Theodore Roosevelt*. Garden City, NY: Doubleday and Company, Inc., 1971.

Skelton, O.D. The *Life and Letters of Sir Wilfrid Laurier*. Toronto: McClelland and Stewart Limited, 1921. Abridged reprint, David M.L. Farr, ed., 1965.

Smith, Allan. "The Continental Dimension in the Evolution of the English-Canadian Mind." *International Journal 31*, 3, 1976, 442–69.

– *Canada – An American Nation? Essays on Continentalism, Identity, and the Canadian Frame of Mind*. Montreal: McGill-Queen's University Press, 1994.

Smith, Gaddis. *The Last Years of the Monroe Doctrine, 1945–1993*. New York: Hill and Wang, 1994.

Smith, Goldwin. *The Political Destiny of Canada*. Toronto: Willing and Williamson, 1878.

– *The Schism in the Anglo-Saxon Race*. An Address Before the Canadian Club of New York, New York, 1887.

– *Canada and the Canadian Question*. New York, 1891.

– "Can Canada Make Her Own Treaties?" *Canadian Magazine 22*, 4, February 1904, 331–5.

– *Reminiscences*. New York, 1911.

– Goldwin Smith Papers. National Archives of Canada.

Spurr, David. *The Rhetoric of Empire: Colonial Discourse in Journalism, Travel Writing, and Imperial Administration*. Durham, NC: Duke University Press, 1993.

Stacey, C.P. *Canada in the Age of Conflict, Volume 1: 1867–1921*. Toronto: University of Toronto Press, 1984.

Stanley, Sir Henry M. "Anglo-Saxon Responsibilities." *Outlook 63*, 30 September 1899, 249–58.

Stead, William T. *The Americanization of the World; or, The Trend of the Twentieth Century*. London: Review of Reviews Annual, 1902, reprinted by Garland Publishing, 1972.

Stephanson, Anders. *Manifest Destiny: American Expansionism and the Empire of Right*. New York: Hill and Wang, 1995.

Stevens, Paul Douglas. "Laurier and the Liberal Party in Ontario," Ph.D. thesis, University of Toronto, 1966.

Strange, T. Bland. "The Nicaragua Canal and the Clayton-Bulwer Treaty." *Canadian Magazine 12*, 5, March 1899, 481.

Strong, Josiah. *Our Country: Its Possible Future and Its Present Crisis*. New York: Baker and Taylor Co., 1885.

– *The New Era; or the Coming Kingdom*. New York: Baker and Taylor Co., 1893.

– *Expansion Under New World Conditions*. New York: Baker and Taylor Co., 1900.

Swainson, Donald, ed. *Oliver Mowat's Ontario*. Toronto: Macmillan of Canada, 1972.

Swift, Morrison I. *Imperialism and Liberty*. Los Angeles: The Ronbroke Press, 1899.

Takaki, Ronald. *Iron Cages: Race and Culture in Nineteenth-Century America*. New York: Alfred A. Knopf, 1979.

– *A Different Mirror: A History of Multicultural America*. Boston: Little, Brown and Company, 1993.

Tansill, Charles Callan. *The Foreign Policy of Thomas F. Bayard, 1885–1897*. New York: Fordham University Press, 1940.

– *Canadian-American Relations, 1875–1911*. New Haven: Yale University Press, 1943.

Tausky, Thomas E., ed. *Sara Jeanette Duncan: Selected Journalism*. Ottawa: The Tecumseh Press, 1978.

– *Sara Jeanette Duncan: Novelist of Empire*. Port Credit, Ontario: P.D. Meany Publishers, 1980.

Thayer, William R. *The Life and Letters of John Hay*, two volumes. Boston and New York, Houghton Mifflin Company, 1915.

Thelen, David. "The Nation and Beyond: Transnational Perspectives on United States History." *Journal of American History* December 1999, 965–75.

Tuchman, Barbara. *A Distant Mirror: The Calamitous Fourteenth Century*. New York, 1978.

Tyrrell, Ian. "Making Nations/Making States: American Historians in the Context of Empire." *Journal of American History* December 1999, 1015–44.

Vahle, Cornelius Wendell, Jr. "Congress, the President, and Overseas Expansion, 1897–1901," Ph.D. thesis, Georgetown University, 1967.

Walden, Daniel. "Race and Imperialism: The Achilles Heel of the Progressives." *Science and Society* 31, 2, 1967, 222–32.

Waldstein, Charles. "The English-Speaking Brotherhood." *North American Review* 167, 501, August 1898, 223–38.

Wallace, Elizabeth. *Goldwin Smith: Victorian Liberal*. Toronto: University of Toronto Press,1957.

Walston, Charles. *The English-Speaking Brotherhood and the League of Nations*. Cambridge: Cambridge University Press, 1919.

Warner, Donald F. *The Idea of Continental Union: Agitation for the Annexation of Canada to the United States, 1849–1893*. Lexington: University of Kentucky Press, 1960.

Wells, David A. "Great Britain and the United States: Their True Relations." *North American Review*, 162, 473, April 1896, 385–405.

White, Henry. Henry White Papers. Manuscript Division, Library of Congress.

Whitely, William N.H. "Canadian Opinion on American Expansionism 1895–1903," M.A. thesis, Queen's University, 1952.

Widenor, William C. *Henry Cabot Lodge and the Search for an American Foreign Policy.* Berkeley: University of California Press, 1980.

Willison, J.S. "Relations between Britain and America." Toronto *Globe,* 24 February 1899.

Winks, Robin W. *The Relevance of Canadian History: U.S. and Imperial Perspectives.* Toronto: Macmillan and Co., 1979.

– "The American Struggle with 'Imperialism': How Words Frighten." Kroes, Rob, ed. *The American Identity: Fusion and Fragmentation,* Amsterdam, 1980, 143–77.

Wise, S.F., and Robert Craig Brown. *Canada Views the United States: Nineteenth-Century Political Attitudes.* Toronto: Macmillan of Canada, 1967.

Woolsley, Theodore. "The President's Monroe Doctrine." *Forum 20,* February 1896, 705–12.

Zeil, Elizabeth. "The United States and the Boer War," M.A. thesis, Columbia University, 1950.

PERIODICALS

American Monthly Review of Reviews
Anglo-Saxon Review
Arena
Atlantic Monthly
Bookman
Canadian Annual Review
Canadian Churchman
Canadian Magazine
Constitution (Atlanta)
Daily Star (Montreal)
Evening Journal (Ottawa)
Forum
Free Press (Manitoba)
Gazette (Montreal)
Globe (Toronto)
Harper's
Herald (Halifax)
Living Age
Mail and Empire (Toronto)
McClure's
Methodist Magazine
Monetary Times
Morang's Annual Register
Nation
New York Times

North American Review
Outlook
Political Science Quarterly
Presbyterian Record
Queen's Quarterly
Saturday Night
Times-Democrat (New Orleans)
Tribune (Chicago)
Tribune (New York)
Yale Review

Index